SUBSIDIA BIBLICA

3

subsidia biblica - 3

JOSEPH A. FITZMYER, S. J.

An Introductory Bibliography
for the
Study of Scripture

Third Edition

EDITRICE PONTIFICIO ISTITUTO BIBLICO — ROMA 1990

1961 – First edition (© Newman Press)
1981 – Second revised edition (© E.P.I.B.)
1990 – Third edition

ISBN 88-7653-592-6

EDITRICE PONTIFICIA UNIVERSITÀ GREGORIANA
EDITRICE PONTIFICIO ISTITUTO BIBLICO
Piazza della Pilotta 35 - 00187 Roma, Italia

To the Memory of
George S. Glanzman, S.J.
1916-1977

Table of Contents

Preface

This introductory bibliography was first published by G. S. Glanzman and myself in 1961, as No. 5 in the series of Woodstock Papers: Occasional Essays for Theology. After a few printings, it soon became outdated. Both Glanzman and I were requested by colleagues to update it; but Glanzman could never arouse enough interest in it to accede to such requests. On 24 October 1977 Glanzman died at Syracuse, NY. During the course of 1979 the question of a revision was again raised, this time by J. Swetnam, S.J., of the Biblical Institute, who had secured permission to revise the work from the Paulist Press (successor to the Newman Press, which published the original bibliography). I decided to attempt the revision of the whole, making use of various OT colleagues as consultants. Their names are listed below. After eight years the book has gone out of print, and a further revision is called for.

The aim of this revision of the annotated introductory bibliography remains what it has always been: to present a list of titles of reasonable length with which the student who is beginning the study of theology or of Scriptutre in a serious way might do well to familiarize himself or herself. It is hoped, not that such students would read through all these books, but that they would acquire some acquaintance with them. In the various disciplines that make up the complex of Scripture studies there are many books to which beginners might turn. But they are often at a loss in trying to decide where to begin or to discover which are the standard, reputable authors in the discipline in which interest is being stirred. It is my hope that this revised and expanded bibliography will guide such beginngers to *basic* titles and enable them to judge other works accordingly, and to become acquainted with the most important *secondary* works.

A selective bibliography such as this is always open to the criticism that it should have included such and such a title. Indeed, reviewers of the first and second editions pointed out at times important titles that were overlooked. An adjustment in this regard has been made in this revision, but I am still all too conscious of this difficulty. Part of the problem remains: Where to draw the line in the selection; what to eliminate and what to introduce. I continue to think, however, that my efforts will have been rewarded if "beginners" were to take two weeks out of their lives, bury themselves in a good library, and browse through the books listed below. Any professor would be happy to find such a "beginner" in his or her course.

The titles have been ordered under convenient headings: *Bibliographies, Periodicals, Series, Introductions*, etc. Under each heading there are often titles which are common to both the OT and the NT; they are followed by what is specifically related to each Testament. The titles have normally been ordered alphabetically in the subdivisions: the more important ones have been listed with an asterisk, and the most important with two asterisks. In many instances references are supplied to reviews of the book in question or to discussions of some aspect of it; they are intended as guides for further judgment about the book. Commonly used abbreviations have been inserted in the lefthand margin to familiarize the student with them.

A number of reviewers of the second edition thought that this bibliography was destined for English-speaking students, and especially for American students. I have tried to remedy this situation, as much as I could, by giving British publishers' names as well as American and by including foreign titles of works translated — in many cases listing them at the head of the entry, when appropriate. I have also introduced a section on the French, German, Italian, and Spanish translations of the Bible. I want to thank in particular professors at the Biblical Institute in Rome (J.-N. Aletti, J. O'Callaghan, and K. Plötz), who sent me suggestions and comments which I have tried to use. A number of reviewers pointed out that some references should have been given to standard works in the study of Phoenician, Ugaritic, Akkadian, and Northwest Semitic languages related to the interpretation of the OT. Again, I have tried to introduce a limited number of such works.

I am indebted to the many reviewers of the second edition who pointed out ways in which to improve the book; a list of the reviews of that edition is found at the end of the book. I am also grateful to many persons who took the time to write to me privately with still further suggestions. I have had the pleasure of consulting many colleagues in the preparation of this third edition. It is my pleasant duty to acknowledge my debt to them: to F. T. Gignac, J. Jensen, A. E. Fitzgerald, of the Catholic University of America; E. W. Bodnar and W. J. Burghardt, of Georgetown University; J. R. Donahue, of the Jesuit School of Theology at Berkeley; P. J. King, of Boston College; E. Rooney, of the Woodstock Theological Center Library, and H. J. Bertels, now of the Biblical Institute Library in Rome. In a special way I am indebted to James Swetnam, of the Biblical Institute, to J. P. M. Walsh, of Georgetown University, who commented on earlier drafts of this revision, and to J. S. Kselman, of Weston School of Theology. I only hope that I have listened correctly to all of them and not garbled their advice.

I shall be grateful to readers of this bibliography who would be kind enough to bring to my attention errors and omissions — as well as ways in which it might still be improved in future revisions.

I hope that this third edition will achieve at least a modicum of the success of the earlier editions. Years ago it was called to my attention by B. M. Metzger, of the Princeton Theological Seminary, that the first edition eventually found its way into a bibliography on the "Bible" in *Bolshaya sovyetskaya entsiklopediya* (Moscow) 3 (1970) 929 (cf. *Great Soviet Encyclopedia* [3d ed.; New York: Macmillan; London: Collier Macmillan, 1973], 3. 249). The bibliography on the "Bible" is headed by K. Marx and F. Engels, *O religii*, and includes O. Eissfeldt's *Introduction* to the OT and W. G. Kümmel's *Introduction* to the NT. This was probably an early manifestation of *Glasnost!*

JOSEPH A. FITZMYER, S.J.
Professor emeritus, Biblical Studies
The Catholic University of America
Washington, DC

Resident at the Jesuit Community
Georgetown University
Washington, DC 20057

List of Abbreviations

For the abbreviations of periodicals, see § 39-90. The standard abbreviations for periodicals, series, and commonly-used (reference) books employed in this bibliography have been adopted by such biblical and theological periodicals as *CBQ* (38 [1976] 446-53), *JBL* (95 [1976] 339-46), *OTA* (1 [1978] 321-28), *TS* (38 [1977] 221-28). The list is repeated each year in the October issue of the *CBQ* and *OTA*. Others not found in the latter list will be explained below. Unabbreviated one-word titles are not listed here. The number following the title in parentheses refers to paragraphs of this book.

AJP	*American Journal of Philology*
ANHW	*Aramäisch-neuhebräisches Handwörterbuch zu Targum, Talmud und Midrasch* (§ 221)
ANTF	Arbciten zur neutestamentlichen Textforschung
APAT	*Die Apokryphen und Pseudepigraphen des Alten Testaments* (§ 559)
APh	*L'Année philologique* (§ 33)
ASAB	*Altjüdisches Schrifttum ausserhalb der Bibel* (§ 561)
AV	*Authorized Version* (= *KJV*)
BAC	Biblioteca de autores cristianos
BAGD	Bauer–Arndt–Gingrich–Danker (§ 225)
B–A	Bauer–Aland (§ 224)
BB	Die Bonnerbibel (§ 399)
BBih	*Bibliographie biblique* (§ 1)
BE	*The Books of Enoch* (§ 548)
BenMon	*Benediktinische Monatsschrift*
BHEAT	Bulletin d'histoire ct d'exégèse de l'Ancien Testament (§ 91)
BJHIL	*Bibliographie zur jüdisch-hellenistischen und intertestamentarischen Literatur* (§ 528)
BL	*Book List* (§ 7)
BNTB	*A Bibliography of New Testament Bibliographies* (§ 15)
DNTC	Black's New Testament Commentaries (§ 405)
CAH	*Cambridge Ancient History* (§ 515)
CahRB	Cahiers de la *RB* (§ 91)
CahThéol	Cahiers théologiques (§ 91)
CBLAA	*Classified Bibliography of Literature of the Acts of the Apostles* (§ 23)
CCD	Confraternity of Christian Doctrine Version (§ 183)
CCHS	*Catholic Commentary of Holy Scripture* (§ 373)
CGL	Coptic Gnostic Library (§ 591)
CGTC	Cambridge Greek Testament Commentary (§ 406)
CHB	*Cambridge History of the Bible* (§ 92)
DBSup	F. Vigouroux, *Dictionnaire de la Bible, Supplément* (§ 318)

DKP	*Der kleine Pauly* (§ 343)
DSSHU	*The Dead Sea Scrolls of Hebrew University* (§ 545)
DSSMM	*The Dead Sea Scrolls of St. Mark's Monastery* (§ 542)
EBB	*Elenchus bibliographicus biblicus* (§ 3)
EtClass	*Etudes classiques* (§ 89)
EWNT	*Exegetisches Wörterbuch zum Neuen Testament* (§ 335)
Expos	*Expositor* (§ 89)
FENHC	Facsimile Edition of the Nag Hammadi Codices (§ 589)
FF	*Forschungen und Fortschritte* (§ 89)
GAT	Grundrisse zum Alten Testament (§ 91)
GB	Gesenius–Buhl (§ 214)
GGPP	*Grammatik der griechischen Papyri aus der Ptolomäerzeit* (§ 275)
GNB, GNBDA	*Good News Bible (with Deuterocanonicals/Apocrypha)* (§ 188)
HSAT	Die Heilige Schrift des Alten Testaments (§ 399)
HSNTA	Hennecke–Schneemelcher, *New Testament Apocrypha* (§ 577)
HZ	*Historische Zeitschrift* (§ 89)
IATG	*Internationales Abkürzungsverzeichnis für Theologie und Grenzgebiete* (§ 38)
IBSS	*Introductory Bibliography for the Study of Scripture* (this book)
IPLAP	*Index to Periodical Literature on the Apostle Paul* (§ 25)
IPLCG	*Index to Periodical Literature on Christ and the Gospels* (§ 18)
IZBG	*Internationale Zeitschriftenschau für Bibelwissenschaft und Grenzgebiete* (§ 4)
JANT	M. R. James, *The Apocryphal New Testament* (§ 578)
JRS	*Journal of Roman Studies* (§ 89)
JSHRZ	Jüdische Schriften aus hellenistisch-römischer Zeit (§ 558)
JSNTSup	*JSNT* Supplements (§ 91)
JSOTSup	*JSOT* Supplements (§ 91)
KEK	Kritisch-exegetischer Kommentar über das Neue Testament (§ 411)
KirSeph	*Kirjath-Sepher*
LCL	Loeb Classical Library
LGNT	F. Zorell, *Lexicon graecum Novi Testamenti* (§ 226)
LHAVT	F. Zorell, *Lexicon Hebraicum et aramaicum Veteris Testamenti* (§ 216)
LR	*Lutherische Rundschau*
LumVie	*Lumière et vie*
MM	Moulton–Milligan, *Vocabulary of the Greek Testament* (§ 228)
MPAT	*Manual of Palestinian Aramaic Texts* (§ 676)
MT	Masoretic Text
NCB	New Century Bible (§ 386)
NHS	Nag Hammadi Studies (§ 590)
NICNT	New International Commentary on the New Testament (§ 414)
NICOT	New International Commentary on the Old Testament (§ 401)
NIDNTT	*New International Dictionary of New Testament Theology* (§ 336)
NIV	*New International Version* (§ 185)
NJV	*New Jewish Version* (§ 187)
NT	New Testament
NTB	C. K. Barrett, *New Testament Background* (§ 678)
OABWA	*Oxford Annotated Bible with the Apocrypha* (§ 182b)

OCD	*Oxford Classical Dictionary* (§ 344)
OSENEBWA	*Oxford Study Edition: New English Bible with the Apocrypha* (§ 186)
OT	Old Testament
OTL	Old Testament Library (§ 402)
PGL	*A Patristic Greek Lexicon* (§ 231)
PNTC	Pelican New Testament Commentaries (§ 416)
PTR	*Princeton Theological Review*
PW	Pauly–Wissowa (§ 342)
RE	*Realencyclopädie* (= PW, § 342)
REG	*Revue des études grecques*
RHW	*Rückläufiges hebräisches Wörterbuch* (§ 223)
RL	*Religion in Life*
RSVCB	*RSV*, Common Bible edition (§ 182a)
RSVCE	*RSV*, Catholic edition (§ 182c)
RTAM	*Revue de théologie ancienne et médiévale*
SBA	Studies in Biblical Archaeology (§ 91)
SBJ	*La sainte Bible de Jérusalem* (§ 189)
ScEccl	*Sciences ecclésiastiques*
SCHNT	Studia ad corpus hellenisticum Novi Testamenti (§ 705)
ScrHier	Scripta hierosolymitana (§ 91)
SPIB	Scripta Pontificii Instituti Biblici
TBC	Torch Bible Commentaries (§ 392)
TBLNT	*Theologisches Begriffslexikon zum Neuen Testament* (§ 336)
TDOT	*Theological Dictionary of the Old Testament* (§ 330)
THAT	*Theologisches Handwörterbuch zum Alten Testament* (§ 331)
TPQ	*Theologisch praktische Quartalschrift*
TynNTC	Tyndale New Testament Commentaries (§ 419)
TynOTC	Tyndale Old Testament Commentaries (§ 403)
ZAPNTG	M. Zerwick, *Analysis philologica Novi Testamenti graeci* (§ 272)
ZBG	M. Zerwick, *Biblical Greek* (§ 271)
ZGB	M. Zerwick, *Graecitas biblica* (§ 271)

Abbreviations of USA State-Names Used in Bibliographical References

AK	Alaska	IA	Iowa	MT	Montana	RI	Rhode Island
AL	Alabama	ID	Idaho	NB	Nebraska	SC	South Carolina
AR	Arkansas	IL	Illinois	NC	North Carolina	SD	South Dakota
AZ	Arizona	IN	Indiana	ND	North Dakota	TN	Tennessee
CA	California	KS	Kansas	NH	New Hampshire	TX	Texas
CO	Colorado	KY	Kentucky	NJ	New Jersey	UT	Utah
CT	Connecticut	LA	Lousiana	NM	New Mexico	VA	Virginia
DC	District of	MA	Massachusetts	NV	Nevada	VI	Virgin Islands
	Columbia	MD	Maryland	NY	New York	VT	Vermont
DE	Delaware	ME	Maine	OH	Ohio	WA	Washington
FL	Florida	MI	Michigan	OK	Oklahoma	WI	Wisconsin
GA	Georgia	MN	Minnesota	OR	Oregon	WV	West Virginia
GU	Guam	MO	Missouri	PA	Pennsylvania	WY	Wyoming
HI	Hawaii	MS	Mississippi	PR	Puerto Rico		

CHAPTER I

Bibliographies

In this initial chapter guidance is given to general bibliographic tools. Much of what is to be found in the rest of this book can be found in such bibliographies as are listed here. The aim is to introduce the bibliography of bibliographies on the Bible and on related general areas. References will be supplied below to more specific bibliographies on certain topics, as occasion arises. In this chapter guidance is given to (A) biblical bibliographies, (B) OT bibliographies, (C) NT bibliographies, and (D) related general bibliographies.

A. Biblical Bibliographies

BBib   **1.** **Langevin, P.-E. (ed.), *Bibliographie biblique. Biblical Bibliography. Biblische Bibliographie. Bibliografia biblica. Bibliografia biblica I: 1930-1970* (Quebec: L'Université Laval, 1972); *II: 1930-1975* (1978); *III: 1930-1983* (1985). With these stout tomes biblical bibliography has entered the computer age. Volume I analyzes the contents of 70 Roman Catholic periodicals written in English, French, German, Italian, Portuguese, and Spanish and containing biblical studies, as well as "a certain number" of Roman Catholic books published on the Bible in the same forty years. It contains 21294 entries. Volume II analyzes the contents of the same 70 Roman Catholic periodicals for the years 1970-1975 and adds entries from 50 other, non-Roman-Catholic journals from 1930-1975 as well as from 812 books published in the same period, of which 325 are of the *Mélanges/Festschrift* sort. In vol. II the entries are numbered from 21295 to 54510. Volume III covers the years 1976-1983 for the same 120 periodicals analyzed in vols. I and II, but it adds the contents of 43 other journals from 1930 to 1983. These new journals deal in large part with ancient Near Eastern archaeology, epigraphy, geography, history, and philology. Volume III further analyzes contributions or articles in 450 books, of which 250 are again of the *Mélanges/Festschrift* sort; many other useful books are likewise analyzed. The entries in vol. III span from a1 to a18604 and from b1 to b17399. The advantage of these volumes is to give quick access to information that one would otherwise have to dig out of the *Elenchus bibliographicus biblicus* (§ 3) year by year. However, the Langevin volumes do not completely replace the *EBB*, which lists reviews of books and much other useful information that these volumes do not contain. *BBib* has introductions in five languages (those of the title) and elaborate indices, which enhance the value of this excellent bibliographic tool. Any work of this sort suffers from a certain amount of inaccuracy; references and titles should always be checked.

See *TS* 40 (1979) 345-47; 47 (1986) 301-3; *CBQ* 35 (1973) 540-41; 42 (1980) 244; *HeyJ* 21 (1980) 111; *JBL* 92 (1973) 312-13; 99 (1980) 125-26; *TRev* 76 (1980) 100-103.

MBTY   **2.** Malamat, A. and H. Reviv, *Mdryk byblywgr'py ltwldwt yśr'l btqwpt hmqr': A Bibliography of the Biblical Period, with Emphasis on Publications in Modern Hebrew* (rev. ed.; Jerusalem: Academon, Hebrew University, 1973). This bibliography first appeared in 1963 and surveys the areas of biblical archaeology, geography, and history and their relations to the ancient Near East in general. Though emphasis is put on publications in modern Hebrew, many of the titles in the bibliography are in European languages.

See *BO* 21 (1964) 256; *Bib* 45 (1964) 462.

EBB   **3.** **Nober, P., *Elenchus bibliographicus biblicus* (Rome: Biblical Institute, 1968-   ). P. Nober died in 1980; since then R. North has compiled *EBB*, having already begun to collaborate with Nober before his death. This extremely valuable index to biblical literature and its secondary material was originally part of the periodical *Biblica* (§ 41), entitled simply "Elenchus bibliographicus." As of *Bib* 49, the elenchus had become so vast in itself that it had to be given an independent existence. For 1968 alone it listed 8879 items. *EBB* appears yearly, but it is always a few years behind the current year. As of 1985, its name has been slightly altered: *Elenchus of Biblica 1985* (appearing in 1988). There are no summaries or abstracts, but *EBB* does list the reviews of books in many languages. Students should learn to make the most of this comprehensive elenchus and its rich indices. The only drawback is that one has to consult it for each year on a given topic. But once the section of the *EBB* is discovered in which one is interested, one finds the same subdivision in it each year (e.g., Matthean materials will be found under section X. Evangelia: 2. Matthaeus; or in the new *Elenchus* under X. Evangelia synoptica, F3). The person who uses the *EBB* for the first time would do well to read the article "Elenchus Elucidated, Or: How to Find Things in Elenchus Bibliographicus," *EBB* 57 (1976) xlvi-xlviii.

IZBG   **4.** *Stier, F. (ed.), *Internationale Zeitschriftenschau für Bibelwissenschaft und Grenzgebiete* (Düsseldorf: Patmos). Begun in 1951, this survey of periodical articles on the Bible and related areas appears yearly. It is a good supplement to articles listed in *EBB* (§ 3). The editor is aided by a team of abstracters, who write in various modern languages. Though the quality of the abstracts varies, the student should not be deterred from using this work simply by the German title. It is similar to *NTA* and *OTA*. In more recent years B. Lang has been the editor.

See *TS* 21 (1960) 133-35.

BYBSL   **5.** Kiehl, E. H., *Building Your Biblical Studies Library: A Survey of Current Resources* (St. Louis, MO: Concordia, 1988). This book provides information and annotated bibliographies on 15 areas of biblical studies: text of the OT; text of the NT; OT grammars, lexica, concordances; NT grammars, lexica, concordances; English versions of the Bible; English concordances, dictionaries, encyclopedias; commentaries; hermeneutics; introductions and Bible history; biblical theology; theological topics; Judaica; geographical resources and atlases; archaeology; culture and society.

BTBE   **6.** Marrow, S. B., *Basic Tools of Biblical Exegesis: A Student's Manual* (Subsidia biblica 2; 2d ed.; Rome: Biblical Institute, 1978). An excellent but brief introductory bibliography for the study of the Bible; in many ways it has sought to accomplish what the first edition of the present bibliography did and has been a welcome substitute for the latter, when it was no longer available. Its main purpose is to help students beginning exegetical work, whether in preparation for the ministry, as part of theological study, or in the technical study of the Bible. Its brief compass, listing some 215 entries, admirably enables students to get a firsthand acquaintance with basic tools.

See *TS* 38 (1977) 196-99; *CBQ* 41 (1979) 164-65.

B. OT Bibliographies

BL   **7.** Rowley, H. H. (ed.), *Eleven Years of Bible Bibliography: The Book Lists of the Society for Old Testament Study 1946-56* (Indian Hills, CO: Falcon's Wing, 1957). A collection of the issues of *Book List* (1946-56), which were prepared for the members of SOTS in England. It is a descriptive and critical bibliography of a large number of books on the OT and closely related fields. It is being continued yearly by *Book List*, which was edited by G. W. Anderson from 1957 to 1966; see his collected volume, *A Decade of Bible Bibliography* (Oxford: Blackwell, 1967). See further P. R. Ackroyd, *Bible Bibliography 1967-1973: Old Testament* (Oxford: Blackwell, 1974). From 1974-79 the editor of *Book List* has been R. N. Whybray of the University of Hull; from 1980-85, M. A. Knibb of King's College, London; from 1986-89, A. G. Auld of New College, Edinburgh. *BL* appears yearly (London: SOTS).

OTBPT   **8.** Childs, B. S., *Old Testament Books for Pastor and Teacher* (Philadelphia, PA: Westminster, 1977). Recommendations are made about the OT text and its translations, about introductions to the OT, its history, and theology. About half of the book (54 pages) is devoted to an evaluation of commentaries on the OT from all periods. This is a helpful tool for OT study.

See *CBQ* 40 (1978) 235-36; *JBL* 97 (1978) 441; *BL* (1978) 11.

OTA   **9.**   ****Old Testament Abstracts.** Published three times a year by the Catholic Biblical Association of America (Washington, DC 20064), it drew its inspiration from the success of *NTA* (§ 14). The first issue appeared in Feb. 1978. Its coverage is now almost the equal of *NTA*. It records and abstracts periodical literature on the OT, its background, archaeology, philology, and theology. It also includes brief notices of books recently published on OT topics.

See *BL* (1979) 24; (1980) 23.

10.   *OT/ANE Permucite Index* (ed. W. T. Claassen; Stellenbosch: Infodex, 1978-   ). This is an exhaustive interdisciplinary indexing system for OT and ancient Near Eastern studies; it is something of a tour de force, but it is useful at times.

C. NT Bibliographies

BibBk   **11.**   Hort, Erasmus (penname), *The Bible Book: Resources for Reading the New Testament* (New York: Crossroad, 1983). The subtitle is more accurate than the main title, for the book is designed to introduce the reader to the study of the NT. It lists and evaluates background books, English versions of the NT, concordances, Greek grammars, dictionaries, encyclopedias, atlases, geographies, books on NT archaeology, handbooks, and commentaries. It concludes with a "Wise Buyer's Guide" and chart giving titles and comparative prices. This is a useful NT handbook, though confined almost exclusively to English titles.

BGNTR   **12.**   France, R. T. (ed.), *A Bibliographic Guide to New Testament Research* (Sheffield, UK: JSOT Press, 1979). This is an annotated brief guide similar to *IBSS*, but it "has been produced primarily with a view to the British scene. English translations of foreign works are listed, where they exist, and the editions cited are British rather than American" (pp. 3-4).

See *RelStRev* 7 (1981) 162.

SVWF   **13.**   Gaffron, H.-G. and H. Stegemann, *Systematisches Verzeichnis der wichtigsten Fachliteratur für das Theologiestudium: Vorausdruck für das Einzelfach Neues Testament gemäss dem Stand im Frühjahr 1966* (Bonn: H. Bouvier u. Co., 1966). A brief annotated list of the essential works to be consulted in the study of the NT, evaluated by the use of circles, crosses, and asterisks for students of varying levels. The data are booked under the following headings: introduction to theological study; commonly used reference works; bibliographies; technical periodicals; editions of the text (of the OT and NT); philological aids (lexica, concordances, grammars); textual transmission of the NT; introductions to the NT; commentaries (in series; major commentaries on individual NT books); standard monographs; collected essays; the NT world.

NTA **14.** **New Testament Abstracts*. Published three times a year by Weston School of Theology (Cambridge, MA 02138), this journal records and abstracts all periodical literature on the NT, its backgrounds, world, and theology. Its abstracts of the most important articles composed in all modern languages are written in English. It also lists in the back, with brief comments about contents, almost all the major books published in the area of NT studies. It is a journal to which every serious student of the Bible or of Christian theology should subscribe. It is subsidized by the Society of Jesus in the U.S.A. and published in cooperation with the Catholic Biblical Association of America. After two experimental issues (one multilithed in Jan. 1956; one printed in May 1956), the first formal issue appeared in the fall of 1956 (vol. 1, no. 1). A cumulative index to vols. 1-15 (1956-71) was published in 1974. The present editor is D.J. Harrington, assisted by a managing and associate editor and a capable staff of abstracters.

See P. Henry, *New Directions in New Testament Study* (Philadelphia, PA: Westminster, 1979) 293

BNTB **15.** Hurd, J.C., Jr., *A Bibliography of New Testament Bibliographies* (New York: Seabury, 1966). Intended to "enable the student to find in the shortest possible time the considerable help which the bibliographies of the New Testament literature afford." The contents of this work include: selective book lists; historical and chronological surveys; comprehensive (research) bibliographies (on the whole NT, on individual books or sections of the NT, on NT words, on special subjects or areas; and on related areas of study). An important final part of this bibliography tells where one can find biographies and bibliographies of modern NT scholars. This is an invaluable work, well-organized, and highly instructive.

See *RB* 73 (1966) 636; *NTA* 11 (1966-67) 144.

IANTEC **16.** Metzger, B.M., *Index of Articles on the New Testament and the Early Church Published in Festschriften* (SBLMS 5; Philadelphia, PA: Society of Biblical Literature, 1951; with a supplement, 1955). A useful index to articles which are often important, but overlooked because they have been "buried" in the limited editions of *Mélanges, Festschriften*, etc.

See *ATR* 33 (1951) 261-62; *ETL* 32 (1956) 87; *RB* 59 (1952) 285-86.

EBNT   **17.**   *Wagner, G. (ed.), *An Exegetical Bibliography of the New Testament* (Macon, GA: Mercer University). Three volumes of this excellent bibliography have appeared so far: *I. Matthew and Mark* (1983); *II. Luke and Acts* (1985); *III. Johannine Writings* (1987). They list interpretations of passages, according to chapter and verse, culled from biblical journals and monographs. The bibliography appeared earlier in card-form (from 1973 on). The compiler is professor of NT at the Baptist Theological Seminary, Rüschlikon, Switzerland.

See *NTA* 21 (1977) 321; *ETL* 65 (1989) 164-66.

IPLCG   **18.**   Metzger, B. M. (ed.), *Index to Periodical Literature on Christ and the Gospels* (NTTS 6: Leiden: Brill, 1966). The counterpart to Metzger's *IPLAP* (§ 25) for the study of the Gospels. It contains 10,090 entries, drawn from 160 periodicals from their inception to the end of 1961 and written in 16 different languages. The main headings under which the entries are booked are the following: bibliographical articles on Christ and the Gospels; historical studies of the life of Jesus; critical studies of the Gospels (textual criticism, literary criticism, form-criticism, *Religionsgeschichte*, demythologization, philological studies, critical and exegetical studies of individual passages in the Gospels, and the Gospels in the NT canon); early non-canonical literature related to Christ and the Gospels; theological studies concerning Jesus Christ and the Gospels (studies classified according to NT books; according to topics); influence and interpretation of Jesus Christ and the Gospels in worship, fine arts, and culture in general. This is an indispensable, but dated, tool for the study of the Gospels.

See *TS* 28 (1967) 140-41; *RB* 73 (1966) 633-34.

JSG   **19.**   Aune, D. E., *Jesus and the Synoptic Gospels: A Bibliographic Study Guide* (Madison, WI: Inter-Varsity Christian Fellowship, 1980). An annotated guide to literature on the various ways of studying the relation of Jesus to the Synoptic Gospels. After an introduction (which lists the basic reference works), the select bibliography is booked under the following headings: literary criticism, tradition criticism, historical criticism, and the theological study of the Gospels. This is the first of a new series of such study-guides; others are to be devoted to Pauline literature, second-century Christianity, intertestamental Judaism, and pentateuchal studies.

See *CBQ* 44 (1982) 504-5.

20. Humphrey, H. M., *A Bibliography for the Gospel of Mark: 1954-1980* (Studies in the Bible and Early Christianity 1; New York/Toronto: Mellen, 1981).

See *RB* 89 (1982) 462.

SJG   **21.** Malatesta, E., *St. John's Gospel 1920-1965: A Cumulative and Classified Bibliography of Books and Periodical Literature on the Fourth Gospel* (AnBib 32; Rome: Biblical Institute, 1967).

See *Bib* 49 (1968) 584-85; *CBQ* 30 (1968) 462-63; *NRT* 90 (1968) 679-80; *RB* 75 (1968) 476.

JohBib   **22.** Van Belle, G., *Johannine Bibliography, 1966-1985* (BETL 82; Louvain: Leuven University, 1988). A bibliographical survey that continues that of E. Malatesta (§ 21).

See *ETL* 65 (1989) 164-66.

CBLAA   **23.** *Mattill, A. J., Jr. and M. B. Mattill (eds.), *A Classified Bibliography of Literature on the Acts of the Apostles* (NTTS 7; Leiden: Brill; Grand Rapids, MI: Ecrdmans, 1966). In general, this bibliography resembles those of B. M. Metzger, *IPLAP* and *IPLCG* (§ 18, 25). It lists 6,646 entries, drawn from 180 periodicals from their inception to the end of 1961 and written in "nearly a score of languages." *CBLAA* differs from the two Metzger bibliographies in that it is not limited to periodical literature, but includes titles of NT introductions and theologies, book reviews, homiletic and devotional works, and dictionary articles. It attempts to "include everything else of scholarly interest that deals with Acts... from the time of the Church Fathers through 1961." Its entries are booked under the following main headings: bibliographic studies, general studies, textual studies, philological studies, literary studies, form-critical studies, historical studies, theological studies, and exegetical studies of individual passages.

See *TS* 28 (1967) 140-41; *RB* 73 (1966) 634-35.

BPLAA   **24.** *Mills, W. E., *A Bibliography of the Periodical Literature on the Acts of the Apostles 1962-1984* (NovTSup 58; Leiden: Brill, 1986). This book picks up the bibliography of periodical literature on Acts from where *CBLAA* (§ 23) left of in 1961. It is limited to periodical articles and is not classified; the arrangement is rather alphabetical by authors.

IPLAP   **25.** Metzger, B. M. (ed.), *Index to Periodical Literature on the Apostle Paul* (NTTS 1; Leiden: Brill; Grand Rapids, MI: Eerdmans, 1960). An excellent (though not exhaustive) bibliography of 2987 articles on the Pauline corpus (13 letters) found in 114 periodicals from their inception to the end of 1957. The entries are grouped conveniently under useful subject headings: bibliographical articles on Paul, historical studies on the life of Paul, critical studies on Pauline literature (broken down according to the individual letters), Pauline apocrypha, theological studies, history of the interpretation of Paul and his letters. This is an indispensable, but dated, tool for the study of the Pauline corpus.

See *TS* 21 (1960) 643-44; *CBQ* 23 (1961) 102-3.

D. Related General Bibliographies

ETLEB   **26.** "Elenchus Bibliographicus" of *Ephemerides theologicae lovanienses*. This is an elaborate bibliography of all theological disciplines. It has a good section on biblical materials and is very useful for the student of Scripture.

IFJS   **27.** Berlin, C., *Index to Festschriften in Jewish Studies* (Cambridge, MA: Harvard College Library; New York [now Hoboken, NJ]: Ktav, 1971). The entries in 243 *Festschriften* have been analyzed and are indexed here not only according to the name of the author of the article, but also according to its subject. Thus one finds more than a dozen articles listed under "Jesus" (p. 225).

See *JBL* 91 (1972) 277-78.

28. "Bibliographie sémitique," *Or* (§ 90). These bibliographies appeared at varying intervals and covered the literature of Northwest Semitic languages. Though the range of them is wider than the interests of most biblical students, they contain references to important extrabiblical materials relating mostly to the OT. Four were prepared by S. Moscati: *Or* 16 (1947) 103-29; 17 (1948) 91-102; 19 (1950) 445-78; 22 (1953) 1*-38*; three by G. Garbini, *Or* 26 (1957) 50*-1115*; 28 (1959) 59*-90*; 30 (1961) 42*-61*; one by P. Matthiae, *Or* 32 (1963) 83*-113*; and one by M. Liverani and P. Matthiae, *Or* 33 (1964) 79*-123*. Unfortunately, no followup of this useful bibliography has appeared in the last years. In its stead one can consult the following entry.

29. Teixdor, J., "Bulletin d'épigraphie sémitique," *Syria* 44 (1967) 163-95; 45 (1968) 353-89; 46 (1969) 319-58; 47 (1970) 357-89; 48 (1971) 453-93; 49 (1972) 413-49; 50 (1973) 401-42; 51 (1974) 299-340; 52 (1975) 261-95; 53 (1976) 305-41; 54 (1977) 251-76; 56 (1979) 353-405. These articles of Teixidor are more than a mere bibliography, being actually a survey that discusses the contents of articles. They have been reprinted in one volume, *Bulletin d'épigraphie sémitique (1964-1980)* (Institut français d'archéologie du Proche Orient — Bibliothèque archéologique et historique 126; Paris: Geuthner, 1986). The articles of *Syria* have been reprinted as they are, but there are addenda and corrigenda (pp. 467-92) and an index of inscriptions cited. It is thus a very useful volume.

CBEBAF   **30.**   **Catalogue de la Bibliothèque de l'Ecole Biblique et Archéologique Française* (13 vols.; Boston: G. K. Hall & Co., 1975). This is a photographic reproduction of the catalogue-cards of the holdings of the library of the Ecole Biblique, which began in 1890 and has specialized holdings of over 50,000 books dealing with the Bible, Palestine, ancient Near Eastern archaeology and geography, as well as with Northwest Semitic epigraphy and philology. Since the Ecole Biblique was the centre of much work done on the Dead Sea Scrolls, its library has all the major publications relating to them. Its catalogue-cards also list secondary literature on the Bible according to books, chapters, and verses; for this reason alone, this catalogue is invaluable. Finally, not only books but articles from journals are included, arranged by author and by subject matter. It was reprinted by the Ecole Biblique in reduced form and with added material (up to 1985) in 12 volumes (1986). Some copies are apparently still available from J. Gabalda, Paris.

COIL   **31.**   **Catalogue of the Oriental Institute Library, University of Chicago* (16 vols.; Boston: G. K. Hall & Co., 1970). A photographic reproduction of the catalogue-cards of the holdings of this famous library, which has so many books and periodicals pertaining to the backgrounds of both the OT and the NT.

BBSSL   **32.**   Hospers, J. H. (ed.), *A Basic Bibliography for the Study of the Semitic Languages* (2 vols.; Leiden: Brill, 1973, 1974). The editor was aided by a team of colleagues in putting this bibliography together. Volume 1 covers Semitic (and other) languages in general (e.g., Sumerian, Akkadian, Anatolian tongues, Hurrian, Urartian, Elamite, Old Persian, Ugaritic, Phoenician-Punic, Amarna-Canaanite, Hebrew, Syriac and Aramaic, South Arabic, Ethiopic); vol. 2 is devoted to Arabic. The bibliography is, however, limited, but the biblical student will at times find things in it that are hard to come by otherwise.

See *JSS* 19 (1974) 269-75.

APh   **33.**   **Marouzeau, J. (ed.), *L'Année philologique: Bibliographie critique et analytique de l'antiquité gréco-latine* (Paris: Société d'édition "Les Belles-Lettres"). Begun in 1928 with a survey of the years 1924-1926 as a supplement to the editor's *Dix années de bibliographie classique 1914-24* (1927-28), it is an important tool (for the NT student in particular), since it covers several areas in which biblical topics and classical subjects overlap. Consult especially the entries under such headings as *Testamenta, Testamentum vetus, Testamentum novum, Archéologie non-classique*. Recent volumes often include materials from earlier years, which may have been overlooked.

AAF   **34.** Rounds, D., *Articles on Antiquity in Festschriften: The Ancient Near East, the Old Testament, Greece, Rome, Roman Law, Byzantium: An Index* (Cambridge, MA: Harvard University, 1962). This invaluable index of articles is based on 1178 *Festschriften* from the years 1863-1954. The student will profit much from the appendix, "Dealing with Festschriften," pp. 549-60.

See *Bib* 44 (1963) 246-47; *JTS* 14 (1963) 573.

IARJHL   **35.** Schwab, M., *Index of Articles Relative to Jewish History and Literature Published in Periodicals, from 1665 to 1900* (rev. ed.; ed. Z. Szajkowski; New York [now Hoboken, NJ]: Ktav, 1971). This index first appeared in French as *Répertoire des articles relatifs à l'histoire et à la littérature juives, parus dans les périodiques, de 1665 à 1900* between 1914 and 1923. It has been augmented and fitted out with a list of abbreviations. It contains many references to older literature on the OT and rabbinic writings.

See *JBL* 91 (1972) 277-78.

BJB   **36.** Shunami, S., *Bibliography of Jewish Bibliographies* (2d ed.; Jerusalem: Magnes, 1965; supplement to the 2d ed., 1975). In 27 chapters all conceivable aspects of Jewish life are categorized, with several of them explicitly devoted to topics of interest to the biblical student. Entries are found in all modern languages. Comments on the entries are provided in English.

See *TLZ* 91 (1966) 350.

DPL   **37.** Thomsen, P. (ed.), *Die Palästina-Literatur* (Berlin: Akademie). This monumental work was issued in six volumes (1908-56), covering bibliographical items from 1895-1939. The manuscript of a seventh volume, covering 1940-45, was prepared and published in 1972. After Thomsen's death in 1954, L. Rost and F. Maass supervised the publication of vol. 6. In 1957-1958, Rost and O. Eissfeldt published two parts of a volume (Band A [appeared 1960]), which had been prepared by Thomsen covering the years 1878-1894. The bibliography embraces the whole range of literature on Palestine, including modern Palestine. Though much of the material will not interest the biblical student, the work is indispensable for reference to older materials.

IATG   **38.** Schwertner, S., *Internationales Abkürzungsverzeichnis für Theologie und Grenzgebiete: Zeitschriften, Serien, Lexika, Quellenwerke mit bibliographischen Angaben. International Glossary of Abbreviations*

*for Theology and Related Subjects: Periodicals, Series, Encyclo-
paedias, Sources with Bibliographical Notes. Index international
des abréviations pour la théologie et matières affinissantes: Périodiques, séries, dictionnaires, éditions de sources avec données biblio-
graphiques* (Berlin/New York: de Gruyter, 1974). An interesting
attempt to impose a uniform system of abbreviation on authors in
the area of theology and the Bible; unfortunately, the system is
too "European" for use by others (e.g., *ThWNT* [instead of
TWNT]); *HThR* [instead of *HTR*]).

See *JBL* 94 (1975) 641-42; *OLZ* 75 (1978) 464-66; *RTL* 6 (1975) 372;
ZAW 87 (1975) 260.

CHAPTER II

Periodicals

This chapter is intended to introduce the student to the most important periodicals in the realm of biblical studies and related areas. Periodicals are important because they are the normal means whereby scholars communicate with one another and disseminate ideas that are not yet developed enough for discussion in a book or monograph. The periodical titles listed below are grouped as (A) biblical, both (a) technical and (b) applied; (B) learned journals and theological periodicals; and (C) periodicals on Palestine and the ancient Near East. Much material pertinent to the study of Scripture is found in such journals as are listed under (B) and (C). Along with the titles will be found the sigla commonly used for them. The sigla are listed alphabetically for convenient consultation under each section. Comments will be made only on the biblical periodicals. See further J. Trinquet, "Revues bibliques," *DBSup* 10. 618-44 (a fuller annotated list of important journals and serials treating biblical topics).

A. Biblical

a. Technical

AusBR   **39.** *Australian Biblical Review* (Melbourne, 1951-   ). Published by the Fellowship for Biblical Studies, in conjunction with Melbourne University, Department of Semitic Studies. Language: English.

AUSS   **40.** *Andrews University Seminary Studies* (Berrien Springs, MI, 1963-   ). Published quarterly by professors of the Seventh-Day Adventist Seminary at Andrews University. Articles on both Testaments and related fields (often archaeological); reviews. Though some important articles have appeared in this journal, the quality is often uneven. Language: English.

Bib   **41.** **Biblica (Rome, 1920-   ). Published quarterly by the professors of the Pontifical Biblical Institute. Articles on both Testaments; shorter notes; reviews. Though the contributions have varied in quality, this has become a very important journal in the area of biblical studies. There is an *index generalis* for vols. 1-25 (A. Bürgi, 1944) and for vols. 26-50 (S. Marrow, 1969). The "Elenchus bibliographicus," which since 1949 has been greatly expanded and improved by P. Nober and R. North, is an indispensable tool. Until vol. 48 (1967) it was part of *Bib*; since 1968 it has appeared separately as *Elenchus bibliographicus biblicus*, and more recently as *Elenchus of Biblica* (§ 3). Languages: English, French, German, Italian, Latin, Spanish.

BM   **42.** *Beth Mikra* (Jerusalem, Israel, 1956-   ). Published by the World Jewish Bible Society, this publication contains articles on the OT in modern Hebrew.

BN   **43.** *Biblische Notizen* (Bamberg, Germany, 1976-   ). A periodical dedicated to short notes on a variety of OT and NT topics, published by professors of the University of Bamberg. Language: Usually German, occasionally English.

BR   **44.** *Biblical Research.* (Chicago, 1957-   ). Published once a year by the Chicago Society of Biblical Research. Articles on both Testaments. Of uneven quality; all the articles are written by members of the CSBR. Language: English.

BT   **45.** *The Bible Translator* (London, later Aberdeen, 1950-   ). Published by the United Bible Societies, this journal is dedicated to problems of translating the Bible into modern languages. Some of its articles are very technical discussions of the meanings of words, phrases, etc. Language: English, occasionally French.

BZ   **46.** **Biblische Zeitschrift* (Freiburg im B., 1903-39; F. Schöningh, Paderborn, 1957-   ). Published semiannually under the editorship of J. Schreiner (earlier V. Hamp) and R. Schnackenburg, it is the leading Roman Catholic biblical journal in the German-speaking world. The old series came to an end in 1939 (vol. 24); a new series (beginning with vol. 1) was started in 1957. Articles on both Testaments, shorter contributions, biblical news, and reviews. Languages: German, English, French.

CBQ   **47.** **Catholic Biblical Quarterly* (Washington, DC, 1939-   ). Published by the Catholic Biblical Association of America. Articles on both Testaments; shorter notes; biblical news; archaeological reports; reviews and short notices on books in the biblical field. In recent years the quality of the journal has greatly improved, and it has become an important biblical periodical. It has a supplementary monograph series, CBQMS (§ 91), and decennial indices. Language: Usually English, occasionally French. For the history of its founding, see G. P. Fogarty, *American Catholic Biblical Scholarship: A History from the Early Republic to Vatican II* (San Francisco, CA: Harper & Row, 1989) 222-80.

ConNT   **48.** *Coniectanea neotestamentica* (Uppsala, 1936-   ). Published sporadically by the NT Seminar of Uppsala University, at first under the direction of A. Fridrichsen. Some issues are monographs; some present a collection of articles by various NT scholars of the Scandinavian tradition. Languages: usually Swedish, occasionally German, French, and English.

DBM   **49.** *Deltio biblikōn meletōn* (Athens, Greece, 1971-   ). A Greek Orthodox periodical devoted to biblical studies. Language: Modern Greek.

EstBib   **50.** *Estudios bíblicos* (Madrid, 1929-   ). Published quarterly by the Association to Foster Biblical Studies in Spain (AFEBE). A series with new numbering began in July-Sept., 1941; vol. 1 represents 1941-42. Articles on both Testaments; shorter notes; reviews. This is the best of biblical journals for Spanish readers. Language: Spanish.

ExpTim   **51.** *Expository Times* (Edinburgh, 1889-   ). Though this journal is intended for more than biblical studies, it often includes many important articles of short compass. There are often good reviews in it.

FN   **52.** *Filología Neotestamentaria* (Córdoba, 1989-   ). Published twice a year by the Departamento de Ciencias de la Antigüedad y de la Edad Media of the University of Córdoba. It is a new journal devoted to all aspects of NT study (philology, textual criticism, lexicography, semantics, semiotics). It has also a monograph series, EFN (§91). Languages: Spanish and English.

IBS   **53.** *Irish Biblical Studies* (Belfast, Northern Ireland, 1979-   ). Published by Union Theological College, this is a new biblical periodical devoted to both OT and NT topics.

Int   **54.** **Interpretation: A Journal of Bible and Theology* (Richmond, VA, 1947-   ). Published quarterly under the editorship of professors of the Union Theological Seminary in Virginia, *Int* is a continuation of *Union Seminary Review*. Articles (exegetical, theological, and expository or homiletic) on both Testaments; reviews, shorter notices. The articles in a given issue are often grouped about one subject, having been written by invited scholars on a given topic. Some articles are of major importance. Language: English.

JBL   **55.** ***Journal of Biblical Literature* (Philadelphia, PA, 1881-   ). Published quarterly by the Society of Biblical Literature ([formerly] and Exegesis), the largest association of biblical scholars in the world. As of Sept. 1986, its place of publication has been changed (Scholars Press, for the SBL, Atlanta, GA). Articles on both Testaments; short notes; reviews; summaries of books of collected essays. The contents have varied in quality over the years; but it has greatly improved in the last decades. There are general indices: for vols. 1-20 (1881-1901), published 1901; for vols. 21-40 (1902-1921), published 1921; for vols. 41-60 (1922-

1941), published 1942; vols. 61-100 (1942-1981), published 1987. It has a supplementary monograph series, SBLMS (§91). Language: English, but occasionally there is a French or German contribution.

See *ETL* 63 (1987) 405.

JSNT   **56.** *Journal for the Study of the New Testament* (Sheffield, UK, 1978-   ). A new NT journal, published by the department of Biblical Studies of the University of Sheffield; its counterpart is *JSOT* (§57). It has a supplementary series of monographs, JSNTSup (§91). Articles and reviews. Language: English.

JSOT   **57.** *Journal for the Study of the Old Testament* (Sheffield, UK, 1976-   ). A new OT journal, published by the department of Biblical Studies of the University of Sheffield. Its NT counterpart is *JSNT* (§56). It too has a supplementary series of monographs, JSOTSup (§91). Articles and reviews. Language: English.

LB   **58.** *Linguistica biblica* (Bonn, Germany, 1970-   ). An interdisciplinary periodical for theology and linguistics.

NTS   **59.** ***New Testament Studies* (Cambridge, UK, 1954-   ). Published quarterly by Studiorum Novi Testamenti Societas, whose *Bulletin* it replaced (three issues of the latter had appeared: 1950, 1951, 1952 [reprinted in one volume, 1963]). Since *NTS* is the organ of the international NT society, its contributors are among the best in the field, representing all faiths. Articles on the NT and related areas (Dead Sea Scrolls, Gnosticism, Hellenistic and Semitic backgrounds, targumic and rabbinic literature); short studies; reviews on rare occasions. A cumulative index of vols. 1-31 (1954-85) and of the *Bulletin* I-III (1950-52), compiled by I. A. Moir, was published in 1986, with *NTS* 32. A list of members and their addresses appears once a year (usually in the second number). There is also a related monograph series, SNTSMS (§91). Languages: English, French, German.

NovT   **60.** *Novum Testamentum* (Leiden, 1956-   ). Published by E. J. Brill, it is a quarterly for NT studies intended for international cooperation. Its initial appearance was sporadic because it seemed to rival *NTS*; its contributions were at the outset very uneven, but it has improved in recent years. Articles; a few reviews. It was intended as the NT counterpart of *VT* (§67). It has a monograph series, NovTSup (§91). Languages: English, French, German.

RB   **61.** **Revue biblique (Paris, 1892-   ). Published quarterly by the Dominicans of L'Ecole pratique d'études bibliques in Jerusalem. After vol. 12 (1903) a new series was begun; this ran to vol. 16

(1919). In 1920 a fresh start was made; the previous collections of 12 and 16 volumes were counted as one series and continued by vol. 29 (1920). During the years 1941-45 the journal appeared under the title *Vivre et penser: Recherches d'exégèse et d'histoire* and ran through three series (= vols. 50-52). In 1946 *RB* was revived with vol. 53. Articles on both Testaments; chronicles of archaeological work in biblical lands; one or two long reviews; an important "Bulletin" of shorter reviews of significant books on both Testaments and allied fields (historical, philological, and archaeological). There exists a very useful additional volume, *Tables générales* (ed. J.-M. Rousée), which appeared in 1976 (Paris: Gabalda) and which contains 693 pages of lists of authors, books reviewed, and a subject index. It covers the period of 1892 to 1968. Language: French, occasionally English (in recent years).

RevQ   **62.** *Revue de Qumran (Paris, 1958-   ). A periodical devoted to studies of the Dead Sea Scrolls, begun by J. Carmignac, who died in 1986. It was published at first by Letouzey et Ané of Paris, but more recently by Gabalda. Its aim was to get scholars who write on the Scrolls to publish in one centralized organ, but it has not succeeded. It contains many articles that bear on biblical topics, because so much of the literature from the Qumran caves is either biblical or parabiblical. Each issue has a valuable bibliography; but the use of it is complicated, since the entries are listed neither alphabetically nor topically, but according to the journals from which they are drawn. Hence one has to page through every last item in the search for material relevant to some topic. However, the index helps in this regard.

RivB   **63.** *Rivista biblica* (Florence, Rome, more recently Brescia, 1953-   ). Published quarterly by the Italian Biblical Association. Articles on both Testaments; short notes, bulletins, reviews. The contributions are sometimes good, but often of uneven quality. Language: Italian.

SEA   **64.** *Svensk exegetisk årsbok* (Uppsala, 1936-   ). Really an annual devoted to exegetical studies of passages in both Testaments, representing the Scandinavian interpretation of them. Language: Usually Swedish, but occasionally English, French, or German.

Semeia   **65.** *Semeia: An Experimental Journal for Biblical Criticism* (Missoula, MT [now Atlanta, GA], 1974-   ). Originally published at irregular intervals, 47 nos. have appeared to date. Articles on both ˙Testaments, from new hermeneutical points of view, utilizing New Criticism, Structuralism, etc. The articles are often grouped about one topic but are uneven in quality. Language: English (some articles have been translated from foreign languages). It has a supplementary series, Semeia Supplements, later Semeia Studies (1975-   ).

SJOT   **66.** *Scandinavian Journal of the Old Testament* (Aarhus, 1987-   ).
           A new journal that publishes studies of OT professors from
           universities in Denmark, Finland, Iceland, Norway, and Sweden.
           Language: English.

VT   **67.** *Vetus Testamentum* (Leiden: Brill, 1951-   ). Published quarterly
           by the International Organization of Old Testament Scholars.
           Articles on OT and (occasionally) on Judaism of pre-Christian and
           early Christian centuries; short notes; reviews. The contributions
           vary greatly in quality. It has a series of supplementary volumes,
           VTSup (§91). Its NT counterpart is *NovT (§60)*. Languages:
           English, French, German.

ZAW   **68.** ***Zeitschrift für die alttestamentliche Wissenschaft* (Giessen, now
           Berlin, 1881-   ). Published semiannually by W. de Gruyter and
           edited by an international group of OT scholars; its main editors
           have been German. It was founded by B. Stade; in 1924 H.
           Gressmann and J. Hempel became the editors and started a new
           series (but the numbering of the volumes remained continuous).
           More recently O. Eissfeldt and G. Fohrer have been the editors.
           The current editor is O. Kaiser. For the years 1942-50 there were
           only four volumes (59-62); with vol. 63 (1951) regular publication
           resumed. Articles on the OT (including the deuterocanonical
           books), intertestamental literature, and Jewish literature of the
           pre-Christian and early Christian centuries; short notes; some
           reviews. A valuable section is devoted to abstracts of important
           OT publications in journals and collections. This is the most
           important German journal devoted to OT studies. 101 vols. have
           appeared to date. For an idea of what such a journal should be,
           see the inside back cover of vol. 71 (1959). It has a supplementary
           monograph series, BZAW (§91). Languages: German, English,
           occasionally French; summaries of articles are often appended in
           the other two languages.

ZNW   **69.** ***Zeitschrift für die neutestamentliche Wissenschaft und die Kunde
           des Urchristentums* [from 1921 on its title has been ... *und die
           Kunde der älteren Kirche*] (Giessen, now Berlin, 1900-   ).
           Published quarterly by W. de Gruyter (formerly A. Töpelmann)
           under the editorship of top-ranking German Protestant NT
           scholars, at first E. Preuschen, later H. Lietzmann, W. Bauer, J.
           Jeremias, E. Lohse; at present E. Grässer. Articles and short notes
           on NT and related fields; a useful "Zeitschriften Bibliographie"
           or "Zeitschriftenschau." The best of German Protestant NT
           contributions are found in this magazine; occasionally Roman
           Catholic scholars also contribute to it. 80 volumes of it have
           appeared to date. The two World Wars interrupted its publication
           somewhat: vols. 18-19 covered the years 1917-20; after vol. 41
           (1942), *ZNW* did not appear for six years; vol. 42 was issued in

1949, vol. 43 covered 1950-51; vol. 44, 1952-53. Since 1954 it has appeared regularly in double issues twice a year. It has a supplementary monograph series, BZNW (§ 91). Language: Usually German, occasionally English.

b. Applied

AsSeign   **70.** *Assemblée du Seigneur* (Paris, 1962-   ). Published by the Benedictine monks of the Abbey of St-André, Bruges, with the collaboration of professors of the Grand Séminaire de Lille, France, in fascicles devoted to the Sundays and feasts of the liturgical calendar, providing an exegetical treatment of the Scripture passages used in liturgical celebrations. Usually one fascicle for each week or major feast. Though the contributions are often uneven, occasionally some are of real value. With the reform of Roman Catholic liturgy, a new series (1968-1976) was instituted and published by Editions du Cerf of Paris. Language: French.

BA   **71.** **Biblical Archaeologist* (New Haven, CT, later Ann Arbor, MI, 1938-   ). Published quarterly by the American Schools of Oriental Research. Articles pertinent to both Testaments; occasionally reviews. An excellent bulletin, less technical than *BASOR* (§ 90), it aims to keep the reader abreast of current archaeological discovery, work, and interpretation, as these bear on the study of the Bible. As of vol. 39 (1976), a larger and improved format (8 ½″ × 11″) was adopted; its editorial office was moved to the University of Michigan, Ann Arbor, MI. Sometimes it contains translations of important essays from similar foreign periodicals. Language: English.

BARev   **72.** *Biblical Archaeology Review* (Washington, DC, 1975-   ). A more popular form of a journal like *BA*, which wanders considerably from the biblical field. Published by the Biblical Archaeology Society.

BeO   **73.** *Bibbia e oriente* (Milan, then Genoa, now Bornato in Franciacorta [Brescia], 1959-   ). Articles on both Testaments; brief philological notes, which sometimes are on the technical side. Published six times a year by "Gruppo biblico milanese." Languages: Italian, occasionally French.

BKir   **74.** *Bibel und Kirche* (Stuttgart, 1946-   ). A quarterly published by Katholisches Bibelwerk and dedicated to the study of the impact of the Bible on church life; an instrument of the Catholic biblical movement in Austria, Germany, and Switzerland. Usually each issue is devoted to a particular theme. Language: German.

BLeb 75. *Bibel und Leben* (Düsseldorf, 1960-1974). Published quarterly by Patmos, this periodical was intended for lay persons, religious, and clergy to stimulate in them a proper understanding of modern biblical interpretation. Haute vulgarisation, presented by top-ranking German Catholic OT and NT scholars. Language: German.

BLit 76. *Bibel und Liturgie* (Klosterneuburg, Vienna, 1927-   ). Published six times a year by the Augustinians of Klosterneuburg, this periodical is dedicated to the study of the relationship between Scripture and Roman Catholic liturgy, destined for clergy and laity. Language: German.

BTB 77. *Biblical Theology Bulletin* (Rome, 1971-76; Siena College, Loudonville, NY, 1977-   ). After the discontinuation of *Verbum Domini* (§ 88), this periodical was begun by L. Sabourin and appeared both in English and French (*Bulletin de théologie biblique*). Appearing at first three times a year, it has become a quarterly only in English and "consists mainly of survey articles" by biblical scholars. Language: English.

BVC 78. *Bible et vie chrétienne* (Paris: Casterman, 1953-1972). Published four to six times a year by the Belgian Benedictines of the Abbey of Maredsous. Articles on both Testaments; reviews. The journal was popular and devoted chiefly to the practical side of biblical studies: preaching, spirituality, liturgy, etc. Language: French.

CahEv 79. *Cahiers Evangile* (Paris, 1972-   ). Published by Service Biblique Evangile et Vie, this is a series of monographs for non-specialists. Language: French.

CulB 80. *Cultura biblica* (Madrid, then Segovia, 1944-   ). Published quarterly by the Association to Foster Biblical Studies in Spain (AFEBE), this is the popular counterpart of *EstBib* (§ 50). It is destined "para toda persona culta" and has articles on both Testaments, biblical news, and reviews. Language: Spanish.

MDB 81. *Le monde de la Bible* (Paris: Bayard, 1978-   ). The French counterpart of *BA*, appearing nine times a year. It is the successor to *Bible et terre sainte* (Paris: 1957-1977). Popular articles, often well written and well-illustrated by good photographs, on topics pertaining to the history and archaeology of both the OT and NT. The title of the new series better characterizes the contents, since there are often articles on the ancient Near East, as the archaeology of other lands turns up material bearing on the OT or NT. Language: French.

Qad

82. *Qadmoniot* (Jerusalem, 1968-   ). A quarterly published in modern Hebrew for the antiquities of Israel and biblical lands. Beautifully illustrated, it surveys each year the archaeological work done at various sites. Several of the articles on Jerusalem have been translated into English and collected in a volume entitled, *Jerusalem Revealed: Archaeology in the Holy City, 1968-1974* (ed. R. Grafman and Y. Yadin; Jerusalem: Israel Exploration Society; New Haven: Yale University, 1975). "No other volume brings together so much up-to-date information on Jerusalem in as authoritative a manner as does this one" (L. T. Geraty).

See *CBQ* 40 (1978) 653-55; *BL* (1976) 26.

RevCB

83. *Revista de cultura bíblica* (São Paulo, Brazil, 1956-   ). Published by the "Liga de estudos bíblicos," this quarterly carries articles on both Testaments and reviews. A new series began in 1964. Language: Portuguese.

RevistB

84. *Revista bíblica* (Buenos Aires, Argentina, 1939-   ). A quarterly, more popular than technical, published by the Sociedad argentina de profesores de Santa Escritura. Articles on both Testaments; reviews; bulletins; biblical news and church documents on Scripture. Language: Spanish.

ScrB

85. *Scripture Bulletin* (London/Twickenham, 1969). Published quarterly by the Catholic Biblical Association of Great Britain, in collaboration with the Bible Reading Fellowship. It is the successor of *Scripture* (London and Edinburgh, 1946-1968). It is a journal for "Biblical news, articles of practical interest about the Bible, information about new archaeological discoveries in the Holy Land, news of pilgrimages to the Bible Lands, book reviews and answers to questions on Biblical matters sent in by readers." Articles on both Testaments; reviews. A popular journal, lightweight in character, with occasional contributions of competent critical quality. Language: English.

TBT

86. *The Bible Today* (Collegeville, MN, 1962-   ). Short articles on both Testaments for popular consumption. Language: English.

TynB

87. *Tyndale Bulletin* (Cambridge, UK/Nottingham: Inter-Varsity, 1956-   ). Published by Tyndale House of Cambridge, it carries articles on the two Testaments. Language: English.

VD

88. *Verbum Domini* (Rome, 1921-69). Originally published six times a year by the Pontifical Biblical Institute, its publication was interrupted in 1945-46, revived in 1947, and finally suspended in 1969 (see *BTB*, §77). Articles on both Testaments; reviews; a rather extensive survey of biblical periodicals and collected works ("Spectator ephemeridum et collectaneorum"). This journal was intended to be less technical than *Bib*; contributions were often written by graduate students of the Institute and were often of good quality and usefulness. Language: Latin.

B. Learned Journals and Theological Periodicals

89.

AJT	*The American Journal of Theology* (Chicago, IL, 1897-1920).
ATR	*Anglican Theological Review* (New York/Evanston, IL, 1918-).
BJRL	*Bulletin of the John Rylands Library* (Manchester, England, 1903-). Renamed in 1972, *Bulletin of the John Rylands University Library of Manchester.*
BLE	*Bulletin de littérature ecclésiastique* (Paris/Toulouse, 1899-).
BSac	*Biblioteca sacra* (New York/London/Andover, MA, then Dallas, TX, 1844-).
CJ	*Classical Journal* (Menasha, WI, 1905-).
CJT	*Canadian Journal of Theology* (Toronto, 1955-70). Having replaced the *Canadian Journal of Religious Thought* (Toronto, 1924-32), it was superseded by *SR* in 1971.
ConJ	*Concordia Journal* (Saint Louis, MO, 1975-).
CP	*Classical Philology* (Chicago, 1906-).
CQR	*Church Quarterly Review* (London 1875-1967).
CRAIBL	*Comptes rendus de l'Académie des Inscriptions et Belles-Lettres* (Paris, 1857-).
CRev	*Classical Review* (Oxford, 1887-1950; ns 1951-).
CTM	*Concordia Theological Monthly* (St. Louis, MO, 1930-72); became *CTM* (1973-74), then *ConJ* (1975-).
CurTM	*Currents in Theology and Mission* (St. Louis, MO, 1974-).
CW	*Classical Weekly* (New York, 1907-57).
CWorld	*Classical World* (New York, 1958-).
EtClass	*Etudes classiques* (Namur, 1932-).
ETL	*Ephemerides theologicae lovanienses* (Louvain, 1924-).
EvQ	*Evangelical Quarterly* (London, then Exeter, England, 1929-).
EvT	*Evangelische Theologie* (Munich, 1934-).
Expos	*The Expositor* (London, 1875-1925).
FF	*Forschungen und Fortschritte* (Berlin, 1925-67).
Gnomon	*Gnomon: Kritische Zeitschrift für die gesamte klassische Altertumswissenschaft* (Berlin, 1925-).
Greg	*Gregorianum* (Rome, 1920-).
GTJ	*Grace Theological Journal* (Winona Lake, IN, 1980-).
HeyJ	*Heythrop Journal* (London, 1960-).
HibJ	*Hibbert Journal* London, 1902-73).
HTR	*Harvard Theological Review* (Cambridge, MA, 1908-).
HZ	*Historische Zeitschrift* (Munich, 1959-1943, 1949-).
JAAR	*Journal of the American Academy of Religion* (Missoula, MT, now Atlanta, GA, 1968-). Replaces the *Journal of Bible and Re-*

ligion (Philadelphia, PA, 1937-66); and *Journal of the National Association of Biblical Instructors* (Wollcott, NY, 1933-36).

JJS   *Journal of Jewish Studies* (London, 1948-   ).

JR   *Journal of Religion* (Chicago, 1921-   ).

JRS   *Journal of Roman Studies* (London, 1911-   ).

JTS   *Journal of Theological Studies* (Oxford, 1899-1949; ns 1, 1950-   ).

Judaica   *Judaica: Beiträge zum Verständnis...* (Zürich, 1945-   ).

KD   *Kerygma und Dogma* (Göttingen, 1955-   ).

MTZ   *Münchener theologische Zeitschrift* (Munich, 1950-   ).

Muséon   *Muséon* (Louvain, 1882-   ).

MUSJ   *Mélanges de l'Université Saint-Joseph* (Beirut, 1922-   ); continues *Mélanges de la faculté orientale de Beyrouth* (Beirut, 1906-21).

NRT   *La nouvelle revue théologique* (Tournai, then Eegenhoven–Louvain, 1869-1979; Namur, 1980-   ).

REJ   *Revue des études juives* (Paris, 1880-   ).

RevExp   *Review and Expositor* (Louisville, KY, 1906-   ).

RevScRel   *Revue des sciences religieuses* (Strasbourg, 1921-40, 1947-   ).

RevThom   *Revue thomiste* (Toulouse, 1893-1939, 1946-   ).

RHPR   *Revue d'histoire et de philosophie religieuses* (Lausanne, 1873-1911, 1913-1950, 1951-   ).

RHR   *Revue de l'histoire des religions* (Paris, 1880-   ).

RSPT   *Revue des sciences philosophiques et théologiques* (Paris, 1907-40, 1947-   ).

RSR   *Recherches de science religieuse* (Paris, 1910-40, 1946-   ).

RTL   *Revue théologiques de Louvain* (Louvain la Neuve, 1970-   ).

RTP   *Revue de théologie et de philosophie* (Lausanne, 1873-1911, 1913-1950, 1951-   ).

RUO   *Revue de l'Université d'Ottawa* (Ottawa, 1931-   ).

SC   *The Second Century: A Journal of Early Christian Studies* (Abilene, TX, 1981-   ).

SJT   *Scottish Journal of Theology* (Edinburgh, 1948-   ).

SR   *Studies in Religion/Sciences religieuses* (Toronto, 1971-   ).

ST   *Studia theologica* (Lund, Sweden, 1948-   ).

TBl   *Theologische Blätter* (Leipzig, 1922-42).

TLZ   *Theologische Literaturzeitung* (Leipzig, 1876-   ).

Theology   *Theology* (London, 1920-   ).

TQ   *Theologische Quartalschrift* (Tübingen/Stuttgart/Munich/Freiburg, 1819-   ).

TRev   *Theologische Revue* (Münster in W., 1902-44, 1948-   ).

TRu   *Theologische Rundschau* (Tübingen, 1897-1917; ns 1929-   ).

TS   *Theological Studies* (New York/Woodstock, MD, 1940-74; Washington, DC, 1974-   ).

TSK   *Theologische Studien und Kritiken* (Hamburg, 1828-1942).

TTKi   *Tidsskrift for Teologi og Kirke* (Oslo, 1930-   ).

TToday   *Theology Today* (Princeton, NJ, 1944-   ).

TTZ   *Trierer theologische Zeitschrift* (Trier, 1947-   ).

TZ   *Theologische Zeitschrift* (Basel, 1945-   ).

VC   *Vigiliae christianae* (Amsterdam, 1947-   ).

WTJ   *Westminster Theological Journal* (Philadelphia, PA, 1938-   ).

ZKT	*Zeitschrift für katholische Theologie* (Innsbruck/Vienna, 1877-1943, 1947-).
ZST	*Zeitschrift für systematische Theologie* (Berlin, 1923-1955).
ZTK	*Zeitschrift für Theologie und Kirche* (Tübingen, 1891-1917; ns 1920-38, 1950-).
ZWT	*Zeitschrift für wissenschaftliche Theologie* (Jena, Leipzig, 1858-1914).

C. Palestine and the Ancient Near East

90.

Abr-N	*Abr-Nahrain*, Melbourne (Leiden, 1959-).
ActOr	*Acta orientalia* (Leiden, 1923-).
Aeg	*Aegyptus* (Milan, 1920-).
AfO	*Archiv für Orientforschung* (Berlin, 1925-44, 1945/51-).
AION	*Annali dell'Istituto orientale di Napoli* (Rome/Naples, 1940-).
AJSL	*American Journal of Semitic Languages and Literatures* (Chicago, 1895-1941; replaced *Hebraica*, 1884-94; replaced by *JNES*).
AO	*Aula orientalis* (Barcelona, 1983-).
ArOr	*Archiv Orientální* (Prague, 1929-42, 1946-).
'Atiqot	*'Atiqot* (Jerusalem, 1955-).
AusJBA	*Australian Journal of Biblical Archaeology* (Sidney, 1968-).
BASOR	**Bulletin of the American Schools of Oriental Research* (New Haven, CT, 1919-1974; Missoula, MT, 1974-78; Ann Arbor, MI, 1978-).
BO	*Bibliotheca orientalis* (Leiden, 1943-).
BSOAS	*Bulletin of the School of Oriental and African Studies* (London, 1940-).
EVO	*Egitto e vicino oriente* (Pisa, 1978-).
FO	*Folia orientalia* (Cracow, Poland, 1959-).
Hen	*Henoch* (Turin, 1978-).
IEJ	*Israel Exploration Journal* (Jerusalem, 1950/51-).
IOS	*Israel Oriental Studies* (Tel Aviv, 1971-).
JA	*Journal asiatique* (Paris, 1822-).
JAOS	*Journal of the American Oriental Society* (New Haven, CT, 1849-).
JCS	*Journal of Cuneiform Studies* (New Haven, CT, 1947-).
JEA	*Journal of Egyptian Archaeology* (London, 1914-).
JNES	*Journal of Near Eastern Studies* (Chicago, Il., 1942-). Superseded *AJSL* and *Hebraica*.
JPOS	*Journal of the Palestine Oriental Society* (Jerusalem, 1920-38, 1946-48).
JQR	*Jewish Quarterly Review* (London, then Philadelphia, PA, 1888-1908, 1910-).
JSJ	*Journal for the Study of Judaism in the Persian, Hellenistic and Roman Periods* (Leiden, 1970-).
JSS	*Journal of Semitic Studies* (Manchester, UK, 1956-).
Leš	*Lešonénu* (Jerusalem, 1928-) [in modern Hebrew].
Maarav	*Maarav: Journal for the Study of Northwest Semitic Languages and Literatures* (Santa Monica, CA; now Rolling Hills Estates, CA, 1978-).
OLZ	*Orientalische Literaturzeitung* (Leipzig/Berlin, 1898-).

Or	*Orientalia* (Rome, 1920-).
OrAnt	*Oriens antiquus* (Rome, 1961-).
OrSyr	*L'Orient syrien* (Vernon, France, 1956-).
PEFQS	*Palestine Exploration Fund, Quarterly Statement* (London, 1869-1937).
PEQ	*Palestine Exploration Quarterly* (London, 1938-). Continuation of *PEFQS*.
Phoenix	*Phoenix* (Leiden, 1955-).
PJ	*Palästina-Jahrbuch* (Berlin, 1905-41).
PSBA	*Proceedings of the Society of Biblical Archaeology* (London, 1878-1918).
QDAP	*Quarterly of the Department of Antiquities of Palestine* (Jerusalem, London, 1931-1950); replaced by ADAJ (§ 91).
RA	*Revue d'assyriologie et d'archéologie orientale* (Paris, 1884-).
RArch	*Revue archéologique* (Paris, seven series, 1844-1957; 8th ser., 1958-).
RSF	*Rivista di studi fenici* (Rome, 1973-).
RSO	*Rivista degli studi orientali* (Rome, 1907-1943; 1946-).
Sef	*Sefarad* (Madrid, 1941-).
SELVOA	*Studi epigrafici e linguistici sul vicino oriente antico* (Verona, 1984-).
Sem	*Semitica* (Paris, 1948-).
SPap	*Studia papyrologica* (Barcelona, 1962-).
Syria	*Syria* (Paris, 1920-).
TA	*Tel Aviv* (Tel Aviv, 1974-).
UF	*Ugarit-Forschungen* (Kevelaer/Neukirchen-Vluyn, 1969-).
WO	*Die Welt des Orients* (Göttingen, 1947-).
WZKM	*Wiener Zeitschrift für die Kunde des Morgenlandes* (Vienna, 1887-1943; 1948-).
ZA	*Zeitschrift für Assyriologie* (Leipzig, 1886-1944; Berlin/New York, 1950-).
ZÄS	*Zeitschrift für ägyptische Sprache und Altertumskunde* (Berlin, 1863-).
ZAH	*Zeitschrift für Althebraistik* (Stuttgart, 1988-).
ZDMG	*Zeitschrift der deutschen morgenländischen Gesellschaft* (Wiesbaden, 1847-).
ZDPV	*Zeitschrift des deutschen Palästina-Vereins* (Leipzig, then Wiesbaden, 1878-1945, 1953-).
ZPE	*Zeitschrift für Papyrologie und Epigraphik* (Bonn, 1956-).

Chapter III

Series

In this chapter are listed the most important monographs and works published in series, which are devoted either wholly or in part to biblical studies. They contain many important essays and collections of articles. The commonly used sigla are also supplied, but no comment is made on their contents.

91.

AASOR	Annual of the American Schools of Oriental Research (New Haven, CT, 1919/1920-).
ADAJ	Annual of the Department of Antiquities of Jordan (Amman, 1951-).
AGJU	Arbeiten zur Geschichte des antiken Judentums und des Urchristentums (Leiden, 1961-).
AKM	Abhandlungen für die Kunde des Morgenlandes (Leipzig, 1957-).
ALBO	Analecta lovaniensia biblica et orientalia (Louvain, 1947-); replaces BHEAT (1934-1947).
ALGHJ	Arbeiten zur Literatur und Geschichte des hellenistischen Judentums (Leiden, 1968-).
ALUOS	Annual of Leeds University Oriental Society (Leeds, Leiden, 1959-).
AnBib	*Analecta biblica (Rome, 1952-).
AnOr	Analecta orientalia (Rome, 1931-).
ANTF	Arbeiten zur neutestamentlichen Textforschung (Berlin, 1963-).
AOAT	*Alter Orient und Altes Testament (Kevelaer/Neukirchen-Vluyn, 1969-).
AOS	American Oriental Series (New Haven, CT, 1925-).
ARM	Archives royales de Mari (Paris, 1941-).
ASAE	Annales du service des antiquites de l'Egypte (Cairo, 1900-).
ASNU	Acta seminarii neotestamentici upsaliensis (Uppsala, 1935-).
ASTI	Annual of the Swedish Theological Institute (Leiden, 1962-).
ATAbh	Alttestamentliche Abhandlungen (Munich, 1908-40).
ATANT	Abhandlungen zur Theologie des Alten und Neuen Testaments (Zürich, 1942-).
BBB	Bonner biblische Beiträge (Bonn, 1950-).
BETL	**Bibliotheca ephemeridum theologicarum lovaniensium (Louvain, 1948-). The series includes the publications of the *Colloquium Biblicum Lovaniense*, the successor to RechBib.
BEvT	Beiträge zur evangelischen Theologie (Munich, 1940-).
BFCT	Beiträge zur Förderung christlicher Theologie (Gütersloh, 1897; ns 1921-).
BGBE	Beiträge zur Geschichte der biblischen Exegese (Tübingen, 1955-).

BHEAT   Bulletin d'histoire et d'exégèse de l'Ancien Testament (Louvain, 1934-47).
BHT   Beiträge zur historischen Theologie (Tübingen, 1929-   ).
BibB   Biblische Beiträge (Einsiedeln, Switzerland, 1952-   ).
BibOr   *Biblica et orientalia (Rome, 1928-   ).
BibS(F)   Biblische Studien (Freiburg im B., 1895-1930).
BibS(N)   Biblische Studien (Neukirchen-Vluyn, 1951-   ).
BKW   Bible Key Words (from G. Kittel, *TWNT*) (London, 1949-65).
BWANT   *Beiträge zur Wissenschaft vom Alten und Neuen Testament (Leipzig/ Stuttgart, 1908-   ).
BZAW   *Beihefte zur *ZAW* (Giessen, then Berlin, 1896-   ).
BZNW   *Beihefte zur *ZNW* (Giessen, then Berlin, 1923-   ).
CahRB   Cahiers de la *RB* (Paris, 1964-   ).
CahThéol   Cahiers théologiques (Neuchâtel, 1943-   ).
CBQMS   Catholic Biblical Quarterly Monograph Series (Washington, 1971-   ).
ConB   Coniectanea biblica (Lund, 1966-   ).
EBib   *Etudes bibliques (Paris, 1903-   ).
EFN   Estudios de filología neotestamentaria: New Testament Philology Studies (Córdoba, 1989-   ).
FBBS   Facet Books, Biblical Series (Philadelphia, PA, 1963-   ).
FB   Forschung zur Bibel (Würzburg/Stuttgart, 1970-   ).
FRLANT   *Forschungen zur Religion und Literatur des Alten und Neuen Testaments (Göttingen, 1903-   ).
GAT   Grundrisse zum Alten Testament (Göttingen, 1975-   ).
GGA   Göttingische gelehrte Anzeigen (unter Aufsicht der Akademie der Wissenschaften) (Göttingen, 1802-1944, 1953-   ).
GNT   Grundrisse zum Neuen Testament (Göttingen, 1969-   ).
GTA   Göttinger theologische Arbeiten (Göttingen, 1975-   ).
HDR   Harvard Dissertations in Religion (Cambridge, MA; Missoula, MT; now Atlanta, GA, 1975-   ).
HSM   *Harvard Semitic Monographs (Cambridge, MA; Missoula, MT; now Atlanta, GA, 1976-   ).
HTS   *Harvard Theological Studies (Cambridge, MA, 1908-   ).
HUCA   Hebrew Union College Annual (Cincinnati, OH, 1924-   ).
JDS   Judean Desert Studies (Jerusalem, 1963-   ).
JQRMS   *JQR* Monograph Series (Philadelphia, PA, 1952-   ).
JSNTSup   *JSNT* Supplement series (Sheffield, UK, 1980-   ).
JSOTSup   *JSOT* Supplement series (Sheffield, UK, 1976-   ).
KIT   Kleine Texte für Vorlesungen und Übungen (Berlin/New York, 1902-   ).
LCL   *Loeb Classical Library (London/Cambridge, MA, 1912-   ).
LD   Lectio divina (Paris, 1946-   ).
MVAAG   Mitteilungen der vorderasiatisch-ägyptischen Gesellschaft (Leipzig, 1896-1944).
NFT   New Frontiers in Theology (New York, 1963-   ).
NHS   Nag Hammadi Studies (Leiden, 1971-   ).
NovTSup   *NovT* Supplements (Leiden, 1958-   ).
NTAbh   *Neutestamentliche Abhandlungen (Münster in W., 1908-   ).

NTF	Neutestamentliche Forschung (Gütersloh, 1923-).
NTTS	*New Testament Tools and Studies (Leiden, 1960-).
OBO	Orbis biblicus et orientalis (Fribourg and Göttingen, 1973-).
OIP	Oriental Institute Publications (Chicago, 1924-).
OLP	Orientalia lovaniensia periodica (Louvain, 1970-).
OTS	Oudtestamentische Studiën (Leiden, 1942-).
PVTG	Pseudepigrapha Veteris Testamenti graece (Leiden, 1964-).
RechBib	Recherches bibliques (Bruges/Paris: Desclée de Brouwer, 1954-74 [tomes 1-8]; Leiden: Brill, 1974 [tome 9]).
SANT	Studien zum Alten und Neuen Testament (Munich, 1960-).
SB	*Sources bibliques (Paris, 1964-).
SBA	Studies in Biblical Archaeology (London/New York, 1955-).
SBB	Stuttgarter biblische Beiträge (Stuttgart, 1969-).
SBFLA	Studii biblici franciscani liber annuus (Jerusalem, 1950-).
SBLASP	Society of Biblical Literature Abstracts and Seminar Papers (Missoula, MT, then Chico, CA, then Atlanta, GA, 1970-).
SBLDS	*SBL Dissertation Series (Missoula, MT, then Chico, CA, then Atlanta, GA, 1972-).
SBLMasS	SBL Masoretic Studies (Missoula, MT, then Chico, CA, then Atlanta, GA, 1974-).
SBLMS	*SBL Monograph Series (Philadelphia, PA. then Missoula, MT, then Chico, CA, then Atlanta, GA, 1946-).
SBLSBS	SBL Sources for Biblical Study (Missoula, MT, then Chico, CA, then Atlanta, GA, 1972-).
SBLSCS	SBL Septuagint and Cognate Studies (Missoula, MT, then Chico, CA, then Atlanta, GA, 1972-).
SBLTT	SBL Texts and Translations (Missoula, MT, then Chico, CA, then Atlanta, GA, 1972-).
SBM	Stuttgarter biblische Monographien (Stuttgart: Katholisches Bibelwerk, 1967-).
SBS	Stuttgarter Bibelstudien (Stuttgart: Katholisches Bibelwerk, 1965-).
SBT	Studies in Biblical Theology (London, 1950-).
SCHNT	Studia ad corpus hellenisticum Novi Testamenti (Leiden, 1970-).
ScrHier	Scripta hierosolymitana (Jerusalem, 1954-).
SJLA	Studies in Judaism in Late Antiquity (Leiden, 1973-).
SJud	Studia judaica (Berlin, 1961-).
SNT	Studien zum Neuen Testament (Gütersloh, 1969-).
SNTSMS	*Society for New Testament Studies Monograph Series (Cambridge, UK, 1965-).
SPB	Studia postbiblica (Leiden, 1959-).
StD	Studies and Documents (London, 1934-).
STDJ	Studies on the Texts of the Desert of Judah (Leiden, 1957-).
StudNeot	Studia neotestamentica, Studia (Bruges/Paris, 1961-).
SUNT	*Studien zur Umwelt des Neuen Testament (Göttingen, 1963-).
SVTP	Studia in Veteris Testamenti pseudepigrapha (Leiden, 1970-).
SymBU	Symbolae biblicae upsalienses (Uppsala, 1943-).
Textus	*Textus: Annual of the Hebrew University Bible Project (Jerusalem, 1960-).

TU   *Texte und Untersuchungen (Berlin, 1882-   ).
UNT   Untersuchungen zum Neuen Testament (Leipzig, 1912-38).
UUÅ   Uppsala Universitetsårskrift (Uppsala, 1861-   ).
VTSup   *VT Supplements (Leiden, 1953-   ).
WdF   Wege der Forschung (Darmstadt, 1956-   ).
WMANT   *Wissenschaftliche Monographien zum Alten und Neuen Testament
            (Neukirchen-Vluyn, 1960-   ).

CHAPTER IV

Introductions to the Biblical Text and Ancient Versions

This chapter aims at gathering the most important titles that introduce the student to the study of the text of the OT and the NT and their ancient versions. See the following chapter for guidance to publications of the texts themselves. What is presented here is intended to set forth the problems that one encounters in studying the original texts or their ancient versions. The items are gathered under the headings: (A) the OT; and (B) the NT.

A. OT

CHB   **92.** *The Cambridge History of the Bible* (Cambridge, UK: University Press). Volume 1, From the Beginnings to Jerome (ed. P. R. Ackroyd and C. F. Evans, 1970); volume 2, The West from the Fathers to the Reformation (ed. G. W. H. Lampe, 1969); volume 3, The West from the Reformation to the Present Day (ed. S. L. Greenslade, 1963). A comprehensive survey of problems of all sorts dealing with the original texts and ancient versions as well as the transmission of the Bible into modern times. The contribu tions of various scholars, which make up the volumes, are, however, uneven at times.

> See *JBL* 83 (1964) 448-50; 89 (1970) 129; 90 (1971) 103-4; *RB* 72 (1965) 287-88; 78 (1971) 155; 79 (1972) 312; *CBQ* 32 (1970) 136-38; 33 (1971) 233-34; *Bib* 45 (1964) 310; *RSR* 59 (1971) 621-24.

93. Würthwein, E., *Der Text des Alten Testaments: Eine Einführung in die Biblia Hebraica* (5th ed.; Stuttgart: Württembergische Bi-belgesellschaft, 1988). This work first appeared in 1952 and served at once as an introduction to the third and later editions of BHK but also as a critique of its deficiencies. In 1957 an English version of it was prepared by P. Ackroyd, *The Text of the Old Testament: An Introduction to Kittel–Kahle's Biblia Hebraica* (Oxford: Blackwell). A translation of the fourth thoroughly revised German edition has been prepared by E. F. Rhodes, *The Text of the Old Testament: An Introduction to the Biblia Hebraica* (Grand Rapids, MI: Eerdmans, 1979). The 5th ed. is a thorough revision with an interesting essay on the pertinence of textual criticism to theology; the bibliography has been updated.

> See *TLZ* 78 (1953) 332-33; *ZAW* 85 (1973) 399; *JSS* 4 (1959) 149-51; *ExpTim* 69 (1957-58) 9-10; *JTS* 9 (1958) 112-13; *RB* 65 (1958) 119; *TRev* 69 (1973) 451.

94. Cross, F. M. and S. Talmon (eds.), *Qumran and the History of the Biblical Text* (Cambridge, MA/London: Harvard University, 1975). A very useful collection of 16 essays on the Hebrew text of the OT and the LXX as these have been affected by the discovery of OT texts in Qumran caves. The essays have been gathered from various publications and were written between 1953 and 1974; two of them have not appeared elsewhere. The last item in the volume is a list of Palestinian Manuscripts, 1947-1972 by J. A. Sanders, similar to that published by him in *JJS* 24 (1973) 74-83.

    See *JBL* 95 (1976) 692-93; *CBQ* 38 (1976) 552-53; *IEJ* 29 (1979) 131-32.

95. Roberts, B. J. *The Old Testament Text and Versions* (Cardiff: University of Wales, 1951). In spite of shortcomings, this has always been a valuable handbook on the text and versions of the OT. Careful descriptions and analyses of older works enable the author to state problems clearly. The bibliography, though rich, is now out of date.

    See *Bib* 32 (1951) 441-47; *TLZ* 76 (1951) 535-39; *VT* 1 (1951) 238-40; *RB* 59 (1952) 439-40.

96. Purvis, J. D., *The Samaritan Pentateuch and the Origin of the Samaritan Sect* (HSM 2; Cambridge, MA: Harvard University, 1968). A modern study of the evidence recently brought to light about the formation of the Samaritan pentateuchal tradition and of its relation to the emergence of the Samaritans as a sect cut off from Judaism.

    See *CBQ* 31 (1969) 453-54; *Bib* 52 (1971) 253-55.

97. Tov, E., *The Text-Critical Use of the Septuagint in Biblical Research* (Jerusalem Biblical Studies 3; Jerusalem: Simor, 1981). This is an important modern study of the LXX and its role in the study of the Hebrew Scriptures. It is a handbook that deals with method.

    See *CBQ* 45 (1983) 468-70; *JBL* 102 (1983) 448-50; *RB* 91 (1984) 134.

98. Jellicoe, S., *The Septuagint and Modern Study* (New York/ London: Oxford University, 1968; repr., Ann Arbor, MI [now Winona Lake, IN]: Eisenbrauns, 1978, 1989). A modern survey of Septuagintal studies, the first in English since the classic by H. B. Swete, *Introduction to the Old Testament in Greek* (Cambridge, UK: University Press, 1900; revised by R. R. Ottley, 1914; repr., New York [now Hoboken, NJ]: Ktav, 1968). Jellicoe's introduction surveys the modern study of the LXX since the edition of Holmes and Parsons up to the critical editions of Cambridge and Göttingen. Part I deals with the origins of the LXX and its transmission history, and Part II with its text and language.

    See *CBQ* 31 (1969) 258-61; *JBL* 88 (1969) 230-32; *RB* 77 (1970) 84-91.

99. Jellicoe, S. (ed.), *Studies in the Septuagint: Origins, Recensions, and Interpretations: Selected Essays with a Prolegomenon* (Library of Biblical Studies; New York [now Hoboken, NJ]: Ktav, 1974). A valuable collection of 35 articles, mostly written in English (but with a few in French or German), presenting surveys of LXX studies, discussion of LXX origins, transmission history, the text of the LXX and its translation techniques, the use of the LXX in the NT and Church Fathers, and the significance of the LXX. A prolegomenon of 42 pp., written before Jellicoe's death in November 1973, introduces the collection.

See *CBQ* 37 (1975) 403-5; *BZ* 22 (1978) 308-9; *BL* (1975) 36; *ExpTim* 86 (1974-75) 220; *ZAW* 87 (1975) 129.

100. Rahlfs, A., *Verzeichnis der griechischen Handschriften des Alten Testaments, für das Septuaginta-Unternehmen* (Berlin: Weidmann, 1914). An old list of approximately 2000 mss. and fragments of the Greek OT, giving their date, size, present location, contents, etc. It has been a very valuable tool for the study of the LXX and other Greek versions of the OT.

See *BZ* 13 (1915) 270.

101. Díez Macho, A., *El targum: Introducción a las traducciones aramaicas de la Biblia* (Barcelona: Consejo Superior de Investigaciones Científicas, 1972). A generic description of targums, their relation to midrashim, their language (Aramaic), their antiquity, their importance, ending with a sketch of the contribution of the Barcelona school of targumic studies. The student will find much that is useful in this book, but he or she must be warned about the claims that Díez Macho makes for the kind of Aramaic found in the targums that he discusses and the dating of them. He also fails to distinguish adequately "el targum" and the various forms of Palestinian targums that are known; they do not all represent *one* targum.

See *CBQ* 35 (1973) 233-35; *RevQ* 8 (1972-75) 437-42; *BZ* 19 (1975) 296-97; *REJ* 133 (1974) 241-42.

102. Le Déaut, R., *Introduction à la littérature targumique: Première partie* (Rome: Biblical Institute, 1966). This introduction was prepared for students at the Biblical Institute in Rome (the title page bears the note, Ad usum privatum), but it has been widely used. It is in many ways the most up-to-date introduction to targumic literature that we have, even though it is not perfect. The student who will use it will find many leads in it to other literature. The second part is still awaited.

103. Grossfeld, B., *A Bibliography of Targum Literature I* (Bibliographica judaica 2; Cincinnati, OH: Hebrew Union College; New

York [now Hoboken, NJ]: Ktav, 1972); *II* (Bibl. jud. 8, 1977). This is a welcome addition to the study of the targums, since it ferrets out of many places a good list to guide the student into the intricacies of targumic literature. The entries are listed under ten headings: General targum; Tg. Onqelos; the Palestinian targums; Tg. Jonathan of the Prophets; targums of the Writings; the targums and the NT; translations of the targums; first editions; lexica, chrestomathies, concordances, and grammars for the study of the targums; reviews of books on targumic literature.

See *JBL* 93 (1974) 135-36; *ZAW* 85 (1973) 265; *Bib* 55 (1974) 281-85; 59 (1978) 419-20; *BO* 32 (1975) 86-89; *ZDMG* 127 (1977) 109-11; *RB* 85 (1978) 456-57.

B. NT

104. *Elliott, J. K., *A Bibliography of Greek New Testament Manuscripts* (SNTSMS 62; Cambridge, UK: University Press, 1989). This work supplies information on particular mss. of the Greek NT, where they are published, where a facsimile, a photographic reproduction, or a collation of their texts can be found, and whether a major study has been undertaken of such texts. It deals with papyri, uncials, cursives, and lectionaries.

See *NTA* 33 (1989) 377; *ExpTim* 101 (1989-90) 29-30.

105. **Aland, K. and B., *Der Text des Neuen Testaments: Einführung in die wissenschaftlichen Ausgaben sowie in Theorie und Praxis der modernen Textkritik* (Stuttgart: Deutsche Bibelgesellschaft, 1982). E. F. Rhodes has translated the book into English, *The Text of the New Testament: An Introduction to the Critical Editions and to the Theory and Practice of Modern Textual Criticism* (Grand Rapids, MI: Eerdmans; Leiden: Brill, 1987). It "gives the basic information necessary for using the Greek New Testament and for forming an independent judgment on the many kinds of variant readings characteristic of the New Testament textual tradition" (p. v). It discusses the modern editions of the NT from Erasmus to the present, the transmission of the Greek text, the manuscripts, the early versions; it supplies an introduction to the use of modern editions, resources, and an introduction to the praxis of NT textual criticism. An Italian translation exists, *Il testo del Nuovo Testamento* (Commentario storico-esegetico dell'Antico e del Nuovo Testamento 2; Genoa: Marietti, 1987).

See *NovT* 25 (1983) 89-90; *CBQ* 50 (1988) 313-15; *JBL* 108 (1989) 139-44; *NovT* 25 (1983) 89-90; *TZ* 39 (1983) 247-49; *BT* 34 (1983) 344-45.

106. **Metzger, B. M., *The Text of the New Testament: Its Transmission, Corruption, and Restoration* (New York/London: Oxford University, 1964). A fascinating account of the study of NT textual criticism and an informative introduction to the science and art of such criticism. It is intended for students of the NT who would like to get interested in this difficult aspect of NT study. An appendix supplies a checklist of the Greek papyrus texts of the NT, and a final bibliography lists chronologically similar introductions to NT textual criticism that preceded Metzger's work. A second, revised, and augmented edition appeared in 1968 (with additional pages 261-73). Highly recommended. Translated into German, *Der Text des Neuen Testaments: Einführung in die neutestamentliche Textkritik* (Stuttgart: Kohlhammer, 1966).

See *TToday* 21 (1964-65) 386-88; *CBQ* 31 (1969) 278-79; *EstBib* 27 (1968) 181; *JTS* 16 (1965) 484-87; 20 (1969) 591.

107. Metzger, B. M., *Manuscripts of the Greek Bible: An Introduction to Greek Palaeography* (New York/Oxford: Oxford University, 1981). This work provides 45 photographic reproductions of pages of papyrus, parchment, and paper manuscripts of the Greek OT and NT. Accompanying them is a one-page description of each text. The specimens range from the second century B.C. to the fifteenth century A.D. An invaluable introduction to Greek palaeography precedes the collection, including a survey of palaeographical study, the pronunciation of ancient Greek, the handling of the tetragram in different texts.

See *BASOR* 260 (1985) 86-87; *JBL* 103 (1984) 307-8; *TS* 43 (1982) 706-7; *CBQ* 45 (1983) 148.

108. Aland, K., *Kurzgefasste Liste der griechischen Handschriften des Neuen Testaments* (ANTF 1; Berlin: de Gruyter, 1963). This work presents a comprehensive listing of the Greek mss. of the NT: Papyri (81-76), uncial mss. (250, numbered in the Gregory system), minuscule mss. (2646), and lectionaries (1997). The content of the texts, their dates, the number of their pages, and the libraries where they are found are all supplied. Comparative tables also set forth the different modes of designation that have been used. A list of libraries is included, stating what mss. they hold. An invaluable tool.

See *BZ* 8 (1964) 116-19; *RB* 71 (1964) 625; *JBL* 82 (1963) 451-52; *NTS* 11 (1964-65) 108-9.

109. Elliott, J. K., *A Survey of Manuscripts Used in Editions of the Greek New Testament* (NovTSup 57; Leiden/New York: Brill, 1987). In separate sections on papyri, uncials, cursives, and lectionaries each page is divided into 15 columns. The first gives the Gregory–Aland number for each NT ms., then that of the editions of the complete Greek NT in chronological order and three of the recent Greek synopses of the Gospels. Lastly, the evidence of the International Greek New Testament Project's work on Luke, data from talismans and ostraca.

See *CBQ* 51 (1989) 558-59.

110. Finegan, J., *Encountering New Testament Manuscripts: A Working Introduction to Textual Criticism* (Grand Rapids, MI: Eerdmans, 1974). This introduction to NT textual criticism seeks to initiate the student directly into work with the Greek mss. themselves. It has been highly praised, but will not replace B. M. Metzger's *Text* (§ 106). Finegan treats of the writing and production of books in antiquity; the history of textual criticism; the techniques of transcribing, collating, and judging various manuscript-traditions; and finally deals with "the future task," i.e., the future of this discipline and the work that remains to be done.

See *CBQ* 37 (1975) 568-69; *BTB* 5 (1975) 216-17; *ATR* 58 (1976) 232-34; *TS* 36 (1975) 381; *ExpTim* 87 (1975-76) 23-24.

111. Gregory, C. R., *Textkritik des Neuen Testaments* (Leipzig: Hinrichs, 1900-9). Though old, this is still a useful account of Greek manuscripts and lectionaries. It goes beyond the prolegomena of Tischendorf's *editio maior* (§ 137). Gregory started a numbering system of Greek mss. that is still used.

See *JTS* 3 (1901-2) 295-96.

112. Kraft, B., *Die Zeichen für die wichtigeren Handschriften des griechischen Neuen Testaments* (3d ed.; Freiburg im B: Herder, 1955). First published in 1926, it was revised in 1934, then again in 1955. It is still an excellent tool for the resolution of the conflict in methods of reference to NT mss. It was meant to be an aid to Von Soden's edition of the NT, but it has useful cross-references to the editions of Tischendorf, Wettstein, and Gregory.

See *JTS* 6 (1955) 347; *CBQ* 17 (1955) 535; *TLZ* 80 (1955) 654-56.

113. Nestle, E., *Einführung in das griechische Neue Testament* (4th ed., rev. by E. von Dobschütz; Göttingen: Vandenhoeck & Ruprecht, 1923). Even though this book has been surpassed in many ways by the works of B. M. Metzger (§ 106) and K. Aland (§ 105), it is retained here as the "classic" in the study of NT textual criticism, written by one whose name is associated with the most widely-used Greek NT in this century. Its three parts contain (1) a history of the text, mss., versions, and printed editions; (2) materials and methods of textual criticism; and (3) 23 photographs of original mss.

See *HTR* 17 (1924) 91-94; *ZNW* 22 (1923) 312-13.

114. Aland, K. (ed.), *Die alten Übersetzungen des Neuen Testaments, die Kirchenväterzitate und Lektionare: Der gegenwärtige Stand ihrer Erforschung und ihre Bedeutung für die griechische Textgeschichte* (ANTF 5; Berlin: de Gruyter, 1972). This is an important collection of 13 essays written by a team of scholars on ancient versions, patristic citations, and lectionary readings in their relationship to the Greek text of the NT. The international team includes B. Fischer (Latin NT), W. Thiele (Latin text of the Catholic Epistles), M. Black (Syriac NT), G. Mink (Coptic NT), L. Leloir (Armenian NT), J. Molitor (Georgian NT), J. Hofmann (Ethiopic NT), E. Stutz (Gothic NT), C. Hannick (Old Church Slavonic NT), P. Prigent (Greek patristic citations), H. J. Frede (Latin patristic citations), B. M. Metzger (Greek lectionaries in general), and K. Junack (Greek lectionaries and the Catholic Epistles).

See *RSR* 62 (1974) 443-45; *RB* 82 (1975) 616-20; *JBL* 93 (1974) 147-48.

115. *Metzger, B. M., *The Early Versions of the New Testament: Their Origin, Transmission, and Limitations* (London/New York: Oxford University, 1977). A highly informative, extremely dependable, and valuable treatment of the ancient versions of the NT, divided into two main parts: Eastern versions (Syriac, Coptic, Armenian, Georgian, Ethiopic, Arabic, Nubian, Persian, Sogdian, and [non-extant] Caucasian–Albanian); Western version (Latin, Gothic, old Church Slavonic, Anglo-Saxon, old High German, and old Low German). Metzger has sought the aid of specialists to alert readers to the limitations of the various languages in their attempt to render the Greek NT text: S. P. Brock (Syriac), J. M. Plumley (Coptic), E. F. Rhodes (Armenian), M. Brière (Georgian), J. Hofmann (Ethiopic), B. Fischer (Latin), G. W. S. Friedrichsen (Gothic).

See *CBQ* 40 (1978) 641-43; *Bib* 60 (1979) 118-21; *TToday* 35 (1979) 210 11.

116. Nickels, P., *Targum and New Testament: A Bibliography together with a New Testament Index* (Rome: Biblical Institute, 1967). The aim of this work is "to acquaint, or further acquaint, exegetes with the work that has been done in the field of Targum–New Testament relationships" (p. v). Nickels's criterion in gathering entries has been "the use of Targumic material in treatment of a New Testament text or theme" (pp. v-vi). *In se*, this is laudable; but it is a little naive, because it presupposes that much of the targumic material to which reference is made actually existed either prior to or contemporaneous with the NT itself. Hence the student must always ask about the date of the targumic material to which reference is being made.

See *CBQ* 30 (1968) 465; *RB* 77 (1970) 139.

Chapter V

Biblical Texts

Here the aim is to list the best critical editions of the original texts of the OT and the NT. However, one runs into a complicated problem, in that the MT contains the protocanonical books of the OT, whereas the deuterocanonical books (apart from Sirach, which is partly preserved in Hebrew) are found in the Greek OT or the so-called Septuagint [LXX]. The latter is in reality an ancient Greek version of the Hebrew and Aramaic writings of the OT, with additional books, among which some are deuterocanonical and others are apocryphal. We shall list the entries under four heads: (A) The MT (the protocanonical books of the OT); (B) the Greek OT (the deuterocanonical and apocryphal books of the OT); (C) the NT; and (D) synopses of the Greek text of the canonical Gospels.

A. The MT (Protocanonical Books of the OT)

BHS   **117.**   **Elliger, K. and W. Rudolph (eds.), *Biblia hebraica stuttgartensia* (Stuttgart: Deutsche Bibelstiftung, 1967-77). Together with a host of collaborators (mostly German, but also some Dutch, English, and French scholars), the editors have produced a greatly improved critical edition of the Hebrew Bible. Over a period of ten years it was issued in fascicles, and the one-volume edition contains prolegomena in German, English, French, Spanish, and Latin. The *Masora parva*, in a form greatly improved, thanks to the labors of G. E. Weil of Nancy, France, is given in the margin. At the foot of the page one finds a short summation of the major comments of the *Masora magna* and then the *apparatus criticus* proper, based on a recent collation of major Hebrew and Aramaic texts of the OT. The Hebrew text of *BHS* is based on the latest hand in the Leningrad Codex. But apparently, all is not yet perfect with this publication and its *apparatus criticus*, even though it is far superior to *BHK* or any other edition of the Hebrew Bible; it will long be used in the critical study of the OT. A supplementary eight-page compendium has been prepared by R. I. Vasholz, *Data for the Sigla of BHS* (Winona Lake, IN: Eisenbrauns, 1983). Cf. R. Wonneberger, *Understanding BHS: A Manual for the Users of Biblia Hebraica Stuttgartensia* (Subsidia biblica 8; Rome: Biblical Institute, 1984; 1990²).

See *CBQ* 31 (1969) 615-16; 32 (1970) 254-55; *ZAW* 81 (1969) 411-12; 83 (1971) 289-91; 85 (1973) 231, 260-61; *Bib* 61 (1980) 126-30; *JBL* 98 (1979) 417-19.

BHK   **118.**   Kittel, R. (ed.), *Biblia hebraica* (9th ed.; Württembergische Bibelanstalt, 1954). Even though this edition of the Hebrew Bible has now been replaced by *BHS*, many still continue to use it. For the first two editions Kittel used the text of ben Ḥayim; beginning with the third edition (1937), he introduced the Leningrad text of ben Asher, reprinted in subsequent editions. After the discovery of the Qumran biblical texts an inadequate attempt was made to include in the *apparatus criticus* variants from 1QIsaᵃ and 1QpHab. Its shortcomings in other respects are notorious; suggested emendations and supposed Hebrew equivalents of LXX readings must be used with great caution.

        See E. Würthwein, *Der Text* (§ 93).

HPS   **119.**   Gall, A. von, *Der hebräische Pentateuch der Samaritaner* (Giessen: Töpelmann, 1914-18; repr., Berlin, 1966). This is an eclectic edition of the Hebrew text of the Pentateuch according to the Samaritan tradition, which differs at times from the MT and is needed in OT textual criticism.

        See *JJS* 2 (1950-51) 144-50; *RB* ns 4 (1907) 314; ns 11 (1914) 542-49; 30 (1921) 616-17.

OTH   **120.**   Snaith, N. H. (ed.), *Old Testament in Hebrew* (London: British and Foreign Bible Society, 1958). A handy edition of the Hebrew Bible based on Spanish mss. in the British Museum. According to the editor, these mss. preserve the authentic ben Asher text, but the text of this edition differs little from *BHK*³⁻⁹, even though the paragraph division and the masorah manifest some divergence. The editor's "preface" can be found in *VT* 7 (1957) 207-8.

        See *BL* (1959) 15; *RB* 66 (1959) 607; *BT* 15 (1964) 142-46.

    121.   Weil, G. E., *Massorah gedolah, iuxta codicem leningradensem B 19a* (Rome: Biblical Institute; Stuttgart: Württembergische Bibelanstalt, 1971). This is the first of a projected four-volume elaborate study of the large masorah of the medieval Hebrew Bible text, based mainly on ms. B 19a of Leningrad (A.D. 1008-9). It is a companion to *BHS* (§ 117) and supplies explanations for the *masora magna* at the bottom of the page above the *apparatus criticus*.

        See *CBQ* 36 (1974) 440-42; *NRT* 94 (1972) 788-89; *ZAW* 84 (1972) 290.

BPM   **122.**   Ayuso Marazuela, T. et al. (eds.), *Biblia polyglotta matritensia* (Madrid: Consejo superior de investigaciones científicas y BAC, 1957-   ). This is a laudable attempt to revive the tradition of polyglot Bibles. The publication, however, is to be made in many volumes. The project was launched when a prooemium was published in 1957, describing the ten projected series: (I) Hebrew

OT; (II) Greek NT; (III) Greek OT; (IV) Aramaic OT (Palestinian targums); (5) Aramaic OT (Tg. Onqelos and Tg. Jonathan); (VI) Syriac OT and NT; (VII) Vetus latina; (VIII) Spanish Vulgate; (IX) Coptic NT; (X) Castilian translation. To date the following volumes have appeared: IV/2 (Palestinian targums of Exodus, 1980); IV/3 (Palestinian targums of Leviticus, 1980); IV/4 (Palestinian targums of Numbers, 1977); IV/5 (Palestinian targums of Deuteronomy, 1980); VI (Tatian's Diatessaron, 1967); VII/21 (Vetus latina, Visigothic-Mozarabic Psalter, 1957); VIII/21 (Vulgata hispana, Jerome's Psalter "iuxta hebraeos," 1960).

See *RB* 63 (1956) 433-36; 69 (1962) 138-39; 85 (1978) 433-36; 90 (1983) 264-71; *CBQ* 24 (1962) 189-91; *JBL* 74 (1955) 52-53; 81 (1962) 203-4.

B. The Greek OT (Deuterocanonical and Apocryphal Books of the OT)

123. *******Septuaginta: Vetus Testamentum graece auctoritate Societatis Göttingensis editum* (Göttingen: Vandenhoeck & Ruprecht, 1931-   ). This great edition of the Greek OT was begun in 1931 under the direction of A. Rahlfs for the Septuaginta-Unternehmen of the Göttingen Academy of Sciences. Its aim is not to present any one Greek text, but, after careful and extensive study of families or groups of texts, to reconstruct a text which will be the oldest and closest to the original Old Greek (see B. J. Roberts, *The Old Testament Text* [§ 95], 164-67). The work is to be completed in 16 volumes; so far the following have appeared: 1 (*Genesis*, ed. J. W. Wevers, 1974); 2/2 (*Leviticus*, ed. J. W. Wevers, 1986); 3/1 (*Numeri*, ed. J. W. Wevers and U. Quast, 1982); 3/2 (*Deuteronomium*, ed. J. W. Wevers and U. Quast, 1977); 8/1 (*Esdrae liber I*, ed. R. Hanhart, 1974); 8/3 (*Esther*, ed. R. Hanhart, 1966); 8/4 (*Iudith*, ed. R. Hanhart, 1979); 8/5 (*Tobit*, ed. R. Hanhart, 1983); 9/1 (*Maccabaeorum liber I*, ed. W. Kappler, 1936; 2d ed. 1967); 9/2 (*Maccabaeorum liber II*, ed. W. Kappler and R. Hanhart, 1959); 9/3 (*Maccabaeorum liber III*, ed. R. Hanhart, 1960); 10 (*Psalmi cum odis*, ed. A. Rahlfs, 1931; 2d ed., 1967); 11/4 (*Job*, ed. J. Ziegler, 1982); 12/1 (*Sapientia Salomonis*, ed. J. Ziegler, 1962); 12/2 (*Sapientia Jesu filii Sirach*, ed. J. Ziegler, 1965); 13 (*Duodecim prophetae*, ed. J. Ziegler, 1943; 2d ed., 1967); 14 (*Isaias*, ed. J. Ziegler, 1939; 2d ed., 1967); 15 (*Ieremias, Baruch, Threni, Epistula Ieremiae*, ed. J. Ziegler, 1957); 16/1 (Ezechiel, ed. J. Ziegler, 1952; 2d ed., 1967); 16/2 (*Susanna, Daniel, Bel et Draco*, ed. J. Ziegler, 1954).

See S. Jellicoe, *The Septuagint* (§ 98), 297-310; *RB* 41 (1932) 289-92; 49 (1940) 264-71; 62 (1955) 117-18; 65 (1958) 292; 66 (1959) 424-30; 68 (1961) 456-57; 70 (1963) 465-66; 73 (1966) 456-57; 74 (1967) 449; *NRT* 104 (1982) 585-86.

OTG **124.** **Brooke, A. E., N. McLean, and H. St. J. Thackeray, *The Old Testament in Greek* (3 vols.; Cambridge, UK: University Press, 1906-40). Vol. 1 (1906-17) contains the Octateuch (Pentateuch, Joshua, Judges, Ruth); vol. 2 (1927-1935) the Later Historical Books (1-2 Samuel, 1-2 Kings, 1-2 Chronicles, 1 Esdras, Ezra, Nehemiah); vol. 3, part 1 (1940) Esther, Judith, and Tobit. This edition does not pretend to restore the original LXX; the text of ms. B, with supplements from other uncial mss., is printed, and an extensive *apparatus criticus* presents the variants of other uncials, cursives, and some versions. This is an indispensable tool for the study of the Greek Bible and for OT textual criticism. But now that some of the same OT books are appearing in the Göttingen LXX (§ 123), it is in part being superseded.

See S. Jellicoe, *The Septuagint* (§ 98), 269-97.

125. *Rahlfs, A., *Septuaginta* (9th ed.; 2 vols.; Stuttgart: Württembergische Bibelanstalt, 1984; editio minor in one vol., 1979). This work was first published in 1935, and all subsequent "editions" of it are merely reprints. The text is Rahlfs's own reconstruction of the "LXX" based on the uncials A, B, and S; a short *apparatus criticus* uses these and a few other mss. The work is intended as a manual edition to serve the needs of clergy and students; as such, it is the most convenient and most popular of all LXX editions. But it labors under obvious defects: an eclectic text and insufficient ms. evidence. The user must be cautioned against drawing ready arguments for textual emendation of the OT or for interpretation of the NT on the basis of Rahlfs's text. For these purposes, the big critical editions of Brooke–McLean–Thackeray and Göttingen are to be preferred.

See *ZAW* 60 (1944) 128-29, *RB* 45 (1936) 140.

126. Swete, H. B., *The Old Testament in Greek* (3 vols.; Cambridge, UK: University Press). This manual edition of the LXX was first published between 1887 and 1894; but various later editions have appeared: Vol. 1 (Genesis—4 Kings, 4th ed., 1909), vol. 2 (1 Chronicles—Tobit, 3d ed., 1905); vol. 3 (Hosea—4 Maccabees, 3d ed., 1907). The text is that of ms. B, with its lacunae supplied from mss. A and S. The *apparatus criticus* supplies from the latter mss. and from a few other early uncials. In contrast to Rahlfs's text, this edition has the advantage of giving the text of a single ms. (with variants from others). But M. L. Margolis, during his study of Joshua, found numerous inaccuracies in Swete's edition; and J. Ziegler, after his study of the Greek text of Amos, concluded that Swete's edition was unsatisfactory for scientific textual criticism.

See *AJSL* 28 (1911-12) 1-55; *ZAW* 60 (1944) 126-28.

127. Schechter, S. and C. Taylor, *The Wisdom of Ben Sira: Portions of the Book Ecclesiasticus from Hebrew Manuscripts in the Cairo Genizah Collection Presented to the University of Cambridge by the Editors* (Cambridge, UK: University Press, 1899). The *editio princeps* of the major Cairo Genizah fragments of Sirach.

> See A. Di Lella, *The Hebrew Text of Sirach* (The Hague: Mouton, 1966); *RB* 9 (1900) 158.

128. **The Book of Ben Sira: Text, Concordance and an Analysis of the of the Vocabulary* (Historical Dictionary of the Hebrew Language; Jerusalem: Academy of the Hebrew Language and the Shrine of the Book, 1973). An excellent modern study of the Hebrew text of Sirach, well described in its title; written in modern Hebrew.

> See *Sef* 34 (1974) 123-25.

129. Vattioni, F., *Ecclesiastico: Testo ebraico con apparato critico e versioni greca, latina e siriaca* (Pubblicazioni del seminario di semitistica, Testi 1; Naples: Istituto orientale di Napoli, 1968). This is the handiest edition of the text of Sirach in various versions, Hebrew, Greek, Latin, and Syriac. The Greek text is that of the *Septuaginta* of Göttingen; the Latin is that of the Vatican polyglott of the Vulgate; the Syriac is that of P. de Lagarde, based on British Museum Codex 12142 (6th century). The Hebrew text is mainly that of the mss. of the Cairo Genizah with readings in the *apparatus criticus* from Qumran and Masada.

> See *ZAW* 81 (1969) 431; *CBQ* 31 (1969) 619-22; *RB* 77 (1970) 626; *JSS* 14 (1969) 273.

130. Yadin, Y., *The Ben Sira Scroll from Masada: With Introduction, Emendations and Commentary* (Jerusalem: Israel Exploration Society and the Shrine of the Book, 1965). Fragments found at Masada contain the Hebrew text of Sir 39:27 – 43:30.

> See *JBL* 85 (1966) 260-62; *RB* 73 (1966) 457-59.

C. The NT

N–A[26]   **131.** **Nestle–Aland, *Novum Testamentum graece* (Stuttgart: Deutsche Bibelstiftung, 1979; 4th rev. repr., 1981). This most widely used pocket edition of the Greek NT was first published in 1898. The first editor, Eberhard Nestle, aimed at constructing a text not based on his own opinions or on the Textus Receptus, but on the critical editions of Tischendorf and Westcott–Hort. When they agreed, he reproduced their agreement; when they differed, he consulted Weymouth's *Resultant Greek Testament* and B. Weiss's *Das Neue Testament* for support. Editions from 1927 on, however, continued by the son Erwin, contain evidence from ms. witnesses

as well. As of the 23d edition, K. Aland became the editor of this
indispensable eclectic text of the Greek NT. The 26th edition,
"Nestle–Aland," has been edited by K. and B. Aland with the
collaboration of M. Black, C. M. Martini, B. M. Metzger, and A.
Wikgren. The Greek text purports to be the same as that of
UBSGNT (§ 132), but the *apparatus criticus* is vastly superior to
that of former editions of Nestle or of *UBSGNT*. The text has
been completely reset with a more pleasing Greek font; the
apparatus criticus is based on readings in mss. (papyri, uncials,
minuscles), versions, patristic citations, and lectionaries. The introduction is a gold mine of technical information. The appendices list the Greek and Latin mss. used in the preparation of
the 26th ed.; the differences in this text from that in other
scholars' editions; the OT passages cited in the NT; and sigla and
abbreviations. The text of N–A[26] is different from the Textus
Receptus, being based on what the editors consider the best
Greek mss. N–A[26] also exists in a form with the Latin of the
Neo-Vulgata (§ 163): *Novum Testamentum graece et latine* (1984);
with the English of the *RSV*, *Greek–English New Testament*
(1981); and with the German: *Novum Testamentum graece (26th
ed.): Deutscher Text, Lutherbibel revidiert 1984 und Einheitsübersetzung 1979* (1986).

See *TRu* 45 (1980) 85-88; 52 (1987) 1-58; *NTT* 34 (1980) 307-22;
JSNT 12 (1981) 53-68; *NTS* 27 (1981) 585-92; 28 (1982) 145-53; *JBL*
100 (1981) 614-18; *GTJ* 9 (1988) 279-85; *TRev* 77 (1981); *ETL* 55
(1979) 331-56; *JTS* 22 (1981) 19-49.

UBSGNT **132.** *Aland, K., M. Black, C. M. Martini, B. M. Metzger, and A.
Wikgren (eds.), *The Greek New Testament* (3d ed.; New York/
London/Edinburgh/Amsterdam/Stuttgart: United Bible Societies,
1975). First issued in 1966, this Greek NT has rapidly become a
widely-used edition, because its 3d ed. bears the same basic text as
N–A[26] (§ 131). The main difference is seen in the *apparatus
criticus*, which has been restricted to the major text-critical problems of the Greek NT. The restriction was made because of the
purpose of this edition, being destined for and adapted to the
needs of Bible translators throughout the world. To assist them,
the *apparatus criticus* uses a system of evaluation for the reading
preferred in the text (from A [a virtually certain reading] to D [a
reading with a very high degree of doubt]). For any problematic
passage represented in the *apparatus criticus* the evidence presented is often far more abundant than in earlier critical editions.
But a comparison of the *apparatus* in *UBSGNT*[3] with that in
N–A[26] quickly reveals the drawbacks of the former. Moreover,
though the evaluative judgment of the committee that worked on
the text is generally good, there are times when the judgments
have been affected by long-standing scholarly prejudices (e.g., the
so-called Western non-interpolations in the last chapters of the

Lucan Gospel; here the judgment is considerably too negative). See also B. M. Metzger, *A Textual Commentary on the Greek New Testament* (London/New York: United Bible Societies, 1971), in which Metzger explains the reasons for the committee's judgments and ratings. In a private communication Metzger has informed me that the evaluations of some readings have been upgraded for the forthcoming 4th ed. of this book.

See *NTS* 14 (1967-68) 136-43; *RB* 74 (1967) 288-89; 83 (1976) 631; *Int* 22 (1968) 92-96; *NovT* 15 (1973) 278-300; 17 (1975) 130-50; *JBL* 95 (1976) 112-21; *TLZ* 104 (1979) 260-70.

133. Merk, A., *Novum Testamentum graece et latine* (9th ed.; Rome: Biblical Institute, 1964). First published in 1933, its Greek text was based on von Soden's text I. But from the fourth and fifth editions on, this text was abandoned, and more recent editions offer an eclectic text based on the evidence of mss., ancient versions, readings in ecclesiastical writers, and critical studies. "Any scholar who seeks to gain as full a picture of the evidence [of NT mss. readings] as possible and neglects Merk, does so at his own peril" (G. D. Kilpatrick). The 9th edition contains a very useful appendix giving variants in recently discovered papyri. The Latin text is the second edition of the Sixto–Clementine Vulgate of 1592. C. M. Martini, who wrote the preface to the 9th ed., subsequently joined the team of editors of N–A[26], and apparently there will be no further editions of this work.

See *JTS* 50 (1949) 142-52; *RB* 53 (1946) 595-97 (reviews of the 5th ed.); *Gnomon* 12 (1936) 429-36; B. M. Metzger, *The Text* (§ 106), 143.

134. Bover, J. M., *Novi Testamenti biblia graeca et latina* (5th ed.; Madrid: Consejo Superior de Investigaciones Científicas, 1968). A resultant text based on the agreements of six main critical editions: Tischendorf, Westcott and Hort, B. Weiss, von Soden, Vogels, and Lagrange (for the Gospels, Romans, Galatians); with added information derived from Merk[2] and the works of Jacquier (Acts), A. C. Clark (Acts), and Allo (1 Corinthians, Revelation). When Bover mentions a reading, he often provides more data from minuscules, versions, and lectionaries than does Nestle[17] and adopts variants which, in his opinion, are supported by the testimony of the most ancient and best codices, versions, and ecclesiastical writers. In general, Bover's text recedes from the Alexandrian type and approaches that of the Byzantine, Western, and Caesarean.

See *NT trilingüe* (§ 135), xxxiii. B. M. Metzger, *Chapters in the History of New Testament Textual Criticism* (NTTS 4; Leiden: Brill; Grand Rapids, MI: Eerdmans, 1963) 135-41.

135. Bover, J. M. and J. O'Callaghan, *Nuevo Testamento trilingüe* (BAC 400; Madrid: La Editorial Católica, 1977). The Greek text of the NT is flanked by that of the Latin Vulgate; beneath them is Bover's latest Spanish translation. An *apparatus criticus* accompanies both the Greek and Latin texts; occasional brief notes explain the Spanish translation. The Latin text used is the "Neo-Vulgata" (§ 163), with the variants of the Sixto–Clementine Vulgate and the Stuttgart edition (§ 162) recorded in the *apparatus criticus*. The Greek text is an improved resultant text, going beyond Bover's 5th ed. (§ 135), listing the readings not only of its six main critical editions, but also of four others (Merk⁹, N–A²⁵, *UBSGNT³* [= N–A²⁶], Tasker). The *apparatus* adds witnesses from all the papyri. The introduction offers a Spanish translation of the majority of Bover's Latin prolegomena.

See *Bib* 59 (1978) 412-17; *BZ* 23 (1979) 290; *EstEcl* 54 (1979) 106-7.

136. Soden, H. von, *Die Schriften des Neuen Testaments in ihrer ältesten erreichbaren Textgestalt hergestellt auf Grund ihrer Textgeschichte* (2 vols. [the first in three parts]; 2d ed.; Göttingen: Vandenhoeck & Ruprecht, 1911, 1913). Von Soden divided the families of NT mss. into three recensions: K (*Koine* (= Antiochene or Syrian), H (*Hesychian* = Egyptian or Alexandrian), I (*Jerusalem* = Palestinian). His text is eclectic; the *apparatus criticus* is abundant, and much information about the text of the NT is to be found only here. Though old, it is still useful; but it must be used with care, since many modern scholars do not agree with the principles upon which the von Soden text is often based, and it contains many errors.

See *JTS* 15 (1914) 307-26; *CQR* 79 (1914-15) 57-68; *Bib* 4 (1923) 180 89; *ZNW* 8 (1907) 34-47; B. M. Metzger, *The Text* (§ 106), 142-43.

137. Tischendorf, C., *Novum Testamentum graece* (8th ed.; 2 vols.; Leipzig: Giesecke und Devrient, 1869, 1872). Volume 3, *Prolegomena* was written by C. R. Gregory (3 parts; Leipzig: Hinrichs, 1884, 1890, 1894). This work contains a thorough *apparatus criticus* that is helpful even today for many problems; but one has to remember that a good number of new texts have come to light since 1894.

See *CQR* 39 (1894-95) 137-59.

138. Vogels, H. J., *Novum Testamentum graece et latine* (2 vols.; Freiburg im B.: Herder, 1949, 1950). For vol. 1 this is the 3d ed.; for vol. 2, the 2d ed. The first edition appeared in 1922; the Greek text alone in 1920. The Greek text is not based on the consensus of modern critical editions, but on a number of original authorities (i.e., the mss. themselves). Its short *apparatus criticus* supplies variants from important majuscules and the chief minuscules, patristic readings, the Old Latin and Syriac versions. The Latin text is that of the Sixto–Clementine Vulgate. The text is somewhat out of date today, but it made its contribution in the early part of this century.

See *Bib* 2 (1921) 78-87; 5 (1924) 86-88; *JTS* 22 (1921) 174-75; *TS* 11 (1950) 141-42.

139. Westcott, B. F. and F. J. A. Hort, *The New Testament in the Original Greek* (2 vols.; rev. ed.; London and Cambridge, UK: Macmillan, 1890-96). The first edition appeared in 1881, and a larger one in 1885. It has been justly recognized as a landmark in the printed editions of the Greek NT. Though the authors distinguished the various NT mss. into four textual forms (the Syrian or Antiochene text, which underlies the Textus Receptus; the Western text, represented mainly by ms. D and the Vetus latina; the Alexandrian; and the Neutral, represented chiefly by Vaticanus and Sinaiticus), they based their edition mainly on the last mentioned. Even though text-critical study has moved far beyond Westcott–Hort, the influence of this edition is still seen in many ways.

See *CQR* 12 (1881) 514-21; 13 (1882) 419-51; B. M. Metzger, *The Text* (§ 106), 129-38.

140. Legg, S. C. E., *Nouum Testamentum graece secundum textum Westcotto–Hortianum: Euangelium secundum Marcum cum apparatu critico nouo plenissimo, lectionibus codicum nuper repertorum additis, editionibus uersionum antiquarum et patrum ecclesiasticorum denuo inuestigatis* (Oxford: Clarendon, 1935). ... *Euangelium secundum Matthaeum I*... (1940). An ambitious project, severely criticized by scholars.

See *RB* 44 (1935) 623-24; *ATR* 17 (1935) 172-73; *Gnomon* 13 (1937) 53; *JTS* 43 (1942) 30-34, 83-92.

OTQNT **141.** Archer, G. L. and G. Chirichigno, *Old Testament Quotations in the New Testament* (Chicago, IL: Moody, 1983). The OT passages quoted in the NT are listed in the order of the *KJV*. For each OT passage four columns are used on two facing pages: (1) the MT, (2) the LXX text [according to Rahlfs], (3) the NT form, and (4) commentary on the variations that the original text has undergone.

See *TS* 45 (1984) 591-92; *ConJ* 11 (1985) 113.

D. Synopses of the Greek Text of the Canonical Gospels

SQE **142.** **Aland, K., *Synopsis quattuor evangeliorum: Locis parallelis evangeliorum apocryphorum et patrum adhibitis* (13th ed. [revised]; Stuttgart: Deutsche Bibelstiftung, 1985). The text of each of the four Gospels is set out in parallel columns in its continuity, and relevant parallels from the other Gospels are given each time they are called for. The result is that the Synopsis is free of any particular theory of source-criticism. Relevant parallels from all parts of the NT, from NT apocrypha, and from patristic writers are cited as occasion offers. The text used is that of N–A[26], and the sigla are taken over from N–A[26]. In the 4th ed. (1967) evidence from 68 uncials not previously used was introduced; from still others in the 9th ed. The *apparatus criticus* consequently is full. In the 13th ed., the *apparatus* has been completely reorganized to cope with all the added material, but the rest of the page layout remains the same. Appendices contain the *Gospel of Thomas* (translated into Latin [by G. Garitte], German [by E. Haenchen], and English [by B. M. Metzger]); the testimony of ancient patristic writers about the origin of the gospel tradition; and tables of parallel passages.

See *JBL* 84 (1965) 436-38; *CBQ* 27 (1965) 265; *SPap* 7 (1968) 76-77; *HTR* 61 (1968) 39-50; *NovT* 21 (1979) 383-84; 29 (1987) 183; *Bib* 61 (1980) 305-29.

SFG **143.** Aland, K., *Synopsis of the Four Gospels: Greek–English Edition of the Synopsis quattuor evangeliorum: Completely Revised on the Basis of Nestle–Aland 26th Edition and Greek New Testament 3rd Edition: The English Text is the Second Edition of the Revised Standard Version* (5th ed.; New York/London: United Bible Societies, 1982). "The Greek part of this diglot edition agrees exactly with the comprehensive edition [§ 142] in its structure, arrangement of parallel texts, and critical apparatus. The last has even been enlarged by the addition of newly discovered papyri and uncials. Omitted are the appendices (the *Gospel of Thomas* and the witnesses of the early Church Fathers concerning the origin of the Gospels) and the additions to the individual pericopes from the apocryphal Gospels and the Church Fathers." The *apparatus criticus* of the English page includes variant readings in the *AV*, American and English *RV*, and the Catholic *RSV*.

See *CBQ* 36 (1974) 243; *Bib* 61 (1980) 305-29.

SDEE **144.** **Huck, A. and H. Greeven, *Synopse der drei ersten Evangelien mit Beigabe der johanneischen Parallelstellen: Synopsis of the First Three Gospels with the Addition of the Johannine Parallels* (13th ed.; Tübingen: Mohr [Siebeck], 1981). This is the updated successor of an old standby with the same title, published earlier by A. Huck and revised in the 9th ed. by H. Lietzmann (1936), of which a form with English titles for the sections was produced by F. L. Cross (Oxford: Blackwell, 1957). An English version of the latter, making use of the *RSV*, was produced by B. H. Throckmorton, Jr. (ed.), *Gospel Parallels: A Synopsis of the First Three Gospels* (4th ed.; London/Toronto/Camden, NJ: Nelson, 1979). "Each of the three Gospels is printed continuously word for word

in its proper column and in unaltered order and the correspond-
ing parallel passages are repeated as many times as this principle
demands. As a result the form is independent of any particular
theory about sources and can be readily used for studies from any
angle" (Cross's Preface). The new synopsis of Huck–Greeven
contains a rich *apparatus criticus*. Moreover, the Greek text of the
NT is not that of N–A[26] or *UBSGNT* but has been constructed
independently from manuscript readings; it merits, then, serious
consideration over against that of N–A[26].

See *RB* 90 (1983) 442-45; *CBQ* 45 (1983) 137-39; *JBL* 102 (1983)
144-46; *ETL* 58 (1982) 123-34, 135-39.

SGQE   **145.**   Boismard, M.-E. and A. Lamouille, *Synopsis graeca quattuor
evangeliorum* (Louvain/Paris: Peeters, 1986). The introduction of
this synopsis is written in French, English, and German and is
followed by a tabula synoptica. The Greek text is disposed in
columns and follows mainly the uncial mss. B, S, C, L and at
times the Western text. Parallels from the Apostolic Fathers,
patristic literature, Oxyrhynchus papyri, and the *Gospel of
Thomas* are cited. A variety of lines separate the columns to
enable the user to follow the texts listed. See also P. Benoit and
M.-E. Boismard, *Synopse des quatre évangiles en français avec
parallèles des apocryphes et des Pères* (3 vols.; Paris: Cerf, 1965,
1972, 1977). Volume 1 presents the basic text of the four Gospels
according to *SBJ*, modified according to the exigencies of the
Greek when put in parallel columns. The text of each Gospel is
repeated completely, and the parallels to a passage in any one are
repeated as often as necessary (the same principle as used in *SQE*
[§ 142]). The second edition of this volume (1972) was corrected
by P. Sandevoir. Volume 2 contains a commentary on the first,
written by M.-E. Boismard with the collaboration of A.
Lamouille and P. Sandevoir. The commentary makes use of a
solution to the synoptic problem, peculiar to the authors (see 2.
15-47). Volume 3 is devoted to *L'Evangile de Jean*.

See *VSpir* 14 (1966) 350-53; *BT* 18 (1967) 50-51; *CBQ* 29 (1967)
132-33; 50 (1988) 707-9; *RB* 79 (1972) 431-35; 96 (1989) 391-94; *JBL*
94 (1975) 128-32; *BZ* 32 (1988) 140-42; especially F. Neirynck, *Jean et
les Synoptiques: Examen critique de l'exégèse de M.-E. Boismard*
(BETL 49; Louvain: Leuven University, 1979); *ETL* 63 (1987) 119-35.

146. *Funk, R. W., *New Gospel Parallels: Volume One, The Synoptic
Gospels; Volume Two, John and the Other Gospels* (Foundations
and Facets 5-6; Philadelphia, PA: Fortress, 1985). This synopsis is
governed by formal narrative analysis of the Gospels. This means
that the gospel has to be read sequentially as well as in parallel
with other gospels. Hence vol. 1 begins with the Matthean Gospel
as a whole and juxtaposes to it the parallels in the other
Synoptics; then the Marcan Gospel is so presented, and finally

the Lucan Gospel. Appendices deal with John the Baptist, the Twelve and the Seventy, and with narrative summaries and transitions. Volume 2 presents the Johannine Gospel and the Gospel of Thomas in similar fashion; then the Infancy Gospels, the Passion Gospels, and the fragmentary Apocryphal Gospels. The text is that of the *RSV*, but it really should have been produced in the original texts of the Gospels themselves. "An intriguing work."

See *ExpTim* 97 (1985-86) 212; *BTB* 17 (1987) 114-15; *CBQ* 48 (1986) 744-46; *JBL* 106 (1987) 713-15.

SFGG   **147.** Orchard, J. B., *A Synopsis of the Four Gospels in Greek Arranged according to the Two-Gospel Hypothesis* (Edinburgh: Clark; Macon, GA: Mercer University, 1983). There exists also an English form of this work: *A Synopsis of the Four Gospels in a New Translation Arranged according to the Two-Gospel Hypothesis* (Macon, GA: Mercer University, 1982). Orchard maintains that the foregoing synopses (§ 142-44) are constructed on the presupposition of Marcan priority and that every synopsis reflects the prejudice of the one who constructs it. (Cf. D. L. Dungan, "Theory of Synopsis Construction," *Bib* 61 [1980] 305-29; F. Neirynck, "Once More: The Making of a Synopsis," *ETL* 62 [1986] 141-54.) Since Orchard favors a form of the Griesbach hypothesis (chronological sequence: Matthew, Luke, then Mark [an abridgement of the two Gospels]) as a solution to the synoptic problem, he has constructed this *Synopsis*, in which the parallel columns have the order: Matthew, Luke, Mark, John.

See *CBQ* 46 (1984) 588; *JBL* 103 (1984) 468-71.

HLSG   **148.** Swanson, R. J., *The Horizontal Line Synopsis of the Gospels (Revised)* (Pasadena, CA: William Carey Library, 1984). This book first appeared in 1975 (Dillsboro, NC: Western North Carolina Press). In part I Matthew is the lead Gospel, and the *RSV* text of Matthew is printed on the top line. Material from Mark and Luke that seem parallel are printed on the second and third lines, and the Johannine material on the fourth. In part II Mark becomes the lead Gospel; in part III, Luke; and in part IV, John. The parallel material is underlined. This mode of constructing a synopsis purports to be the most neutral.

See *JBL* 96 (1977) 138-39; *CBQ* 38 (1976) 422-23; *RB* 83 (1976) 633; 93 (1986) 471.

CHAPTER VI

Ancient Versions

In this chapter the aim is to list the most important editions of the ancient versions of the Bible. Since the Greek version of the OT, the so-called LXX, has already been listed in chap. V, the reader is referred to that part of this book. Here we shall list: (A) the Aramaic versions of the OT; (B) the Latin versions of the OT and the NT; (C) the Syriac versions of the OT and the NT; and (D) the Coptic versions of the OT and the NT. In the last three sections the entries will be given alphabetically, without distinction of the OT and NT.

A. Aramaic Versions of the Old Testament (the Targums)

149. *Sperber, A., *The Bible in Aramaic Based on Old Manuscripts and Printed Texts* (4 vols.; Leiden: Brill, 1959-73). This work contains a critical edition of various "official" targums: Vol. 1, The Pentateuch according to Tg. Onqelos (1959); vol. 2, The Former Prophets according to Tg. Jonathan (1959); vol. 3, The Latter Prophets according to Tg. Jonathan (1962); vol. 4a, The Targums of Chronicles, Ruth, Canticles, Lamentations, Ecclesiastes, and Esther (1968); vol. 4b, a study of "the targum and the Hebrew Bible" (1973). This is the best edition to date of these targums, but it is not without its defects.

See *VT* 10 (1960) 383-84; *JSS* 5 (1960) 286-88, 430-31; 9 (1964) 379.

150. Díez Macho, A. (ed.), *Neophyti 1, Targum palestinense, Ms de la Biblioteca Vaticana: Tomo I, Génesis: Edición príncipe, introducción general y versión castellana* (Textos y estudios 7-11; Madrid/ Barcelona: Consejo Superior de Investigaciones Científicas, 1968); *Tomo II, Exodo* (1970); *Tomo III, Levítico* (1971); *Tomo IV, Números* (1974); *Tomo V, Deuteronomio* (1978); *Tomo VI, Apéndices* (1979). A deluxe edition of an Aramaic translation of the Pentateuch, with accompanying translations into Spanish (A. Díez Macho), French (R. Le Déaut) and English (M. McNamara and M. Maher). The editor has at times tampered with the text so that it is not always clear just what the ms. itself reads. For any serious text-critical work, it must be controlled either by consulting a microfilm (available from the Vatican Library) or by using the facsimile edition, *The Palestinian Targum to the Pentateuch: Codex Vatican Neofiti I* (Jerusalem: Makor, 1970).

Vol. 1 = Codex Neofiti 1, fols. 1r-109v; vol. 2 = fols. 110r-200v; vol. 3 = fols. 201r-257v; vol. 4 = fols. 258r-355v; vol. 5 = fols. 356r-end.

> See *CBQ* 32 (1970) 107-12; *JBL* 91 (1972) 575-78; 95 (1976) 315-17; *RB* 77 (1970) 253-59; 78 (1971) 270-74; 80 (1973) 106-12; 81 (1974) 450-57; 86 (1979) 468-72; 88 (1981) 420-21.

151. Kahle, P., *Masoreten des Westens* (2 vols.; Stuttgart: Kohlhammer, 1927, 1930; repr. in one volume, Hildesheim/New York: Olms, 1967). The second volume contains the text of five fragmentary targums of the Pentateuch and of two Aramaic liturgical texts which quote pentateuchal passages. They come from the Cairo Genizah and are said to be Palestinian in origin and older than the texts preserved in the so-called Fragmentary Targum (§ 152).

> See R. Le Déaut, *Introduction* (§ 102), 109-13; *RB* 38 (1929) 266-71; 40 (1931) 464-65.

152. Klein, M. L., *The Fragment-Targums of the Pentateuch: According to Their Extant Sources* (AnBib 76; 2 vols.; Rome: Biblical Institute, 1980). A critical edition of the so-called Fragmentary Targum of the Pentateuch. Volume I presents the texts, indices, and introductory essays; volume II, the English translation.

> See *RB* 89 (1982) 599-605; *CBQ* 44 (1982) 651-52.

153. Clarke, E. G. (with the collaboration of W. E. Aufrecht, J. C. Hurd, and F. Spitzer), *Targum Pseudo-Jonathan of the Pentateuch: Text and Concordance* (Hoboken, NJ: Ktav, 1984). This is a critical edition of the targum according to the British Museum ms. Add. 27031. It reproduces the errors of the manuscript itself. It thus supersedes the editions of Tg. Ps.-Jonathan of M. Ginsburger and D. Rieder (§ 154). It is also accompanied by a Key-Word-in-Context concordance of the targum.

> See *RB* 93 (1986) 605-8; *JBL* 106 (1987) 154-55; *TS* 46 (1985) 712-14; *CBQ* 49 (1987) 108-9.

154. Rieder, D., *Pseudo-Jonathan, Targum Jonathan ben Uziel on the Pentateuch Copied fron* [sic] *the London MS. (Britich* [sic] *Museum add. 27031)* (Jerusalem: Private publication [now out of print], 1974). This edition of Tg. Pseudo-Jonathan is superior to that of M. Ginsburger, *Pseudo-Jonathan* (Berlin: Calvary, 1903; repr., Hildesheim/New York: Olms, 1971), but it is far from a perfect reproduction of the London ms. A good French translation of this targum can be found in R. Le Déaut and J. Robert, *Targum du Pentateuque* (SC 245, 256, 261, 271; 4 vols.; Paris: Cerf, 1978, 1979, 1979, 1980), with that of Neofiti 1 facing it. See also J. W. Etheridge, *The Targums of Onkelos and Jonathan ben Uzziel on* *the Pentateuch with the Fragments of the Jerusalem Targum* (2 vols. in one; New York [now Hoboken, NJ]: Ktav, 1968); but this translation must always be checked against the texts themselves. See *JBL* 94 (1975) 277-79.

155. Le Déaut, R. and J. Robert, *Targum des Chroniques* (AnBib 51; 2 vols.; Rome: Biblical Institute, 1971). This edition contains an introduction, the Aramaic text, a French translation, and a glossary of a targum of Chronicles preserved in the Vatican ms. Urb. ebr. 1.

      See *RB* 80 (1973) 313-14; *Bib* 53 (1972) 132-37.

156. Lagarde, P. de, *Hagiographa chaldaice* (Leipzig: Teubner, 1873; repr., Osnabrück: Zeller, 1967). This edition contains an Aramaic translation of the Psalter, Job, Proverbs, Canticles, Ruth, Lamentations, Ecclesiastes, Esther I and II, Chronicles, and the Dream of Mordechai. For some of these books the edition of A. Sperber (§ 149) is to be preferred; but this edition still has to be used for OT books not included by Sperber, until better (critical) editions of the targums of the Writings are prepared.

157. McNamara, M. (director), *The Aramaic Bible: The Targums* (19 vols.; Wilmington, DE: Glazier, 1987-   ). This is a fresh English translation of all the known targums based on the best critical editions available. Each volume contains a brief introduction, a translation, and notes of varying sorts (often calling attention to divergences of the targumic rendering from the MT). To date nine volumes have appeared: 6 (Tg. Onqelos of Genesis [B. Grossfeld], 1988); 7 (Tg. Onqelos of Exodus [B. Grossfeld], 1988); 8 (Tg. Onqelos of Leviticus and Numbers [B. Grossfeld], 1988); 9 (Tg. Onqelos of Deuteronomy [B. Grossfeld], 1988); 10 (Tg. Jonathan of the Former Prophets [D. J. Harrington and A. J. Saldarini], 1987); 11 (Tg. Isaiah [B. D. Chilton], 1987); 12 (Tg. Jeremiah [R. Hayward], 1987); 13 (Tg. Ezekiel [S. H. Levey], 1987); 14 (Tg. of the Minor Prophets, 1989). The English translations are of uneven quality.

      See *TS* 49 (1988) 735-39; *RB* 95 (1988) 612-14.

B. Latin Versions of the OT and the NT

VL   158. *Vetus latina: Die Reste der altlateinischen Bibel nach Petrus Sabatier neu gesammelt und herausgegeben von der Erzabtei Beuron* (Freiburg im B.: Herder, 1949-   ). This monumental work is eventually to be completed in 27 vols., covering both the OT and the NT. In 1949, B. Fischer published the first volume, *Verzeichnis der Sigel für Handschriften und Kirchenschriftsteller*. A third edition of this volume was prepared by H. J.

Frede, *Kirchenschriftsteller: Verzeichnis und Sigel* (1981). The following volumes have appeared: 2 (*Genesis*, 1949-54); 11/1 (*Wisdom*, 1977-85); 11/2 (Sirach [fasc. 1-2, introduction], 1987-88); 12 (Isaiah [fasc. 1-4, up to Isa 10:19], 1987-89); 24/1 (*Ephesians*, 1962-64); 24/2 *Philippians and Colossians*, 1966-71); 25/1-2 (*Thessalonians, Timothy, Titus, Philemon, and Hebrews*, 1975-82 [fasc. 1-6 of part 2, up to Heb 7:10]); 26/1 (*Catholic Epistles*, 1956-69). This work is proving to be a very important tool for the study of the Latin Bible prior to the Vulgate tradition. There is also an accompanying *Ergänzende Schriften-reihe* of nine vols.

> See *RB* 58 (1951) 455-56; 59 (1952) 279-80; 60 (1953) 308-9; 62 (1955) 275-76; 71 (1964) 443-44; 96 (1989) 312, 606-7; *FF* 29 (1959) 46-57; *CBQ* 31 (1969) 137-42; 33 (1971) 147-50.

159. Julicher, A., *Itala, das Neue Testament in altlateinischer Ueber-lieferung* (Berlin: de Gruyter, 1938-   ). The publication of the Vetus Itala, begun by A. Jülicher, has been continued by W. Matzkow, and more recently by K. Aland. So far four volumes have appeared, and the first three have been revised. Volume 1 contains the Matthean Gospel (1938, rev. ed. 1972); vol. 2, the Marcan Gospel (1940, rev. ed., 1970); vol. 3 the Lucan Gospel (1954, rev. ed., 1976); vol. 4, the Johannine Gospel (1963).

> See *RB* 48 (1939) 126-27; 63 (1956) 456-57; 71 (1964) 442-43; *Bib* 41 (1960) 441; 45 (1964) 104-5; *JTS* 40 (1939) 281-83.

160. *Wordsworth, J. and H. J. White (eds)., *Nouum Testamentum domini nostri Jesu Christi latine secundum editionem s. Hieronymi ad codicum manuscriptorum fidem* (3 vols.; Oxford: Clarendon, 1889-1954). This is the critical edition of the Latin Vulgate text of the NT. The Gospels appeared fairly rapidly between 1889 and 1895, but the rest of the NT was slow in being published (Acts, 1905; Romans, 1911; the rest of the Pauline corpus, 1941; the remaining part, 1954). The tedious work was slowed up by the consultation of many more mss. after the publication of the Gospels, and then by the death of Wordsworth in 1911 and of White in 1934. Prominent English scholars collaborated in various phases of the work; after 1934 it was under the direction of H. F. D. Sparks. It is an indispensable *instrument de travail* for the study of the Latin Bible; its high scientific value and merits have often been pointed out.

> See *ZNW* 46 (1955) 178-96; *JTS* 43 (1942) 98-99; *NRT* 76 (1954) 544; B. M. Metzger, *Early Versions* (§ 115), 285-374; K. Aland, *Die alten Übersetzungen* (§ 114), 49-79.

161. *Biblia sacra juxta latinam Vulgatam versionem ad codicum fidem ... cura et studio monachorum abbatiae pontificiae s. Hieronymi in Urbe ordinis sancti Benedicti editu* (Rome: Vatican

Polyglot Press, 1926-   ). So far 14 volumes, covering most of
the OT, have appeared (only Ezekiel, Daniel, and the Minor
Prophets are missing). The edition was launched in 1907 under
the direction of Card. Gasquet (cf. "Vulgate, Revision of,"
Catholic Encyclopedia 15 [1912] 515-20, for Gasquet's own
description of the undertaking). Its aim was "to determine as
accurately as possible the text of St. Jerome's Latin translation,
made in the fourth century." H. Quentin was appointed editor,
and he established the principles on which the work proceeds.
While the principles of editing have been criticized, and though
the resulting text cannot be called the original Vulgate of Jerome,
this edition has very great importance for the history of the
Vulgate and for the textual criticism of the OT and the NT. A
cursory comparison of this text with the Sixto–Clementine
Vulgate will convince the student that many readings have been
going erroneously by the name "Vulgate."

See *Bib* 11 (1930) 458-64; B. J. Roberts, *Old Testament Text* (§95),
260-62; *RB* 96 (1989) 607.

162. *Weber, R. (ed.), *Biblia sacra juxta vulgatam versionem* (2 vols.;
Stuttgart: Württembergische Bibelanstalt, 1969; 2d ed., 1975). The
editor of this manual edition of the Vulgate was aided by an
interconfessional team of collaborators (B. Fischer, J. Gribomont,
H. F. D. Sparks, and W. Thiele). The text presents the Latin
Vulgate version of the protocanonical and deuterocanonical books,
and in an appendix that of the Prayer of Manasseh, 3 Ezra, 4 Ezra,
Psalm 151, and the Epistle to the Laodiceans. The Psalter is that of
both "iuxta LXX" and "iuxta hebraicum." The prefaces of Jerome
precede various books, and useful cross-references are supplied in
the margins. The text of the Vulgate is based on critical editions
(that of the Benedictines of San Girolamo for the OT; that of J.
Wordsworth and H. J. White for the NT).

See *RB* 77 (1970) 469-70.

163. *Nova Vulgata bibliorum sacrorum editio* (Vatican City: Libreria
editrice Vaticana, 1979). A new edition of the Latin Vulgate, or
the "Neo-Vulgata," ordered after the Second Vatican Council by
Pope Paul VI in 1966 (*AAS* 59 [1967] 53-54) for use in the
revision of the Roman Catholic liturgy. It appeared piecemeal, in
several fascicles from 1969-1977; but it has now been issued in
one volume. It contains only the books in the Roman Catholic
canon and does not have in an appendix the pseudepigraphical
books often associated with the Vulgate tradition. Its aim was to
correct the Vulgate in use, taking into account the critical work of
the Benedictines of San Girolamo (§161), but also other factors
(e.g., readability in public, singability in choir).

See *RB* 85 (1978) 470; *OTA* 3 (1980) 4-5; *EstBib* 38 (1979-80) 115-38;
39 (1981) 177-78.

C. Syriac Versions of the OT and the NT

164. Dirksen, P. B., *An Annotated Bibliography of the Peshitta of the Old Testament* (Monographs of the Peshitta Institute 5; Leiden/ New York: Brill, 1989). 532 books and articles are analyzed under nine headings: general; surveys and catalogues of mss.; individual mss.; text editions; publications concerning printed editions; collections of variant readings; concordances and word lists; studies about separate (groups of) books; specific subjects.

165. The Peshitta Institute of the University of Leiden, *List of Old Testament Peshitta Manuscripts (Preliminary Issue)* (Leiden: Brill, 1961). A handy list of Peshitta mss., prepared for the use of co-workers of the project to publish a critical edition of the Peshitta OT.

OTSPV   **166.** *The Peshitta Institute of the University of Leiden, *The Old Testament in Syriac according to the Peshitta Version* (Leiden: Brill, 1972-   ). This critical edition of the Syriac OT is being published on behalf of the International Organization for the Study of the Old Testament. It is to be a multivolume work. So far there have appeared a general preface (describing the project, 1972), a sample edition (containing the Song of Songs, Tobit, 4 Esdras, 1966), Part I/1 (rewritten preface, Genesis, Exodus, 1977), II/1a (Job, 1982), II/2 (Judges, 1-2 Samuel, 1978), II/3 (Psalms, 1980), II/4 (1-2 Kings, 1976), II/5 (Proverbs, Wisdom, Qohelet, Song of Songs, 1979), III/1 (Isaiah, 1987), III/3 (Ezekiel, 1985), III/4 (Dodeka-propheton, Daniel-Bel-Draco, 1980), IV/3 (Apocalypse of Baruch, 4 Esdras, 1973), IV/6 (Canticles or Odes, Prayer of Manasseh, Apocryphal Psalms, Psalms of Solomon, Tobit, 1[3] Esdras, 1972). The unpointed Estrangela form of Syriac is used.

   See *JBL* 94 (1975) 454-55; 103 (1984) 107-8.

167. *Ceriani, A. M., *Translatio syra pescitto Veteris Testamenti ex codice ambrosiano sec. fere vi photolithographice edita* (2 vols., Milan: A. della Croce, 1876). A photographic reproduction of an ancient Syriac ms. of the OT, the only one to be used for most problems, when there is not yet a volume in the critical edition of the Peshitta OT (§ 166).

168. Dominicans of Mossul, *Biblia sacra juxta versionem simplicem quae dicitur Pschitta* (3 vols.; Beirut: Imprimerie catholique, 1951). This is a corrected, photographically reduced offset edition of that originally published in Mossul, 1886-91. Volumes 1-2 contain the OT, vol. 3 the NT. The Nestorian form of Syriac is used. This is not a critical edition of the Syriac Bible, but its usefulness in manual form has long been recognized.

169. *Ketābā' qaddîšā': Diyatîqî' 'attîqā'* (London: Trinitarian Bible Society, n.d.; repr., 1954). A manual edition of the Syriac text of 39 books of the Hebrew canon. The Nestorian form of Syriac is used. The text is that of the Peshitta. This publication is inferior to that of the Mossul Dominicans (§ 168).

170. Burkitt, F. C., *Evangelion da-Mepharreshe: The Curetonian Syriac Gospels, Re-edited, together with the Readings of the Sinaitic Palimpsest...* (2 vols.; Cambridge, UK: University Press, 1904). The is the standard publication of the Old Syriac "Gospel of the Separated" (syr^cur), which dates from the 5th century A. D.

171. Lewis, A. S., *The Old Syriac Gospels or Evangelion da-Mepharreshe: Being the Text of the Sinai or Syro-Antiochian Palimpsest, Including the Latest Additions and Emendations, with the Variants of the Curetonian Text* (London: Williams & Norgate, 1910). This is the standard publication of the Old Syriac "Gospel of the Separated" (syr^sin), which probably dates from the end of the 4th century A.D.

See B. M. Metzger, *Early Versions* (§ 115), 36-48.

172. *Pusey, P. E. and G. H. Gwilliam, *Tetraeuangelium sanctum juxta simplicem Syrorum versionem ad fidem codicum, massorae, editionum denuo recognitum* (Oxford: Clarendon, 1901). The Serta form of Syriac is used in this critical edition of the Syriac Gospels in the Peshitta version. The text is accompanied by a list of Syriac codices, tables of the Eusebian canons, a Latin translation of the Syriac text, and an *apparatus criticus* (mixed with occasional notes of another sort).

See B. M. Metzger, *Early Versions* (§ 115), 48-63; K. Aland, *Die alten Übersetzungen* (§ 114), 120-59; *CQR* 56 (1903) 143-71.

173. Kilgour, R. (ed.), *The New Testament in Syriac* (London: British and Foreign Bible Society, 1950). "In 1905 the British and Foreign Bible Society published an edition of the Gospels in Syriac, reprinted by permission from a revised text of the Peshitta Version which had been prepared by the late Rev. G. H. Gwilliam [§ 172].... To these have now [i.e., 1919] been added the books from Acts to Revelation, thus completing the New Testament" (p. iii). The text of Acts, James, 1 Peter, 1 John, and the Pauline Epistles (including Hebrews) "follows a critical revision of the Peshitta originally undertaken by Mr. Gwilliam for the Clarendon Press as a completion of his edition of the Gospels" (ibid.). These 18 books are arranged in the order found in many of the oldest Syriac mss. In an appendix one finds 2 Peter, 2-3 John, Jude, Revelation, which were not canonical in the Peshitta. The text of Revelation is derived from an 1897 edition published by J. Gwynn; and the text of the four epistles follows the Philoxenian Version. The Serta form of Syriac is used.

D. Coptic Versions of the OT and the NT

174. Lagarde, P. de, *Der Pentateuch koptisch* (Leipzig: Teubner, 1867; repr., Osnabrück: Zeller, 1967). Not a critical edition of the Coptic OT, but convenient for consultation, in lieu of something better.

175. Peters, M.K.H., *A Critical Edition of the Coptic (Bohairic) Pentateuch: Volume 5, Deuteronomy* (SBLSCS 15; Atlanta, GA: Scholars, 1983). Peter's edition is based on eight Coptic mss., diligently studied for their relationships.

See *CBQ* 47 (1985) 332-33; *RB* 91 (1984) 468-69.

176. Kosack, W., *Proverbia Salomonis achmimisch, sahidisch, bohairisch und arabisch* (Vetus Testamentum coptice 1; Bonn: R. Habelt, 1973). This is the beginning of an important attempt to publish in better form what remains of various Coptic dialects as translations of OT books, but it is not without its problems.

177. Horner G.W. (ed.), *The Coptic Version of the New Testament in the Northern Dialect, Otherwise Called Memphitic and Bohairic, with Introduction, Critical Apparatus, and Literal English Translation* (4 vols.; Oxford: Clarendon, 1898-1905).

See *RB* 8 (1899) 148-50; 14 (1905) 457-59.

178. (Horner, G.W. [ed.]), *The Coptic Version of the New Testament in the Southern Dialect, Otherwise Called Sahidic and Thebaic, with Critical Apparatus, Literal English Translation, Register of Fragments and Estimate of the Version* (7 vols.; Oxford. Clarendon, 1911-24).

See *RB* 30 (1921) 278-82; 32 (1923) 302-7; 34 (1925) 623-24.

179. *Quecke, H., *Das Markusevangelium saïdisch: Text der Handschrift PPalau Rib. Inv.-Nr. 182 mit den Varianten der Handschrift M 569* (Papyrologica castroctaviana, studia et textus 4; Barcelona: Papyrologica castroctaviana, 1972 [distributed by Biblical Institute Press, Rome]). The Sahidic text of Mark's Gospel is presented according to two main manuscripts which preserve it. The same has been done for Luke's Gospel, *Das Lukasevangelium saïdisch: Text der Handschrift PPalau Rib. Inv.-Nr. 181 mit den Varianten der Handschrift M 569* (Papyrologica castroctaviana, studia et textus 6; Barcelona: Papyrologica castroctaviana, 1977); and for John's Gospel, *Das Johannesevangelium saïdisch: Text der Handschrift PPalau Rib. Inv.-Nr. 183 mit den Varianten der Handschriften 813 und 814 der Chester Beatty Library und der Handschrift M 569* (Papyrologica castroctaviana, studia et textus 11; Barcelona: Papyrologica castroctaviana, 1984). This is the best set of texts to consult for these Gospels.

See *Bib* 59 (1978) 439-42; 67 (1986) 407-9; *JBL* 93 (1974) 118-19; 98 (1979) 446-47; *RB* 88 (1981) 313-14; 96 (1989) 460; *JTS* 25 (1974) 164-65; 37 (1986) 301-2.

CHAPTER VII

Modern Versions

In earlier editions of this book this chapter was devoted to English versions of the Bible. Now we are including some entries on other modern translations in French, German, Italian, and Spanish. It would be impossible and really needless to give here an account of the modern translations of the Bible which have appeared in the last 450 years. In general, one may consult the *Cambridge History of the Bible* (§ 92), especially vol. 3, where a survey is given of the versions in many languages. A few are selected for comment because they are in modern use and invite comparison.

A. **English**

180. For details on earlier versions and on the history of the English Bible, one should consult the convenient summaries in such books as H. W. Robinson, *The Bible in Its Ancient and English Versions* (Oxford: Clarendon, 1954) 128-74 (with bibliography for important older materials); F. F. Bruce, *History of the Bible in English: From the Earliest Versions* (3d ed.; New York: Oxford University, 1978); earlier editions of this book had a different title (*The English Bible*). Cf. A. S. Herbert, *Historical Catalogue of Printed Editions of the English Bible 1525-1961: Revised and Expanded from the Edition of T. H. Darlow and H. F. Moule, 1903* (London: British and Foreign Bible Society; New York: American Bible Society, 1968). See also L. A. Weigle, *The New Testament Octapla: Eight English Versions of the New Testament in the Tyndale–King James Tradition* (New York: Nelson, 1962); it contains Tyndale, Great, Geneva, Bishops, Rheims, *KJV, RV, RSV*. S. Kubo and W. Specht have written a frank adssessment of 15 English versions of the Bible produced in this century: *So Many Versions? Twentieth Century English Versions of the Bible* (Grand Rapids, MI: Zondervan, 1975).

See L. R. Bailey (ed.), *Duke Divinity School Review* 44 (1979) 67-195 (assessment of *RSV, JB, NEB, NAB, Living Bible, GNB, NIV,* and *NJV*).

181. *The Complete Bible: An American Translation* (rev. ed.; Chicago, IL: University of Chicago, 1939). This is an independent translation of the OT and the NT, often called the "Chicago Bible," the excellence of which is not to be underestimated, even though it has not been recognized for official church-usage. In 1923, E. J.

Goodspeed published a translation of the NT in modern English, based on the Greek text of Westcott–Hort, *The New Testament: An American Translation* (Chicago, IL: University of Chicago). Of it J. L. McKenzie once wrote: "A comparison of the modern versions raises one's esteem of G as nothing else will. He was the first to break out of the chains of 'Bible English,' and he not only broke out, he shattered the chains." In 1927, a translation of the OT was issued by a group of scholars under the editorship of J. M. Powis Smith; this edition contained nearly 100 pages of closely printed textual notes justifying the translation, but unfortunately they have been omitted in later editions. In 1935, this OT translation was revised by T. J. Meek with the assistance of L. Waterman. In 1938, Goodspeed published *The Apocrypha: An American Translation* (Chicago, IL: University of Chicago). Finally, all these independently produced translations were combined in the edition of 1939. An edition of Goodspeed's NT translation facing the Greek text of Westcott–Hort was produced in 1954, *The Student's New Testament—The Greek Text and the American Translation* (Chicago, IL: University of Chicago, 1954).

See *ExpTim* 35 (1923-24) 110-11; *CBQ* 16 (1954) 382; *JBL* 37 (1954) 86-91.

RSV

RSVWA

182. *******The Holy Bible: Revised Standard Version, Containing the Old and New Testaments, Translated from the Original Tongues, Being the Version Set Forth A.D. 1611, Revised A.D. 1881-1885 and A.D. 1901; Compared with the Most Ancient Authorities and Revised A.D. 1946-1952. — The Apocrypha of the Old Testament: Revised Standard Version* New York: Nelson, 1952, 1956, 1957). These parts of the *RSV* are available separately or in one volume. The translation of the OT (according to the Hebrew canon) and of the NT was prepared under the direction of the Division of Christian Education of the National Council of Churches of Christ in America. It represents the third authorized revision of the *KJV* or *AV* of 1611, being preceded by the *American Standard Version* of 1901 and the English *Revised Version* of 1881-1885. A second edition of the *RSV* NT appeared in 1971, and further revision of both the OT and the NT is under way. The translation of the OT Apocrypha includes the seven deuterocanonical books (Judith, Tobit, Wisdom, Ecclesiasticus, Baruch, and 1-2 Maccabees [mnemonic: J. T. Web and the Two MacCabes]), the five deuterocanonical parts of three books (Additions to Esther, Epistle of Jeremy, Prayer of Azariah and Song of Three Young Men, Susanna, Bel and the Dragon), and apocryphal writings (Prayer of Manasseh, and 1-2 Esdras). The Hebrew text on which the revision of the OT was based was BHK^3, with an eye on the ancient versions; the Greek text used for most of the Apocrypha is that of Rahlfs's LXX; for 2 Esdras, the text is that of the Vetus Latina, ed. by R. L. Bensly. The Greek text used at first for the

NT translation differed little from Westcott–Hort's, but it has gradually approached more and more that of Nestle. The 1946-1952 translators were prominent Protestant OT and NT scholars, but in recent years Jewish and Roman Catholic scholars have been added to the committee. A brochure, prepared by 12 members of the revision committee under the direction of L. A. Weigle, *An Introduction to the Revised Standard Version of the Old Testament* (New York: Nelson, 1952), furnishes the general reader with some idea of the principles which guided the revision. Being a revision of former versions, the *RSV* is not "a new translation in the language of today," but retains much "Bible English." A forthcoming revision is to eliminate much of this (e.g., the use of "thou" and "thee" when God is addressed). Yet this translation is generally preferred in many circles because of its fidelity to the original texts and its suitability in pedagogic settings. A new edition of the Apocrypha includes the apocryphal Psalm 151 and 3 Maccabees; these are "canonical" in the Greek Orthodox tradition, toward which the *RSV* has now been adjusted. (The apocryphal 4 Maccabees is included in an appendix.)

Since the *RSV* is published in different forms, the Roman Catholic student should use a form "with the Apocrypha" (*RSVWA*), which contains the deuterocanonical books and parts of books in the Roman Catholic canon. In fact, such a form is recommended to serious Bible students of any confessional background because of the accessibility of these intertestamental Jewish writings here, often important for the interpretation of the NT. However, attention may be called to three specific forms of

RSVCB

the *RSV*: (a) *The Holy Bible: Revised Standard Version, Containing the Old and New Testaments with the Apocrypha/ Deuterocanonical Book: An Ecumenical Edition* (New York/ Glasgow: Collins, 1973). This popularly-called "Common Bible" clearly distinguishes the deuterocanonical and apocryphal books of the OT, but prints them both between the translations of the OT and the NT. A form also exists in which the Greek Orthodox can find Psalm 151 and 3 Maccabees.

OABWA

(b) **May, H. G. and B. M. Metzger (eds.), *The New Oxford Annotated Bible with the Apocrypha: Revised Standard Version: Containing the Second Edition of the New Testament and an Expanded Edition of the Apocrypha* (New York: Oxford University, 1977). This is the "expanded edition" of an ecumenical study Bible. R. Card. Cushing, Abp. of Boston, gave an imprimatur to the first edition of *OABWA*; and Athenagoras, Orthodox Abp. of Thyateira and Great Britain, his approval of this expanded edition (which includes an Engl. tr. of Psalm 151 and 3-4 Maccabees, the first two of which are canonical for the Greek Orthodox).

RSVCE

(c) *The Holy Bible: Revised Standard Version: Catholic Edition* (London: Catholic Truth Society, 1966). The form of the *RSV* bears the imprimatur of the Abp. of St. Andrews and Edinburgh, Scotland. No changes were introduced in the text of the OT by the members of the Catholic Biblical Association of Great Britain, who prepared it for publication; but the separate publication of the *RSVCE* NT in 1965 (Collegeville, MN: St. John's Abbey) contains a "list of changes" in Appendix 2, which fills about 3½ pages of fine print in columns (not always full). There are 66 changes modifying both the text and the footnotes of the *RSV*; some of the changes are highly questionable. Fortunately, such tampering with the *RSV* text was not the condition for the imprimatur given to *OABWA*.

For the OT, see *JQR* 43 (1952-53) 381-84; *Int* 7 (1953) 338-44; *ATR* 36 (1954) 111-23; *CBQ* 17 (1955) 88-90; *Eleven Years* (§ 7), 485-86. — For the NT, see *JBL* 66 (1947) 361-84; *TS* 7 (1946) 321-25; *JTS* 49 (1948) 118-24. — For the Apocrypha, see *RB* 66 (1959) 607; *TToday* 14 (1957) 420-26; *JBL* 78 (1959) 253-55. — For *RSVCE* NT, see *TS* 26 (1965) 672-75.

NAB   **183.** **Members of the Catholic Biblical Association of America, *The New American Bible: Translated from the Original Languages with Critical Use of All the Ancient Sources: With Textual Notes on Old Testament Readings* (2 vols. in one; Paterson, NJ: St. Anthony Guild, 1970). This is an authorized English translation of the OT and the NT, sponsored by the Bishops' Committee of the Confraternity of Christian Doctrine in the U.S.A. It replaces an

CCD   earlier form of the same translation-project, *The Holy Bible: Confraternity of Christian Doctrine* (Paterson: St. Anthony Guild, 1941-1969), which appeared in five volumes: *The New Testament of Our Lord and Savior Jesus Christ, Translated from the Latin Vulgate* (1941); and four volumes of the OT ("Genesis to Ruth," 1952 [after a trial edition, "Genesis," 1948]; "Isaiah to Malachi," 1955; "Job to Sirach," 1960 [after a trial edition, "Psalms," 1950]; and "Samuel to Maccabees," 1969).

The *NAB* represents the first attempt to provide English-speaking Roman Catholics with a complete Bible translated from the original Hebrew, Aramaic, and Greek, and not from the Latin Vulgate, as was formerly the custom since the Council of Trent. Some non-Roman-Catholic scholars (F. M. Cross, D. N. Freedman, J. Knox, and J. A. Sanders) were invited to help in preparing parts of the translation. The rendering of the OT in the *NAB* was more successful than that of the NT, which was

NABNTRE   criticized at times. The latter has now been revised: *The New American Bible: The New Testament Revised Edition* (New York: Catholic Book Publishing Co., 1987). Serious students of the OT should use the original printing of the Paterson edition of the *NAB*, which contains a list of textual notes on readings adopted in it (see 2. 323-451). These notes include variant readings of the Hebrew of 1-2 Samuel from texts of Qumran Cave 4, prepared by

F. M. Cross (2. 342-51). Unfortunately, these textual notes have not been reproduced in subsequent printings of the Paterson edition or in other printings of thc *NAB* (by other publishers). But they are still available as an offprint, *Textual Notes on the New American Bible* (pp. 124; $1.30), from the Catholic Biblical Association of America, Washington, DC 20064.

See *JBL* 92 (1973) 275-78; *CBQ* 33 (1971) 405-9.

NJB   **184.** **The New Jerusalem Bible* (ed. H. Wansbrough; London: Darton, Longman & Todd; Garden City, NY: Doubleday, 1985). This is the successor to *The Jerusalem Bible* (ed. A. Jones, 1966), which retained the excellent notes of the one-volume French *SBJ* (§ 189), but the translation of the biblical text itself in the *JB*, often quite readable, was at times miserable; most of the Pauline letters were a paraphrase rather than a translation, and crucial phrases were often badly rendered (e.g., 1 Cor 7:2; Luke 1:34). (See the review of *JB* by W. J. Harrington, *RB* 75 [1968] 450-52, published in French to spare the sensibilities of English-speaking admirers of *JB*.) The new French one-volume *SBJ* (1973) has now been translated into English, and it is a vast improvement, even though not perfect. The English translation has been based on the original Hebrew, Aramaic, or Greek, but when the text tolerates more than one interpretation, that of the French *SBJ* has normally been followed.

See *RB* 94 (1987) 124-27; *ScrB* 16 (1985) 2-3; *CBQ* 51 (1989) 358-59; *Furrow* 57 (1986) 476-77; *Greg* 67 (1986) 149-50; *NovT* 28 (1986) 381; *Theology* 39 (1986) 309-10.

NIV   **185.** *The Holy Bible: New International Version: Containing the Old Testament and the New Testament* (London: Hodder and Stoughton; Grand Rapids, MI: Zondervan, 1978). This is a good modern English translation of the OT (according to the Hebrew canon) and of the NT, produced by over 100 scholars of conservative, evangelical bent from many Christian denominations (Anglican, Assemblies of God, Baptist, Brethren, Christian Reformed, Church of Christ, Evangelical Free, Lutheran, Mennonite, Methodist, Nazarene, Presbyterian, Wesleyan, etc.). Very brief notes explain difficulties in the original text or suggest alternate translations; cross-references are sparse. Conservative positions are adopted in the translation of disputed passages (e.g., Isa 7:14; Luke 1:34). The deuterocanonical books of the OT are missing. Cf. B. L. Goddard, *The NIV Story: The Inside Story of the New International Version* (New York: Vantage, 1989).

See *JBL* 93 (1974) 591-94; *JETS* 21 (1978) 239-49; *Christianity Today* 23 (1978) 76-77; *BT* 30 (1979) 345-50; 31 (1980) 325-36.

REBWA   **186.** *The Revised English Bible with the Apocrypha* (Oxford/Cambridge, UK: University Press, 1989). This is a revision of *The New*

NEB

English Bible, the NT of which was first published by the same presses in 1961, and the whole Bible in 1970. The *NEB* was, in general, an excellent fresh translation of the OT and the NT, produced by famous British scholars from various universities, planned and directed by representatives of nine non-Roman-Catholic Christian churches of Great Britain. The first edition of the NT was too "British" for American ears; some of this was remedied in the second edition. The OT of the *NEB* suffered at times from the eccentric influence of G. R. Driver (compare the first edition of Josh 15:18 or Judg 1:14 with the second edition). Now the *REB* remedies much of that. However, in general there is more translation by dynamic equivalence than one will find in the *RSV* or the *NAB*. An annotated form of the *NEB* can be found in the *Oxford Study Edition: The New English Bible with the Apocrypha* (ed. S. Sandmel et al.; New York/London: Oxford University, 1976). The annotators have been Catholic, Jewish, and Protestant scholars from the U.S.A. and Canada. It is the counterpart of the *OABWA* (§ 182b), using a more modern English translation.

OSENEBWA

See *CBQ* 23 (1961) 321-24; 32 (1970) 426-28; *RB* 69 (1962) 147-49.

NJV

187. **The Torah: The Five Books of Moses: A New Translation of the Holy Scriptures according to the Masoretic Text, First Section* (Philadelphia, PA: Jewish Publication Society of America, 1962); *The Prophets Nevi'im: Second Section* (1978). *The Writings Kethubim: Third Section* (1982). Popularly called "the New Jewish Version" (*NJV*), this translation is intended to replace *The Holy Scriptures according to the Masoretic Text* (Philadelphia, PA: JPSA, 1917). This excellent English version is not simply a revision of the 1917 publication, but a fresh translation, done by competent Jewish scholars and rabbis of the U.S.A. and Israel. Though the *NJV* closely follows the MT, notes call attention to problems in that text, variants in Hebrew mss., and differences in ancient versions. Cross-references are added for clarification at times. The student who uses the *NJV* would wisely consult H. M. Orlinsky, *Notes on the New Translation of the Torah* (Philadelphia, PA: JPSA, 1969), which explains decisions of the translation committee.

See *ETR* 45 (1970) 417-19; *BT* 26 (1975) 148-52.

GNBDA

188. *Good News Bible with Deuterocanonicals/Apocrypha: The Bible in Today's English Version* (Cleveland/New York: Collins, 1978). The principle followed in this translation is "dynamic equivalence." The foreword explains: It "seeks to state clearly and accurately the meaning of the original texts in words and forms that are widely accepted by all people who use English as a means of communication." This means that this translation was produced with a view to those whose second language is English. Its paraphrastic text has caught on in the U.S.A. because of the prevalent low level of comprehension of the English language. It will be used by the serious student of the Bible or of theology only with caution. It reflects what happens when linguists with little historical or theological sense work on a text as complicated as the Greek NT. A form of this work also exists without the deuterocanonicals and Apocrypha: *Good News Bible: The Bible in Today's English Version* (New York: American Bible Society, 1976). This is, in fact, the original publisher of this version.

B. French

SBJ   **189.**   **La Sainte Bible (Paris: Cerf, 1948-54). After the Second World War the Dominicans of the Ecole Biblique undertook a new translation of the Bible into French, which appeared in fascicles; most of the fascicles were subsequently revised at least once. The notes of this presentation of the Bible were excellent, reckoning with the documentary hypothesis of the Pentateuch and with the historical-critical method. A one-volume edition, which abbreviated its excellent introductions and notes, appeared in 1961, and was eventually translated into many foreign languages. A new edition of the latter, *La Bible de Jérusalem: La Sainte Bible traduite en français sous la direction de l'Ecole Biblique de Jérusalem* (Paris: Cerf) became available in 1973. It is a remarkable revision, based on the subsequent revisions of the fascicle edition and utilizing a more critical approach in the notes. The one-volume *SBJ* (of 1973) has been translated into English (§ 184), Spanish, *Biblia de Jerusalén* (new ed.; ed. J. A. Ubieta; Bilbao: Ed. Española Desclée de Brouwer, 1977); Portuguese, *A Bíblia de Jerusalém: Novo Testamento* (São Paulo: Ediçôes Paulinas, 1976); German, *Die Heilige Schrift des Alten und Neuen Bundes: Deutsche Ausgabe mit dem Erläuterungen der Jerusalemer Bibel* (ed. D. Arenhoevel et al.; Freiburg im B.: Herder 1969; new ed., ed. U. Schütz, 1979); Italian, *La Bibbia di Gerusalemme* (Bologna: Dehoniane, 1985).

TOB   **190.**   **Traduction œcuménique de la Bible* (édition intégrale, 2 vols.; ed. J. Potin; Paris: Cerf/Les Bergers et les Mages, 1975; repr., 1985). A collaborative translation of the whole Bible. The NT is fitted out with excellent notes; the translation of the OT is not as good as that of the NT. The order of the OT books does not follow that of the LXX, but rather that of the MT (Torah, Prophets, Writings), to which the deuterocanonicals are appended. A form of this Bible has been produced in Italian, M. Galizzi (ed.), *Bibbia TOB* (Turin: Elle Di Ci, 1978).

> See *NRT* 91 (1969) 876; *RevThom* 69 (1969) 245-46; *RTL* 7 (1976) 337-53; *BT* 18 (1967) 101-3, 103-7; 28 (1977) 343-44.

191. *La Bible: L'Ancien Testament* (Bibliothèque de la Pléiade 120, 139; Paris: Gallimard). Known popularly as "La Bible de la Pléiade," because of the series in which it appears, these two volumes were published in 1956 and 1959, under the editorship of E. Dhorme. The work is an excellent critical translation of the OT with introductions and philological notes, largely from the pen of Dhorme himself. The translation has been highly praised, and the scholarship and sobriety of judgment displayed in these volumes are noteworthy. Though intended for the layman, the work can be used with great profit by students. There is an edition with a translation of the NT, which cannot claim the excellence of that of the OT.

See *RA* 51 (1957) 114-15; *TLZ* 83 (1958) 411-12; *ETR* 34 (1959) 101-20; *BT* 9 (1958) 151-53.

192. Segond, L., *La Sainte Bible, qui comprend l'Ancien et le Nouveau Testament traduite sur les textes originaux hébreu et grec* (Oxford, UK: Oxford, 1880). The OT had been published earlier in Geneva (Cherbuliez, 1874). This famous Protestant translation of the Bible was produced by a renowned Swiss theologian. It was largely a revision of an older version of D. Martin (Amsterdam, 1696-1707) and J.-F. Osterwald (Amsterdam: Chatelain, 1724[?]). "La Bible Segond" was slightly revised in 1910; another revision (*NVSR*) was produced in 1962-64. Yet another: *La Sainte Bible: Nouvelle Version Segond Revisée avec notes, références et glossaire* (Paris: Alliance biblique universelle, 1978).

See *BT* 8 (1957) 80-85; 31 (1980) 135-40; 32 (1981) 145-48

193. Crampon, A., *La Sainte Bible traduite en français sur les textes originaux, avec introductions et notes et la Vulgate latine en regard* (Paris/Tournai: Desclée, 1894-1904). This is a renowned Catholic translation of the Bible into French, accompanied by summary notes. It appeared at first in seven volumes, and then the French translation was issued in a manual form. It was revised in 1923 by unnamed French Jesuits and Sulpicians: *La Sainte Bible: Traduction d'après les textes originaux par l'Abbé A. Crampon.* In 1956 it was again revised, and its title was changed: *La Sainte Bible du Chanoine Crampon: Traduction d'après les textes originaux.* Most of the OT was revised by J. Bonsirven, but the Psalms by A. Robert; A. Tricot preferred to make a new translation of the NT, which was more concise and direct than that of Crampon's original translation.

See *ETL* 30 (1954) 465-66; *NRT* 75 (1953) 413; *BT* 13 (1962) 184-88.

194. Osty, E. with the collaboration of J. Trinquet, *La Bible: Traduction française sur les textes originaux, introductions, notes* (17 vols.; Lausanne: Rencontre, 1970-72; Paris: Desclée de Brouwer, 1977).

This is an excellent translation of the Bible, with notes more historical and philological than theological. "La traduction de M. Osty se place parmi les meilleures que l'exégèse française ait offertes au public ce siècle-ci" (M. Gilbert, *NRT* 103 [1971] 1093).

See *ETL* 47 (1971) 510; *JBL* 92 (1973) 279-80; *RB* 79 (1972) 465-66; 80 (1973) 299-300.

C. German

195. *Lutherbibel: Revidierte Ausgabe* (Stuttgart: Privilegierte Württembergische Bibelanstalt, 1984). A modern revision of the famous translation of the Bible by M. Luther. His original translation has been critically edited by H. Volz in the Weimarer Ausgabe of his works: *Die Deutsche Bibel*, vols. 1-12 (Weimar: Böhlau, 1906-61). A modern revision of his translation was published in 1956; further revision was undertaken between 1957-1975, especially that of the NT. There also exists a Hebrew–German edition of the revised *Lutherbibel*, using the 16th ed. of *BHK* (1976). This edition enables readers to orient themselves to the original text with the aid of Luther's translation. The revision of 1984 is also used in the Greek–German form of N–A^{26} (§ 131).

See *ZAW* 71 (1959) 254; 73 (1961) 126; *BT* 8 (1957) 155-60; 11 (1960) 178-81; *TRu* 25 (1959) 87; *TLZ* 87 (1962) 108-10; *ZTK* 76 (1979) 241-60.

EÜ   **196.** Knoch, O. et al. (eds.), *Die Bibel: Einheitsübersetzung der Heiligen Schrift, Altes und Neues Testament* (Stuttgart: Katholisches Bibelanstalt/Deutsche Bibelstiftung, 1979-80). This project of a common translation was launched in 1962, and work on it began seriously in 1969. The NT first appeared in 1972; the OT in 1974; revised in 1979-80. This translation was sponsored by the episcopal conferences of Germany, Austria, Switzerland, Luxemburg, and Liège and by the Council of Evangelische Kirche in Deutschland. It has been prepared for use in the liturgy, preaching, schools, and study. This translation is accompanied by notes, cross references, an appendix, and indices to persons and subjects.

See *TPQ* 129 (1981) 57-64; *ZAW* 87 (1975) 251; *ZKT* 98 (1976) 196-97; *BKir* 32 (1977) 24; 33 (1978) 93-97; *TRE* 6. 274-75.

197. Buber, M. with F. Rosenzweig, *Die Schrift* (Berlin: Schocken, 1926-38; Cologne: Hegner, 1926-29; Heidelberg: L. Schneider, 1955-57). A highly-prized literary translation of the OT. The 9th ed. of the Pentateuch (Die fünf Bücher der Weisung) appeared in 1976; the 7th ed. of the historical books in 1979; the 7th ed. of the Prophets (Bücher der Kündigung) in 1978; and the 8th ed. of the Psalms (Das Buch der Preisungen) in 1975. The 11th revised ed. of the whole OT appeared in 1984; repr. 1987.

See *TGl* 49 (1959) 55-57; *BLeb* 4 (1963) 147-54; *BL* (1980) 50; *GLeb* 53 (1980) 79; *BZ* 26 (1982) 93-97.

198. Menge, H., *Die Heilige Schrift Alten und Neuen Testaments* (11th ed.; Stuttgart: Privilegierte Württembergische Bibelanstalt, 1949; often repr.). An excellent German translation based on the original texts, which began to be produced in 1923 (NT) and 1926 (OT). Philologically precise, it rendered the biblical text into excellent German. It has good division titles and a careful presentation that enables one to grasp the meaning. The use of parentheses, brackets, and brief notes helps to this end.

See *TRE* 6. 273.

199. Kautzsch, E., *Die Heilige Schrift des Alten Testaments* (ed. A. Bertholet; Tübingen: Mohr [Siebeck], 1909; 4th ed., 1922-23). A careful, highly-regarded translation of the OT, which was begun in 1894. Each book has a brief introduction and two types of notes: one critical, the other concerned with historical, chronological, and theological matters. A useful index aids the reader to understand the world of the OT.

200. Karrer, O., *Neues Testament, übersetzt und erklärt* (new ed.; Munich: Ars Sacra Josef Müller, 1967). A good German translation, accompanied by brief notes, which explain difficult passages and bring out the religious meaning of the text. It first appeared in 1950; revised in 1953 and in 1959. The 3d ed. was a complete reworking of the text. Karrer was not *ex professo* a Scripture scholar, but he sought and got good advice. However, some of his exegetical comments remain those of another vintage.

See *TPQ* 117 (1969) 165-66; *ZKT* 91 (1969) 120.

201. Kürzinger, J., *Das Neue Testament nach dem Grundtext neu übersetzt* (Aschaffenburg: Pattloch, 1953; 24th ed., 1979). A translation noted for its fidelity to the original Greek, its clarity, and its good German. It became part of the so-called *Pattloch-Bibel* when V. Hamp and M. Stenzel translated the OT, *Die Heilige Schrift des Alten und Neuen Testaments nach den Grundtexten neu übersetzt* (Aschaffenburg: Pattloch; Zurich: Christiana, 1956).

See *Bib* 41 (1960) 439; *BLit* 23 (1955-56) 252, 270-73.

D. Italian

CEI 202. Garofalo, S. (ed.), *La Sacra Bibbia: Versione italiana per l'uso liturgico a cura della Conferenza Episcopale Italiana* (Vatican City: Libreria Editrice Vaticana, 1971). Commonly referred to as *La Bibbia della CEI*, it was produced with the aid of many scholars. The three vols. have been collected in one (Turin: Marietti, 1980). A special form of it is *La Bibbia a cura de la Civiltà Cattolica* (Rome: Civiltà Cattolica, 1974; 2d ed., 1978).

See *BT* 24 (1973) 344-46; *Greg* 60 (1979) 747-48; *BeO* 16 (1974) 211.

203. Cipriani, S. et al. (eds.), *La Bibbia Concordata: Tradotta dai testi originali, con introduzione e note* (Milan: Mondadori, 1968). This is a modern Italian ecumenical translation, produced by Catholic, Jewish, Orthodox, and Protestant members of the Società Biblica Italiana, and approved by Patriarch Athenagoras, the Archbishop of Ravenna, and the Grand Rabbi of Rome. But the work is uneven; scholars from the different communities produced the translations of books assigned to them, and they were then gathered into one volume, without a real coordination. Nor is it clear that the best critical texts were always used.

See *BeO* 11 (1969) 221-22; *JBL* 88 (1969) 491-92.

204. Galbiati, E. et al. (eds.), *La Sacra Bibbia: Tradotta dai testi originali e commentata* (3 vols.; Turin: Unione Tipografica-Editrice Torinese, 1973). This is commonly known as "Bibbia UTET," and it is in its 3d ed. for the OT.

205. *Nuovissima versione della Bibbia* (48 brochures; Rome: Edizioni Paoline, 1967-80). A form of this translation was produced in 3 vols. in 1984.

206. Vaccari, A. (ed.), *La Sacra Bibbia* (8 vols.; Florence: Salani 1942-50; in one volume, 1958). The professors of the Biblical Institute in Rome were collaborators with Vaccari.

See *Palestra del clero* 22 (1943) 1-3; 62 (1983) 892-95; *VD* 23 (1943) 159-60; *Bib* 28 (1947) 293-302; *RSO* 22 (1947) 139-40.

E. Spanish

207. Alonso Schökel, L. and J. Mateos, *Nueva Biblia española: Traducción de los textos originales* (Madrid: Cristiandad, 1974; 2d ed., 1977). In general, this Castilian translation is a highly literary production generally faithful to the original texts, but it often makes use of the principle of "dynamic equivalence." It is also used in the commentary series, LSS (§ 384).

See *BT* 22 (1971) 38-44; *Sal Terrae* 63 (1975) 232-33; especially J. O'Callaghan, *El Nuevo Testamento en las versiones españolas* (Subsidia biblica 6; Rome: Biblical Institute, 1982).

208. Cantera Burgos, F. and M. Iglesias González, *Sagrada Biblia: Versión crítica sobre los textos hebreo, arameo y griego* (BAC Maior 10; Madrid: Editorial Católica, 1975). This Castilian translation is noted for its literal character, which in the OT is at times a bit obscure, but more successful in the NT.

See *CulB* 33 (1976) 75-79; *Sef* 36 (1976) 145-49.

209. *La Biblia: Traducida de los textos originales* (9th ed.; Madrid: Casa de la Biblia, 1976). This translation purports to be in the language of the ordinary person of today, plain and simple, avoiding rare words and long sentences. The translation has been produced by a group of Spanish and Latin American scholars. It is often called *La Biblia Hispano-Americana.*

210. Nácar Fuster, E. and A. Colungo, *Sagrada Biblia: Versión directa de las lenguas originales* (BAC; Madrid: Editorial Católica, 1944; 16th ed., 1965). This is the first Spanish Catholic translation of the Bible based on the original texts. It is a good modern translation that has been widely used.

See *Bib* 25 (1944) 382-84.

211. *La Santa Biblia: Antiguo y Nuevo Testamento: Antigua versión de Casiodoro de Reina (1569), revisada por Cipriano de Valera (1602) y cotejada posteriormente con diversas traducciones y con los textos hebreo y griego, con referencias y concordancias* (Madrid, 1974; Dallas, TX: Associación Biblica International, 1976; revised, Barcelona: Terrassa, 1977). This Protestant translation of the Bible is noted for its clarity, even though it is quite literal. The revision was first published in 1960.

See *BT* 1 (1950) 155-57; 2 (1951) 89-91, 168-77; 12 (1961) 107-19.

CHAPTER VIII

Lexica

Serious work on the original texts of the Bible and its ancient versions can only be done by the student who makes use of the best tools for such work. In this and the following chapters guidance will be given to such tools for study. Here the aim is to list the best lexica for the study of the original text of the OT and the NT and their versions. They will be grouped under five headings: (A) Hebrew and Aramaic lexica (taken together because OT lexica often group, in separate parts, both biblical Hebrew and biblical Aramaic vocabulary); (B) Greek lexica (for the study of the LXX and the NT); (C) Latin lexica; and (D) Syriac and Coptic lexica; (E) Lexica of other Northwest Semitic Languages.

A. Hebrew and Aramaic Lexica

HALAT   **212.**   **Baumgartner, W. (ed.), *Hebräisches und aramäisches Lexikon zum Alten Testament* (5 vols.; Leiden: Brill, 1967, 1974, 1983, 1990, 19??). This excellent lexicon purports to be the 3d ed. of KB (§ 213), but it is really an independent, greatly improved work. Baumgartner originally had the collaboration of L. Koehler (until his death in 1956) and then that of B. Hartmann and E. Y. Kutscher (until the latter's death in 1971). Baumgartner himself died in January 1970. Since that time the production of this lexicon has been under the direction of B. Hartmann, assisted by P. Reymond and J. J. Stamm. The first volume covers '–*ṭbḥ* (pp. 1-352); the second, *ṭbḥ–nbṭ* (pp. 353-624); the third, *nbṭ–r'h* (pp. 625-1080); the fourth is still awaited. It follows more or less the principles of KB, but the English translations have been eliminated, the parallels in cognate Semitic languages have been multiplied, a great number of references to secondary literature have been added, and the etymologies and meanings greatly improved. It is currently the best Hebrew lexicon available for the study of the OT. An abbreviated English form of KB was prepared by W. L. Holladay, *A Concise Hebrew and Aramaic Lexicon of the Old Testament, Based upon the Lexical Work of L. Koehler & W. Baumgartner* (Leiden: Brill, 1971); it used as much of *HALAT* as was available at the time and supplied the rest from KB. It is intended for students beginning their study of Biblical Hebrew and Aramaic and is well suited for that purpose.

See *RB* 76 (1969) 111; 82 (1975) 296-97; *VT* 34 (1984) 500-506; *VTSup* 16 (1967) 158-75; *JBL* 92 (1973) 448-50; *ETR* 47 (1972) 229-30; *ZAW* 84 (1972) 122; 96 (1984) 148.

KB 213. *Koehler, L. and W. Baumgartner, *Lexicon in Veteris Testamenti libros* (2d ed.; Leiden: Brill, 1958). The second edition is a reprint of the 1953 edition, together with an important supplement of over 225 pages, incorporating a German–Hebrew and German–Aramaic index of words and a vast number of corrections and additions made to the main text. The lexicon was originally issued in fascicles. Meanings and discussions are given in both German and English; but the latter are at times weak and untrustworthy. The Hebrew and Aramaic words are listed in strictly alphabetical order. The Aramaic part is usually thought to be superior to the Hebrew part. If constant reference is made to the supplement, this can be an indispensable tool.

> See the reviews of the fascicle edition by P. Humbert, *TZ* 5 (1949) 81-92; 6 (1950) 58-63, 307-9; 7 (1951) 65-70; 10 (1954) 51-53; *VT* 5 (1955) 214-23; *JSS* 4 (1959) 147-48.

GesRMD 214. **Gesenius, W., *Hebräisches und aramäisches Handwörterbuch über das Alte Testament* (18th ed.; ed. U. Rüterswörden, R. Meyer, and H. Donner; Berlin/New York: Springer-V., 1987-   ). This is a new edition of the famous OT dictionary of Gesenius. It replaces

GB the 17th ed., rev. by F. Buhl (1921). Its first part (1987) covers '–g.

BDB 215. Brown, F., S. R. Driver, and C. A. Briggs, *A Hebrew and English Lexicon of the Old Testament* (corrected impression; Oxford: Clarendon, 1952). The dictionary includes both Biblical Hebrew and Aramaic; words are not arranged alphabetically, but according to roots, sometimes more putative than real. Though the etymologies usually need scrutiny and many translations must now be corrected, this work is still valuable for its abundance of references to biblical passages and its listing of Hebrew or Aramaic idioms, which more modern lexica often curtail. For the corrected impression, G. R. Driver inserted only those corrections which could be made without resetting the sheets. This lexicon was based on an English translation of one by W. Gesenius, which in later editions has been a valuable reference tool (§ 214). BDB has been reissued: *The New Brown–Driver–Briggs–Gesenius Hebrew and English Lexicon with an Appendix Containing the Biblical Aramaic* (Peabody, MA: Hendrickson, 1979). The *Addenda* and *Corrigenda* grouped previously in an appendix have been moved to the bottom margin of pages to which they refer. The Hebrew or Aramaic words have been coded to the numbering system of Strong's *Concordance* (§ 317e), and an important index has been added. All of this makes this old lexicon a still valuable tool for study.

> See *RB* 8 (1899) 460-61.

LHAVT 216. *Zorell, F., *Lexicon hebraicum et aramaicum Veteris Testamenti* (Rome: Biblical Institute, 1940-54). This work never sought to rival the lexica of GB or BDB, but it has its own virtues, not the least being the inclusion of the vocabulary of the Hebrew text of Ben Sira. Zorell died in 1947, and the lexicon was continued by his colleagues at the Biblical Institute. Despite the title, it contains no section on Biblical Aramaic, as this eventually appeared separately (§ 217). It has many good observations, to be missed only by those who are Latin-less or do not turn to it.

See *CBQ* 3 (1941) 377-79.

LLAVT　　**217.**　**Vogt, E., *Lexicon linguae aramaicae Veteris Testamenti documentis antiquis illustratum* (Rome: Biblical Institute, 1971). This is unquestionably the best lexicon available for Biblical Aramaic. It was originally supposed to be the Aramaic section of F. Zorell, *LHAVT* (§ 216), but because of the adopted format and type of lexicon that it became, it was rightly decided to publish it on its own. It lists all the words in Biblical Aramaic, illustrating them abundantly with usages of the same words in earlier and contemporary Aramaic texts. It is something like MM (§ 228) for the study of NT Greek vocabulary. Modern secondary literature is referred to. The book is being translated into English so that the modern Latin-less student can profit from it.

See *Bib* 54 (1973) 131-35; *RB* 79 (1972) 614-17; *JBL* 91 (1972) 552-53; *CBQ* 34 (1972) 394-95; *Or* 44 (1975) 116-25; *ZDMG* 129 (1979) 375-77.

218.　Ben-Yehuda, E., *Millôn hallāšôn ha'ibrît hayyĕšānāh wĕhaḥădāšāh: Thesaurus totius hebraitatis et veteris et recentioris* (16 vols.; Berlin-Schöneberg: Langenscheidt, 1908-　　; repr. in 8 vols.; New York: Yoseloff, 1960; Tel-Aviv: La'Am Publ. House, 1940; Jerusalem: La'Or, 1948). This is a classic lexicon of the Hebrew language, composed in Hebrew. In its own way, it often helps to solve problems in the interpretation of the biblical text because of the history of the word that it can supply. The basic meaning of the word is also given in German, French, and English.

See *RB* 15 (1906) 659.

219.　Levy, J., *Chaldäisches Wörterbuch über die Targumim und einen grossen Theil des rabbinischen Schriftthums* (2 vols. bound in one; 3d ed.; Leipzig: Baumgartner, 1881; repr., Cologne: J. Melzer, 1959). This lexicon of targumic and rabbinic Aramaic writings first appeared in 1867-68. It is a valuable tool because it supplies abundant references to the literature from which the words are culled. But students must learn to use it with caution, checking the passages cited. This dictionary is of use to the biblical student because it reveals the uses of Aramaic words in the postbiblical period; it is often needed in the interpretation of Qumran texts.

220. Levy, J., *Neuhebräisches und chaldäisches Wörterbuch über die Talmudim und Midraschim* (4 vols.; Leipzig: Brockhaus, 1876, 1879, 1883, 1889). This lexicon contains the vocabulary of rabbinic Hebrew and Aramaic which is found in the Babylonian and Jerusalem talmuds, the Tosephta, and the Midrashim (both halakhic and haggadic). Abundant citations are supplied for all the words cited; meanings are given in German. A supplement was published in 1924 by J. Levy and L. Goldschmidt, *Nachträge und Berechtigungen zu Jacob Levy/Wörterbuch über die Talmudim und Midraschim* (Berlin/Wien: B. Harz). Since there is no dictionary of Hebrew texts of the intertestamental period, the biblical student will often find himself or herself consulting this dictionary in the study of such literature.

ANHW **221.** *Dalman, G. H., *Aramäisch–neuhebräisches Handwörterbuch zu Targum, Talmud und Midrasch* (3d ed.; Göttingen: E. Pfeiffer, 1938; repr., Hildesheim/New York: Olms, 1967). A handy lexicon of post-biblical Hebrew and Aramaic, useful also for the study of Hebrew and Aramaic texts of Qumran. Though it is lean on references, it usually books words according to their normative Hebraic or Aramaic forms, thus making it an easier lexicon to use than Jastrow (§ 222). The first edition appeared in 1901.

See *AJSL* 15 (1898-99) 57-60.

Jastrow **222.** Jastrow, M., *A Dictionary of the Targumim, the Talmud Babli and Yerushalmi, and the Midrashic Literature* (London: Luzac; New York: Putnam, 1886-1900; often reprinted, sometimes 2 vols. in one: New York/Berlin: Choreb; London: Shapiro, Vallentine & Co., 1926; New York: Pardes, 1950). This is the English counterpart of the two lexica of J. Levy (§ 219, 220). It is better than Dalman's *ANHW* (§ 221) in that it gives more references to rabbinic and targumic literature; but it is confusing for beginners because the words are often booked with rabbinic *scriptio plena*, which demands a time-consuming search to find out where Jastrow has entered the words.

See *AJSL* 18 (1901-2) 56-58.

DJPABP **222a.** Sokoloff, M., *A Dictionary of Jewish Palestinian Aramaic of the Byzantine Period* (Dictionaries of Talmud, Midrash and Targum 2; Ramat-Gan: Bar Ilan University, 1990). This is a new dictionary of Palestinian Jewish Aramaic that replaces both *ANHW* (§ 221) and Jastrow (§ 222).

RHW **223.** Kuhn, K. G., *Rückläufiges hebräisches Wörterbuch* (Göttingen: Vandenhoeck & Ruprecht, 1958). This is a reverse index, listing the Hebrew words of the MT, Ben Sira, and (non-biblical) texts of Qumran Cave 1 and booking them in backward spelling. Its purpose is to aid students of fragmentary texts to fill in lacunae, when only the last letters of a word are found. It is a useful tool, but it has to be used with caution. If a student cannot find what he or she is looking for in this *Wörterbuch*, the search is not to be given up; when one does find here what might seem satisfactory, the task of restoration is not necessarily over.

See *Bib* 39 (1958) 376; *ZAW* 70 (1958) 129; *JBL* 77 (1958) 269-70; *TZ* 15 (1959) 61-62; *JSS* 4 (1959) 148; *TLZ* 84 (1959) 824-25.

B. Greek Lexica

B–A   **224.**   **Bauer, W., *Griechisch–deutsches Wörterbuch zu den Schriften des Neuen Testaments und der frühchristlichen Literatur* (6th ed.; ed. K. and B. Aland; Berlin/New York: de Gruyter, 1988). Internationally recognized as the best NT dictionary, Bauer's lexicon is a reworking of an older one by E. Preuschen. Its value lies in the attempt to give succinctly the history of the Greek word, indicating its terminus a quo in Greek literature, its use in the LXX, papyri, and later Greek, as well as the NT occurrences themselves. Abundant bibliographical references to articles and books on the word concerned are also supplied. Though primarily a lexicographical tool, the theological significance of this lexicon should not be underestimated. The sixth ed. is based on N–A[26]. The occurrences of Greek words in the Apostolic Fathers have been thoroughly checked, and vocabulary from NT apocrypha (from the first half of the second century) have been added: as a result, 250 new word-articles appear. However, to accommodate this new material, much of the secondary literature has been eliminated (making the use of Bauer's 5th ed. [1958] still indispensable).

See *TLZ* 53 (1928) 541-42; 84 (1959) 52-53; *NTS* 9 (1962-63) 3-10; *JTS* 30 (1928-29) 201; *RB* 37 (1928) 618-20; *ZNW* 43 (1950-51) 266; *TTZ* 67 (1958) 373-74; *ZKG* 69 (1958) 138-41. For the 6th ed. (Bauer–Aland): *TS* 50 (1989) 576-78; *ETL* 64 (1988) 450-54; *GGA* 241 (1989) 103-46.

BAGD   **225.**   **Bauer, W., F. W. Gingrich, and F. W. Danker, *A Greek–English Lexicon of the New Testament and Other Early Christian Literature* (2d ed.; Chicago, IL/London: University of Chicago, 1979). Originally, W. F. Arndt and F. W. Gingrich translated and adapted the fourth, revised edition of Bauer (§224) under the same English title as that given above (1957). When the BAG first English edition was published, Bauer was completing his work on the 5th German ed., which he published in nine fascicles (1957-58). The second English edition has lost an editor (W. F. Arndt) and acquired a new one (F. W. Danker); it has utilized much of the new material that Bauer introduced into his 5th ed. and added some other matter that the American editors had gathered on their own. Though completely reset in smaller type, it is still readable. But only with the use of it over a period of time does one realize that all is not yet perfect. Much more secondary literature could have been introduced, and entries on old material could have been updated. There exists an index to BAGD, listing biblical passages in it according to books, chapters, and verses to enable the student to find a meaning quickly, when working on a given passage: J. R. Alsop, *An Index to the Revised Bauer–Arndt–Gingrich Greek Lexicon* (2d ed.; Grand Rapids, MI: Zondervan, 1982).

See *TS* 40 (1979) 533-35; *CBQ* 42 (1980) 555-58; *Bib* 38 (1957) 355-56; *ExpTim* 68 (1956-57) 262-63; *JBL* 100 (1981) 290-91.

LGNT   **226.** Zorell, F., *Lexicon graecum Novi Testamenti* (3d ed.; Cursus sacrae Scripturae, pars prior, libri introductorii 7; Paris: Lethielleux, 1961). When it was first published in 1911, this was the only NT lexicon that had made use of the material coming from the papyri: "a careful compilation quite up to the level of modern research" (Richards). It is a lexicon of the canonical NT writings only and thus differs from BAG or BAGD, which include early Christian Greek writings. The second edition, which made use of the researches of Preuschen, Bauer, Preisigke, Moulton and Milligan was highly praised. The third edition added only a "supplementum bibliographicum" of 40 pages. Unfortunately, it has not been kept up to date; but in many ways it is still quite useful.

See *JTS* 15 (1914) 87; 33 (1931-32) 297-98; *TLZ* 56 (1931) 344; *OrChr* 22 (1931) 249-51; *ETL* 8 (1931) 740-41; *RHPR* 11 (1931) 223-25; *RB* ns 8 (1911) 476-77; ns 9 (1912) 157; 40 (1931) 637-38; 69 (1962) 146.

227. Preisigke, F., *Wörterbuch der griechischen Papyrusurkunden mit Einschluss der griechischen Inschriften Aufschriften Ostraka Mumienschilder usw. aus Ägypten.* Vollendet und herausgegeben von E. Kiessling (3 vols.; Berlin: Privately published, 1925, 1927, 1931). There is also a fourth volume, begun in 1944, of which only three fascicles have appeared (1958, 1966, 1971). But another volume has been published, *Supplement I* (ed. W. Rübsam; Amsterdam: Hakkert, 1969-71). This is a very important comprehensive dictionary of non-literary Greek texts found in papyri and inscriptions from Egypt; though dated, it is still an indispensable tool for a thorough study of NT Greek.

See *Bib* 6 (1925) 482-85; *OLZ* 34 (1931) 16-18; *Aegyptus* 48 (1968) 167-244; 49 (1969) 203-57; *SPap* 6 (1967) 141-42; 11 (1972) 63.

MM   **228.** *Moulton, J. H. and G. Milligan, *The Vocabulary of the Greek Testament, Illustrated from the Papyri and Other Non-Literary Sources* (2d ed.; London: Hodder and Stoughton, 1957). Begun in 1914, the one-volume form first appeared in 1930 and has been reprinted several times (1949, 1952, 1980). It is not a complete lexicon of the NT, but lists only those Greek words of NT vocabulary which are found in non-literary papyri and other non-literary sources (inscriptions, etc.). It thus attests some of the ordinary usages of NT Greek words in extrabiblical texts. Since it gives the context of this usage, it is quite valuable in its own right, a welcome companion to BAG or BAGD. However, it should be noted that many new Greek texts have come to light since 1930, sometimes with meanings of words not listed here (e.g., the sense of *apolyein*, "divorce" in a Greek document from a Murabba'at cave in ancient Palestine [Mur 115:3-4; see DJD 2. 248; *TS* 37 (1976) 211-13]). An updating of MM is being planned. Meanwhile, much similar information can be found in G. H. R. Horsley, *New Documents Illustrating Early Christianity* (5 vols.; North Ryde, N.S.W.: Ancient History Documentary Research Centre, Macquarie University, 1981, 1982, 1983, 1987, 1989). Volume 5 contains cumulative indices for the whole series.

See *RB* ns 12 (1915) 262-65; ns 14 (1917) 591-92; 29 (1920) 462-63; *RB* 93 (1986) 309-10; 95 (1988) 468-69; *TLZ* 56 (1931) 223-24; *CRev* 45 (1931) 49; *JTS* 34 (1983) 578-79; *VC* 37 (1983) 200-202; *NovT* 25 (1983) 191-92.

229. Schleusner, J. F., *Novus thesaurus philologico-criticus: sive, Lexicon in LXX, et reliquos interpretes graecos ac scriptores apocryphos Veteris Testamenti* (3 vols.; London: J. Duncan, 1829). This remains the only lexicon of the Greek OT in existence. Though it retains some value, students will most often do better to refer to LSJ[9] or various modern lexica of NT Greek.

LSJ

230. **Liddell, H. G. and R. Scott, *A Greek–English Lexicon: A New Edition Revised and Augmented throughout* by H. S. Jones, assisted by R. McKenzie (9th ed.; 2 vols. [later bound in one]; Oxford: Clarendon, 1925-40; repr., 1966). This excellent lexicon, mainly devoted to classical Greek, frequently includes references to the LXX and the NT. It is especially useful for tracing the early history of a NT word or for determining its etymology. In 1968 *A Supplement* of 153 pp. was published by E. A. Barber et al. (Oxford: Clarendon), the product of 12 years' work, which sought to take account of new material in the publications of more recently discovered inscriptions and papyrus texts or new critical editions. It includes the "Addenda et corrigenda" to the two main volumes, accumulated since 1940. New word entries are prefixed with a superscript x. Attention should also be called to R. Renehan, *Greek Lexicographical Notes: A Critical Supplement to the Greek-English Lexicon of Liddell–Scott–Jones* (Hypomnemata 45; Göttingen: Vandenhoeck & Ruprecht, 1975). Half of the entries discussed in these *Notes* were previously published in *Glotta* between 1968 and 1972; they are presented here in a revised and expanded form. — There exists an abridgement of earlier editions, "intended chiefly for use in Schools," but it dates from 1871, *A Lexicon Abridged from Liddell and Scott's Greek–English Lexicon* (Oxford: Clarendon, repr., 1979).

LSJSup

See *CP* 37 (1942) 96-98; *JHS* 62 (1942) 94; *CRev* 55 (1941) 1-13, 28-30.

PGL   **231.** ****Lampe, G. W. H.** (ed.), *A Patristic Greek Lexicon* (Oxford: Clarendon, 1961). This is the important counterpart to LSJ⁹, since the latter normally excludes specific data from early Christian and Byzantine Greek writers; its aim is to present the vocabulary of Greek Christian writers "from Clement of Rome to Theodore of Studium [d. A. D. 826]" (Preface, vii). This is a top-notch lexicon, produced in the good Oxford tradition, edited by a professor of Cambridge University. Some of its data overlap with BAG and BAGD, but it is useful in tracing the development of specifically Christian vocabulary from the NT onward. At the end there is a list of "addenda et corrigenda" (pp. 1559-68).

See *JTS* 14 (1963) 400-20; 18 (1967) 213-17; 19 (1968) 311-21; *JBL* 81 (1962) 290-93; 82 (1963) 246; 83 (1964) 342; 85 (1966) 129; 88 (1969) 512; *RB* 69 (1962) 631-32; 71 (1964) 153; *TRu* 29 (1963) 178-81.

DGF   **232.** **Bailly, A.,** *Dictionnaire grec français* (rev. by L. Séchan and P. Chantraine; Paris: Hachette, 1950). The French counterpart of LSJ, issued between the 9th ed. of the latter and its Supplement. An appendix supplies useful tables on Greek numbering, coins, names of months, and measurements of length, weight, and capacity. Some reprintings also have a supplement on Greek mythology and religion.

See *EtClass* 19 (1951) 267-68.

            233. **Chantraine, P.,** *Dictionnaire étymologique de la langue grecque: Histoire des mots* (4 vols.; Paris: Klincksieck, 1968, 1970, 1974, 1977, 1980). The 4th vol. exists in two parts. Chantraine died in 1974, having finished 3/4 of vol. 4 (up to *phainō*); the rest has been completed by a team of colleagues.

See *EtClass* 40 (1972) 437-38.

            234. **Frisk, H.,** *Griechisches etymologisches Wörterbuch* (Indogermanische Bibliothek 11. Reihe; 3 vols.; Heidelberg: C. Winter, 1960, 1970, 1972). Volume 1 covers *a–kopsichos*; vol. 2, *krabbatos–ōps*; vol. 3, additions, corrections, indices, and a *Nachwort*. This and the Chantraine title (§233) are the two standard etymological dictionaries, to which the student may have to turn from time to time, as questions arise about the historical etymology of Greek words.

See *EtClass* 29 (1961) 339-40.

            235. **Greenlee, J. H.,** *A New Testament Greek Morpheme Lexicon* (Grand Rapids, MI: Zondervan, 1983). This book provides a "systematic analysis of Greek words according to morphemes and components (prefixes, root words, suffixes, and terminations)" (p. vii). The first part "lists each word from BAGD with its component parts." The second part lists the same words according to prefixes, roots, suffixes and terminations. It is a useful compilation.

See *NovT* 27 (1985) 382-84.

236. Sophocles, E. A., *Greek Lexicon of the Roman and Byzantine Periods (from B.C. 146 — A.D. 1100)* (rev. ed.; New York: Scribner's, 1887; repr. 1957). An old, not carefully constructed, lexicon, which may still help in certain problems, where no other lexica cover the same matter (e.g., some Greek intertestamental writings). The first edition appeared in 1870.

237. Daris, S., *Spoglio lessicale papirologico* (3 vols.; Milan: Istituto di papirologia dell'Università cattolica del Sacro Cuore, 1968). A work intended to update the Preisigke *Wörterbuch* (§ 227), but which has to be used with great caution; one must always check the references.

C. Latin Lexica

OLD   **238.** **Glare, P. G. W. (ed.), *Oxford Latin Dictionary* (Oxford: Clarendon, 1968-1982). Launched in 1931, it has taken over 50 years to produce this book. In this excellent Latin dictionary over 40,000 words are not only defined and distinguished according to uses, but abundant references are supplied to classical writings from the beginning of Latin literature to the end of the second century A.D.

> See *New York Times Book Review*, 9 October 1983, 12, 26-27; *AJP* 105 (1984) 101-2; *CWorld* 77 (1984) 190-91; *Revue de philologie* 55 (1981) 367; *Greece & Rome* 29 (1982) 198.

239. Lewis, C. T. and C. Short, *A New Latin Dictionary Founded on the Translation of Freund's Latin–German Lexicon* (New York: American Book Co., 1907). This dictionary is often popularly referred to as "Harper's Latin Dictionary," a subtitle that also appears on it, since it was originally published by Harper & Bros. (1879). It covers the writings of authors as late as A.D. 600 and includes references to Jerome's Vulgate. Hence though it is in many ways superseded by *OLD*, it covers later Latin writings than it.

240. Klotz, R. et al. (eds.), *Handwörterbuch der lateinischen Sprache* (2 vols.; 7th ed.; Graz: Akademische Druck- u. Verlagsanstalt, 1963). Unchanged reprint of the 3d rev. ed. (Braunschweig: Westermann, 1879).

D. Syriac and Coptic Lexica

241. **Payne Smith, R., *Thesaurus syriacus* (2 vols.; Oxford: Clarendon, 1879, 1901). These two massive tomes were based on the earlier work of E. M. Quatremère, G. H. Bernstein, and others. The meanings of Syriac words are given in Latin, along with abundant references. R. Payne Smith died in 1895, and the *Thesaurus* was completed by his daughter Jessica and her husband, D. S. Margoliouth. *A Supplement to the Thesaurus* *syriacus of R. Payne Smith, S.T.P., Collected and Arranged by His Daughter J. P. Margoliouth* (Oxford: Clarendon) was published in 1927. This is a reference work of no little merit; but a modern Syriac lexicon, covering works that have been discovered or published in the last 60 years, is badly needed.

See *ZDMG* 37 (1883) 469-76; 41 (1887) 359-64; 45 (1891) 697-705; 47 (1893) 514-37; and later vols.

242. Brockelmann, C., *Lexicon syriacum* (2d ed.; Halle an d. S: Niemeyer, 1928; repr., Hildesheim/New York: Olms, 1966). An excellent one-volume lexicon of Syriac, prepared by a distinguished Semitist, who supplies Semitic cognates for the words entered. The words are grouped under a basic noun or verb. A Latin index to the meanings of the Syriac words is supplied in an appendix.

See *RB* 4 (1895) 633-34.

243. Payne Smith, J. (Mrs. Margoliouth), *A Compendious Syriac Dictionary: Founded upon the Thesaurus syriacus of R. Payne Smith D.D.* (Oxford: Clarendon, 1930; often reprinted, latest 1976). This abridgement of her father's *Thesaurus syriacus* (§ 241) by Mrs. Margoliouth is intended for beginners. It uses an "alphabetical rather than scientific order" of words and gives the meanings in English. It is devoid of references to Syriac writings, for which one must consult the *Thesaurus*, or of etymologies and Semitic cognates. But it often includes Syriac idioms.

See *RB* 8 (1899) 461-62.

244. **Crum, W. E., *A Coptic Dictionary* (Oxford: Clarendon, 1939). An excellent, comprehensive Coptic lexicon of words in Sahidic, Bohairic, and the "lesser dialects" of the language, which began to be published in 1931. No effort has been made to associate the Coptic words with their hieroglyphic, hieratic, or demotic etymologies. For these one has to consult W. Spiegelberg, *Koptisches Handwörterbuch*, or more recently, W. Westendorf, *Koptisches Handwörterbuch* (§ 246). Crum's appendix contains very useful indices (in English, Greek, and Arabic). For supplementary material one should consult R. Kasser, *Compléments au dictionnaire copte de Crum* (Bibliothèque d'études coptes 7; Cairo: Institut français d'archéologie orientale, 1964).

See *RB* 73 (1966) 158-59; *JTS* 34 (1933) 331-32; 36 (1935) 220-21; 39 (1938) 217-22; 42 (1941) 119-22.

245. Cerný, J., *Coptic Etymological Dictionary* (Cambridge, UK: University Press, 1976). The entries contain references to W. E. Crum's, *Coptic Dictionary* (§ 244), give the meanings of words, and supply the earlier hieroglyphic and demotic words to which the Coptic words are related, as well as Semitic, Persian, or Greek words to which they may be cognate.

See *JNES* 41 (1982) 139-40; *BSOAS* 41 (1978) 358-62; *JEA* 64 (1978) 186-89.

246. Westendorf, W., *Koptisches Handwörterbuch* (Heidelberg: C. Winter, 1965-77). This modern Coptic lexicon, issued in nine fascicles, is a revision of an older one by W. Spiegelberg (1921 [same title and publisher]). It has an advantage over Crum's dictionary in that it explains the Coptic vocabulary in relation to older forms of Egyptian.

See *BO* 24 (1967) 131-35; 25 (1968) 336-38; 30 (1973) 424-28; 33 (1976) 31-33; *Or* 35 (1966) 459-64; 37 (1968) 255-57; 41 (1972) 321; 42 (1973) 471-72; 44 (1975) 466; 49 (1980) 126-28.

E. Lexica of Other Northwest Semitic Languages

DISO   **247.** *Jean, C.-F. and J. Hoftijzer, *Dictionnaire des inscriptions sémitiques de l'ouest* (Leiden: Brill, 1965). This lexicon books the Northwest Semitic vocabulary of Old Canaanite, Phoenician, Punic, Moabite, Hebrew, Ya'udi, Old Aramaic, Imperial Aramaic, Nabatean, Palmyrene, Hatran, and Jewish Aramaic inscriptions. It is an important publication, even though it lumps together under one entry so many different languages.

See *JSS* 12 (1967) 111-12; *VT* 16 (1966) 364-66.

248. Tomback, R.S., *A Comparative Semitic Lexicon of the Phoenician and Punic Languages* (SBLDS 32; Missoula, MT [now Atlanta, GA]: Scholars, 1978). A useful tool for the comparative study of Phoenician and Punic inscriptions.

See *Bib* 60 (1979) 429-35; *BO* 36 (1979) 201-3; *CBQ* 41 (1979) 324-25; *EstBib* 37 (1978) 135-36; *Greg* 60 (1979) 377-79.

WUS   **249.** Aistleitner, J., *Wörterbuch der ugaritischen Sprache* (Berichte über die Verhandlungen der sächsischen Akademie der Wissenschadften zu Leipzig, Philol.-histor. Kl., 106/3; Berlin: Akademie, 1963; 3d ed., 1967). This is a small dictionary of Ugaritic, but it is not really very adequate for the literature.

See *BASOR* 184 (1966) 39; *BO* 23 (1966) 307-8.

250. Vinnikov, I.N., "Slovar arameiskich Nadpisey," *Palestinskii Sbornik* 3 (66, 1958) 171-216; 4 (67, 1959) 196-240; 7 (70, 1962) 192-237; 9 (72, 1962) 141-58; 11 (74, 1964) 189-232; 13 (76, 1965) 217-262. This is a valuable "Dictionary of Aramaic Inscriptions," which lists all the vocabulary of Old Aramaic and Imperial Aramaic. It includes also proper names, which *DISO* (§ 247) does not. Even if one cannot read Russian, the references are listed in roman characters, and so the dictionary is helpful.

See *ArOr* 35 (1967) 463-66.

CAD   **251.**   **Oppenheim, A. L. et al. (eds.), *The Assyrian Dictionary* (so far 18 vols.; Chicago, IL: University of Chicago; Glückstadt: J. J. Augustin, 1956-   ). This is a very important comprehensive lexicon for the study of Assyrian and Babylonian texts, which supplies abundant examples in the history of the words booked. Cognates are provided from other Semitic languages, and select secondary literature is given. The completed vols. cover the letters A/1-2, B, D, E, G, H, I/J, K, L, M/1-2, N/1-2, Q, S, Ṣ, Z.

   See *AJSL* 38 (1921-22) 288-305; *Or* 18 (1949) 376-77; 21 (1952) 358-59; 53 (1984) 72-124; *OLZ* 79 (1984) 31-34.

AHW   **252.**   *Soden, W. von, *Akkadisches Handwörterbuch* (3 vols.; Wiesbaden: Harrassowitz, 1965, 1972, 1981). This excellent dictionary gives the vocabulary of important Assyrian and Babylonian texts often needed in the interpretation of the OT.

   See *JSS* 12 (1967) 105-9; *Or* 35 (1966) 304-18; *RB* 73 (1966) 486.

   253.   Cohen, D., *Dictionnaire des racines sémitiques ou attestées dans les langues sémitiques* (Paris/The Hague: Mouton, 1970-   ). For comparative study of the Semitic languages, this is a very valuable dictionary. It is issued in fascicles and is not yet complete.

   See *AION* 33 (1973) 271-74; *JQR* 63 (1972-73) 175-77; *Leš* 40 (1975-76) 185-89.

CHAPTER IX

Grammars

In this chapter are listed the best grammars for the study of the languages connected with the Bible. The entries are collected under the following headings: (A) Hebrew grammars; (B) Aramaic grammars; (C) Greek grammars; (D) Syriac and Coptic grammars; (E) grammars of other Northwest Semitic languages; (F) comparative Semitic grammars. Under some of these headings titles will be listed that go beyond the biblical books because they pertain either to the ancient versions or to extrabiblical texts of importance for the linguistic context of the language in question.

A. Hebrew Grammars

254. **Bauer, H. and P. Leander, *Historische Grammatik der hebräischen Sprache des Alten Testaments* (Halle an d. S.: Niemeyer, 1922). Only the first volume of this work ever appeared, treating the orthography, phonology, and morphology of Biblical Hebrew; an appended set of paradigms accompanied it. Though recent developments in the study of Hebrew (and its NW Semitic cognate languages) have dated many aspects of the work, many others in it can still be used, especially the classes of verbs, noun-types, etc.

See *ZAW* 45 (1927) 235-36.

GKB   **255.** *Gesenius, W., *Hebräische Grammatik* (29th ed., rev. G. Bergsträsser; Leipzig: Vogel [Part I: Einleitung, Schrift- und Lautlehre, 1918]; Hinrichs [Part II: Verbum, 1929]; repr. in one volume, Hildesheim/New York: Olms, 1962). This revision was never finished, but it was a great improvement over the 28th ed. of Gesenius' *Grammatik*. Though it is the best reference grammar for the part of the Hebrew language that it covers, it has to be supplemented by modern studies of the historical development of the language and of its counterparts in the NW Semitic languages to which it is cognate. An index to Hebrew forms and OT passages occurring in it can be found in L. G. Running, *Hebräisches Wortregister zur hebräischen Grammatik von G. Bergsträsser* (Hildesheim/New York: Olms, 1968).

See *ZAW* 45 (1927) 236-38; 48 (1930) 224.

GKC   **256.** *Gesenius, W. and E. Kautzsch, *Gesenius' Hebrew Grammar* (tr. A. E. Cowley; 2d ed.; Oxford: Clarendon, 1910). The English translation was based on the 28th German edition, translated by Cowley in 1909. It remains the best Biblical Hebrew reference grammar in English, but its treatment is antiquated at times.

GHB   **257.** **Joüon, P., *Grammaire de l'hébreu biblique* (2d ed.; Rome: Biblical Institute, 1947; repr., 1982). The first edition of this valuable Hebrew grammar appeared in 1923; the second was merely a corrected reprint. Though dependent on Gesenius' *Grammatik*, it constantly shows its independence. A brief introductory section ("Histoire de la grammaire hébraïque") contains a critical evaluation of earlier grammars and lexica. Joüon's *Grammaire* is rightly recognized for its treatment of syntax; it is the only full reference grammar that treats it so well, even though one has to admit today that the study of Hebrew syntax has gone beyond it. Students who will immerse themselves in the study of Hebrew as presented in this grammar will never regret it.

See *RB* 33 (1924) 314-15.

258. **Meyer, R., *Hebräische Grammatik* (Sammlung Göschen 763, 763a-b; 764, 764a-b; 5765; 4765; 4 vols.; Berlin: de Gruyter, 1966, 1969, 1972, 1972). These four small volumes constitute a compact reference grammar of Biblical Hebrew (originally started by G. Beer) for students who already have an elementary knowledge of the language. Forms and syntax are explained from both a comparative and historical point of view. Account is taken of the data come to light in Ugaritic tablets and in the Hebrew texts of Qumran. Volume 1 is devoted to introduction, orthography, and phonology; vol. 2 to morphology; vol. 3 to syntax; vol. 4 contains the index to the first three. There is also a companion volume of texts for reading, *Hebräisches Textbuch* (Sammlung Göschen 769, 769a, 1960).

See *RB* 61 (1954) 305-6; 63 (1956) 619-20; 67 (1960) 633-34; 73 (1966) 468-69; *Bib* 35 (1954) 117-21; 38 (1957) 95-98; *ArOr* 22 (1955) 488-90; 24 (1956) 153-55; *Eleven Years* (§ 7), 532, 782.

259. Brockelmann, C., *Hebräische Syntax* (Neukirchen: Erziehungsverein, 1956). The plan of this book follows almost section for section that of the author's older comparative syntax in the second volume of *Grundriss der vergleichenden Grammatik der semitischen Sprachen* (2 vols.; Berlin: Reuther und Reichard, 1908, 1913; repr., Hildesheim/New York: Olms, 1966). The work is a good modern treatment of Hebrew syntax, incorporating material from recent discoveries of Hebrew inscriptions and of the Qumran scrolls. Some points, however, are treated all too briefly, and others are open to debate. But it is nevertheless a very useful work, containing a rich bibliography (now somewhat out of date).

See *ZAW* 68 (1956) 265; *JSS* 2 (1957) 389-91; *TLZ* 83 (1958) 346-47.

260. Waltke, B. K. and M. O'Connor, *An Introduction to Biblical Hebrew Syntax* (Winona Lake, IN: Eisenbrauns, 1989). This is a modern linguistic study of Biblical Hebrew syntax, intended for self-study and also as a reference grammar. Some 3500 examples illustrate the points of syntax discussed.

B. Aramaic Grammars

GBA   261. **Bauer, H. and P. Leander, *Grammatik des Biblisch-Aramäischen* (Halle an d. S.: Niemeyer, 1927; repr., Hildesheim/New York: Olms, 1962). Though old and in need of some correction on minor points, this grammar remains the best comprehensive study of Biblical Aramaic. An abbreviated form of it exists: *Kurzgefasste biblisch-aramäische Grammatik mit Texten und Glossar* (Halle an d. S.: Niemeyer, 1929).

See *ZAW* 45 (1927) 235-36; *RB* 37 (1928) 310-11.

SGBA   262. Johns, A. F., *A Short Grammar of Biblical Aramaic* (Berrien Springs, MI: Andrews University, 1966). This short introductory grammar of Biblical Aramaic is intended for those who already know Biblical Hebrew. It borrows certain features from Bauer–Leander *Kurzgefasste... Grammatik* (§ 261) and is less complicated than F. Rosenthal, *A Grammar* (§ 263), organizing the material for sessions of classroom presentation, with graduated vocabulary and Aramaic-to-English exercises (drawn verbatim or in modified form from the OT).

See *JBL* 87 (1968) 234-35; *ZAW* 80 (1968) 278; *BO* 25 (1968) 378-39.

GBibAr   263. *Rosenthal, F., *A Grammar of Biblical Aramaic* (Porta linguarum orientalium ns 5; Wiesbaden: Harrassowitz, 1961; repr., 1974). This small grammar is intended "to provide the beginner with the elements of the language, and... to prepare him... for possible research in the problems of Aramaeology" (p. 1). It does not presuppose that the student has already acquired a good knowledge of Biblical Hebrew, but tries to treat Biblical Aramaic as a language in its own right. An index to the biblical passages quoted in it, prepared by G. H. Wilson, can be found in *JSS* 24 (1979) 21-24. An excellent introductory grammar, written by a famous Aramaist.

See *JBL* 80 (1961) 386-87; *Bib* 42 (1961) 245-46; *RB* 69 (1962) 280-81; *BO* 19 (1962) 266.

AGBCG   264. Segert, S., *Altaramäische Grammatik mit Bibliographie, Chrestomathie und Glossar* (Leipzig: VEB Verlag Enzyklopädie, 1975). This is a comprehensive reference grammar of the Aramaic language fitted out with bibliography, chrestomathy, and glossary, intended to cover not only Old Aramaic (925-700 B.C.), but also Official or Imperial Aramaic (700-200 B.C.), and Middle Aramaic (200 B.C. – A.D. 200). Lumping together the Aramaic evidence from these three periods of the language makes use of the grammar somewhat difficult. A treatment of Biblical Aramaic is included. The "decimal" numbering system (e.g., 5.1.4.1.5) is an encumbrance.

See *JSJ* 8 (1977) 99-105; *JBL* 96 (1977) 573-75; *JNES* 37 (1978) 197-99; *BO* 34 (1977) 92-97; *IEJ* 28 (1978) 205-6.

GJPA   **265.** Dalman, G., *Grammatik des jüdisch-palästinischen Aramäisch nach den Idiomen des palästinischen Talmud, des Onkelostargum und Prophetentargum und der jerusalemischen Targume* (2d ed.; Leipzig: Hinrichs, 1905; repr., Darmstadt: Wissenschaftliche Buchgesellschaft, 1960, 1981). Often reprinted with it is the author's *Aramäische Dialektproben* (2d ed.; Leipzig: Hinrichs, 1927). This is still the best reference grammar for the study of the targums; but it has its problems (see E. Y. Kutscher, *Studies in Galilean Aramaic* [tr. M. Sokoloff; Bar-Ilan Studies in Near Eastern Languages and Culture; Ramat-Gan: Bar-Ilan University, 1976]).

See *AJSL* 15 (1898-99) 116-20.

C. Greek Grammars

266. Thackeray, H. St. J., *A Grammar of the Old Testament in Greek according to the Septuagint* (vol. 1; Cambridge, UK: University Press, 1909; repr., 1978). Only the first volume, covering orthography, phonology, and morphology, ever appeared. The grammatical material is drawn almost exclusively from the uncial mss. A, B, S and a few others, which had been collated for Swete's manual edition of the LXX (§ 126). Abundant use was also made of papyri. This work, though outdated, remains the one indispensable grammar of the Greek OT; it is entirely independent of and superior to the slightly earlier grammar of R. Helbing, *Grammatik der Septuaginta: Laut- und Wortlehre* (Göttingen: Vandenhoeck & Ruprecht, 1907; repr., 1979), which was harshly criticized by J. Wackernagel, *TLZ* 33 (1908) 635-42.

See *JTS* 11 (1910) 293-300; *TRu* 15 (1912) 352.

BDR   **267.** *Blass, F. and A. Debrunner, *Grammatik des neutestamentlichen Griechisch* (14th ed.; rev. F. Rehkopf; Göttingen: Vandenhoeck & Ruprecht, 1976). The last thorough revision of BD was the 9th ed. (1954), which was simply reprinted in the intervening years up to the 13th ed. (1970). In 1965 D. Tabachovitz issued an *Ergänzungsheft* for the 12th ed. The 14th edition represents a reworking of the 9th, utilizing the material of Tabachovitz and other matters that Rehkopf had gathered. No mention is made here of the supplementary notes of A. Debrunner, to which R. W. Funk had access (§ 268). It is a mystery why Rehkopf did not use more material from BDF; because he has not, this means that BDR has not entirely replaced BDF. The 16th ed. appeared in 1984. An Italian translation exists, *Grammatica del Greco del Nuovo Testamento* (ed. G. Pisa; Brescia: Paideia, 1982).

See *CRev* 28 (1978) 98-100; *NRT* 98 (1976) 688-89.

BDF **268.** **Blass, F. and A. Debrunner, *A Greek Grammar of the New Testament and Other Early Christian Literature* (Chicago, IL: University of Chicago, 1961). This is a translation and revision of the 9th-10th German edition, *Grammatik des neutestamentlichen Griechisch* (Göttingen: Vandenhoeck & Ruprecht, 1954, 1959), in which the translator, R. W. Funk, incorporated the supplementary notes of A. Debrunner and much of his own material. Of an earlier edition of the German original, P. Benoit once wrote: "Un ouvrage de première valeur dont l'éloge n'est plus à faire." Funk's English version has also won its place in the sun. It is at present the most authoritative NT Greek grammar.

See *RB* 62 (1955) 447; *TLZ* 82 (1957) 110-15; *HibJ* 54 (1955-56) 93-94; *JBL* 82 (1963) 436-38; *CBQ* 24 (1962) 233-34; *Bib* 43 (1962) 237-38; *TS* 23 (1962) 272-74.

GNTG **269.** *Moulton, J. H. and F. W. Howard, *A Grammar of New Testament Greek* (4 vols.; Edinburgh: Clark). Volume 1, prolegomena, 3d ed., 1949; vol. 2, accidence and word formation, 1929; vol. 3, syntax, by N. Turner, 1963; vol. 4, style, by N. Turner, 1976. Though this grammar was written over a long period of time, it is a good comprehensive grammar of NT Greek; parts of it would not be as up-to-date as BDF (§ 268).

See *RB* ns 3 (1906) 658; 32 (1923) 146-48; 40 (1931) 130-31; *ExpTim* 41 (1929-30) 113; *JBL* 82 (1963) 439-41; *CBQ* 39 (1977) 165-67.

270. Robertson, A. T., *A Grammar of the Greek New Testament in the Light of Historical Research* (4th ed.; London: Hodder and Stoughton, 1923). A vast tome of 1454 pp. which treat thoroughly many NT grammatical problems. It first appeared in 1914 and is outdated in many ways.

See *RB* 12 (1915) 587-93.

ZGB² **271.** *Zerwick, M., *Graecitas biblica Novi Testamenti exemplis illustratur* (SPIB 92; 5th ed.; Rome: Biblical Institute, 1966). A compact summary in Latin of NT syntax, stressing mainly its difference from that of classical Greek; it presupposes therefore a knowledge of classical Greek and is not intended for beginners. But it is a useful companion to *ZAPNTG* (§ 272), and it has been highly praised for its good sense and enlightening comments on various NT passages. An adapted English version of the 4th ed. (1963)

ZBG

exists, *Biblical Greek Illustrated by Examples* (tr. J. Smith; SPIB 114; Rome: Biblical Institute, 1963). The English form has been criticized for ponderous English style and tampering with the section on moods and tenses. It is better to use the original *ZGB*.

See *RB* 53 (1946) 473; *TLZ* 76 (1951) 231-32; *JBL* 93 (1964) 332-33; *CBQ* 26 (1964) 406-7.

ZAPNTG **272.** Zerwick, M., *Analysis philologica Novi Testamenti graeci* (3d ed.; Rome: Biblical Institute, 1966). This work is neither a lexicon nor a grammar, but rather a handy companion to Merk's Greek text (§ 133), supplying a running lexical and grammatical analysis of NT words and phrases, together with frequent exegetical comments. It imitates and improves on F. Rienecker, *Sprachlicher Schlüssel zum griechischen Neuen Testament* (Giessen: Brunnen-V., 1957); in an expanded English translation: C. L. Rogers, Jr. (ed.), *A Linguistic Key to the Greek New Testament: Volume I, Matthew through Acts* (Grand Rapids, MI: Zondervan, 1976); *Volume II, Romans through Revelation* (1980; repr. two vols. in one, 1980). *ZAPNTG* is clearly intended for beginners, to enable them to get some rapid-reading experience of the Greek NT text; but it is not to be taken as a substitute for personal research or the consultation of standard grammars and lexica. It exists in an expanded and improved English translation, M. Zerwick and M. Grosvenor, *A Grammatical Analysis of the Greek New Testament* (2 vols.; Rome: Biblical Institute, 1974, 1979); vol. 1 covers the Gospels and Acts; vol. 2, the rest of the NT. All variants mentioned in the *RSV* are explained; the Greek text is now that of *UBSGNT*[3]. There is an unabridged, revised edition in one volume (1981), 3d ed. (1988)

See *RB* 62 (1955) 135; *ZKT* 76 (1954) 360; *CBQ* 17 (1955) 108-11; 37 (1975) 617.

IBNTG **273.** Moule, C. F. D., *An Idiom-Book of New Testament Greek* (2d ed.; Cambridge, UK: University Press, 1959). Without pretending to be a thorough and systematic treatment of NT syntax, this book is a readable and useful survey of many of its features not always adequately covered in other standard grammars. It is "an attempt to provide a syntactical companion to the interpretation of the NT" (p. vii). It first appeared in 1953.

See *ExpTim* 65 (1953-54) 104; *NTS* 1 (1954-55) 62-65; *JTS* ns 5 (1954) 243-44.

274. **Schwyzer, E., *Griechische Grammatik auf der Grundlage von Karl Brugmanns griechischer Grammatik* (Handbuch der Altertumswissenschaft II/I.1-3; 3 vols.; 2d. ed.; Munich: Beck, 1953, 1959). This is the topnotch German grammar for the study of Greek of all periods. Volume 3 (1953) is an index to the other two, prepared by D. J. Georgacas.

See *TLZ* 64 (1939) 7-9; 79 (1954) 239-41; *AJP* 73 (1952) 319-22; 76 (1955) 110.

GGPP   **275.**   Mayser, E., *Grammatik der griechischen Papyri aus der Pto-lemäerzeit: Mit Einschluss der gleichzeitigen Ostraka und der in Ägypten verfassten Inschriften* (2d ed.; Berlin/Leipzig: de Gruyter). The fascicles of this grammar were issued in a complicated order: Vol. 1/1-2 (1938); 1/3 (1936); 2/1 (1926); 2/2 (1934); 2/3 (1934). The work was never finished, but it constitutes a partial reference grammar of Greek non-literary writings of the Ptolemaic and early Roman periods of Egypt inscribed on papyrus, potsherds, and stone monuments. Gignac's *GGPRBP* (§ 276) treats similar texts from the Roman and Byzantine periods.

See *BSac* 84 (1927) 234-35; *RB* 36 (1927) 435-39.

GGPRBP   **276.**   *Gignac, F. T., *A Grammar of the Greek Papyri of the Roman and Byzantine Periods* (Testi e documenti per lo studio dell'antichità 55; 4 vols.; Milan: Istituto Editoriale Cisalpino–La Goliardica, 1976, 1981, 19??). Only two volumes of this important grammar have appeared so far; they treat respectively the phonology and the morphology of the Greek language in these papyri. Volumes 3 and 4 will be devoted to the syntax. "The corpus of texts analyzed in this grammar is the total number of the documentary papyri and ostraca from Egypt from the beginning of the Roman period in 30 B.C. to the end of the papyri ca. A.D. 735" (p. 1). A total of 32,284 documents has been analyzed in this study. It acts as the successor to E. Mayser's *Grammatik* (§ 275).

See *CBQ* 40 (1978) 272-73; 46 (1984) 156; *Gnomon* 51 (1979) 114-17; *Aegyptus* 58 (1978) 303-4; *REG* 91 (1978) 208-9; *CW* 72 (1978) 41-43; *EtClass* 45 (1977) 289; *JBL* 102 (1983) 350-52.

D. Syriac and Coptic Grammars

277.   *Nöldeke, T., *Compendious Syriac Grammar* (tr. J. A. Crichton; London: Williams & Norgate, 1904). This is a translation of the German, *Kurzgefasste syrische Grammatik* (2d ed.; Leipzig: C. H. Tauchnitz, 1898). Though Nöldeke expresses his satisfaction with Crichton's translation, there are some "howlers" in it. Otherwise it remains for English-speaking students the best reference grammar for the study of Syriac for either NT or OT interpreta-tion, even though it is hardly up to date.

278.   *Ungnad, A., *Syrische Grammatik mit Übungsbuch* (Clavis lin-guarum semiticarum 7; 2d ed.; Munich: Beck, 1932). Even though this book is out of print and hard to find, it remains the best elementary Syriac grammar.

See *RB* 41 (1932) 644; *ZAW* 50 (1932) 207.

279.   Brockelmann, C., *Syrische Grammatik mit Paradigmen, Litera-tur, Chrestomathie und Glossar* (Porta linguarum orientalium 5;

6th rev. ed.; Leipzig: Harrassowitz, 1951; repr., Leipzig: VEB
Verlag Enzyklopädie, 1976). This is the widely used introductory
grammar of classical Syriac. Its chrestomathy is better than
Ungnad's (§ 278), but its explanations of Syriac forms and other
phenomena in the language do not rival that of Ungnad.

See *RB* 8 (1899) 639.

280.   Steindorff, G., *Lehrbuch der koptischen Grammatik* (Chicago, IL:
University of Chicago, 1951). This grammar was posthumously
published by a team of scholars who knew Steindorff well; but
they did not succeed in eliminating all the typographical errors
that his failing health could not cope with. Yet it remains one of
the best reference grammars for the study of Coptic and its
various dialects. It is mainly a grammar of Sahidic, but with other
dialectal forms supplied for comparison. In the area of Coptic
studies, certain refinements in the study of grammar have been
made, which are not found here; but it is still an excellent
reference grammar.

See *Or* 23 (1954) 152-69; *JAOS* 74 (1954) 62-63; *BO* 11 (1954) 103-7.

281.   Till, W. C., *Koptische Grammatik (Sahidischer Dialekt): Mit
Bibliographie, Lesestücken und Wörterverzeichnissen* (Lehrbücher
für das Studium der orientalischen Sprachen 1; Leipzig: Harrassowitz, 1955). An excellent introductory grammar for the study of
the classical dialect of Coptic. The author has marked with an
asterisk those paragraphs which are of special importance for
beginners.

See *RB* 64 (1957) 316-17.

282.   Lambdin, T. O., *Introduction to Sahidic Coptic* (Macon, GA:
Mercer University, 1983). This grammar provides a concise introduction to the basic elements of Sahidic Coptic grammar.
After an introductory chapter on orthography and phonology,
the chapters deal with morphology and syntax. The chrestomathy
contains passages from the OT and NT and from "the Sayings of
the Fathers."

See *CBQ* 47 (1985) 322-23.

283.   Vergote, J., *Grammaire copte* (2 vols.; Louvain: Peeters, 1973).
See *Muséon* 91 (1978) 476-80.

E. Grammars of Other Northwest Semitic Languages

PPG   284.   *Friedrich, J. and W. Röllig, *Phönizisch–Punische Grammatik*
(AnOr 46; 2d ed.; Rome: Biblical Institute, 1970). The first edition,
authored by Friedrich alone, appeared in 1952 (AnOr 38). Its

Anhang included a sketch of the Aramaic dialect of the Zenjirli inscriptions (Ya'udi), which was later dropped.

See *Or* 41 (1972) 315-17; *Syria* 48 (1971) 529-30; *ZAW* 83 (1971) 420.

285. Branden, A. van den, *Grammaire phénicienne* (Bibliothèque de l'Université Saint-Esprit Kaslik–Liban 2; Beirut: Librairie du Liban, 1969).

See *BL* (1971) 67; *BeO* 11 (1969) 216; *BO* 27 (1970) 376-79.

286. Segert, S., *A Grammar of Phoenician and Punic* (Munich: Beck, 1976).

See *OLZ* 75 (1980) 150-53; *JNES* 37 (1978) 197-99.

287. Harris, Z. S., *A Grammar of the Phoenician Language* (AOS 8; New Haven, CT: American Oriental Society, 1936; repr., 1971). A standard English grammar for Phoenician and Punic, but it is now somewhat out of date and superseded by Segert's grammar (§ 286).

UT 288. *Gordon, C. H., *Ugaritic Textbook: Grammar, Texts in Transliteration, Cuneiform Selections, Glossary, Indices* (AnOr 38; Rome: Biblical Institute, 1965). This is the successor to the author's *Ugaritic Grammar* (AnOr 20, 1940), *Ugaritic Handbook* (AnOr 25, 1947), and *Ugaritic Manual* (AnOr 35, 1955). It is the standard grammar for Ugaritic, which teaches a mode of vocalizing the texts.

See *JBL* 69 (1950) 385-93.

289. Segert, S., *A Basic Grammar of the Ugaritic Language with Selected Texts and Glossary* (Berkeley, CA: University of California, 1984). A select bibliography is included.

See *BL* (1986) 140; *JRAS* (1986) 258-60; *Lešonénu* 48-49 (1984-85) 291-96.

GAG 290. **Soden, W. von, *Grundriss der akkadischen Grammatik* (AnOr 33; Rome: Biblical Institute, 1952); *Ergänzungsheft zum Grundriss der akkadischen Grammatik* (AnOr 47, 1969). This is the authoritative modern grammar for the study of Assyrian and Babylonian texts.

See *BO* 12 (1955) 96-98.

291. Ungnad, A. *Grammatik des Akkadischen* (5th ed., rev. L. Matouš; Munich: Beck, 1969). A very useful introductory grammar for the study of Akkadian.

See *BO* 23 (1966) 293-96; *JNES* 27 (1968) 74-75; *Syria* 44 (1967) 204-5.

292. Caplice, R., *Introduction to Akkadian* (Studia Pohl, ser. maior 9; Rome: Biblical Institute, 1983).

293. Riemschneider, K. K., *Lehrbuch des Akkadischen* (3d ed.; Leipzig: VEB Verlag Enzyklopädie, 1978). An English translation of the 2d ed. of this introductory grammar exists: J. F. X. Sheehan, *An Akkadian Grammar* (Milwaukee, WI: Marquette University, 1978).

     See *JANES* 2 (1969) 58-65.

F. Comparative Semitic Grammars

294. *Brockelmann, C., *Grundriss der vergleichenden Grammatik der semitischen Sprachen* (2 vols.; Berlin: Reuther und Reichard, 1908, 1913; repr., Hildesheim/New York: Olms, 1966, 1982). Though old, and in need of revision, this is still the standard grammar for the comparative study of Semitic languages. Volume 1 is devoted to phonology and morphology; vol. 2, to syntax.

295. Harris, Z. S., *Development of the Canaanite Dialects: An Investigation in Linguistic History* (AOS 16; New Haven, CT: American Oriental Society, 1939). This is a comparative study of some Northwest Semitic dialects.

296. Moscati, S. (ed.), *An Introduction to the Comparative Grammar of the Semitic Languages: Phonology and Morphology* (Porta linguarum orientalium ns 6; Wiesbaden: Harrassowitz, 1964). This is the latest attempt to present a comparative study of the Semitic languages. Though it has summarized and retained many of the good points in older comparative grammars, it is woefully inadequate because of its failure to record differences of languages and dialects now recognized, the historical development of forms within a given (or related) language, etc. Though Moscati had the assistance of reputable scholars (A. Spitaler, E. Ullendorff, and W. von Soden), one realizes that the shortcomings of this — the only modern comparative grammar that we have — are not all to be ascribed to them.

     See *Or* 34 (1965) 35-44; *JSS* 10 (1965) 267-69; *RSO* 39 (1964) 320-24; 40 (1965) 1-8; *BSOAS* 29 (1966) 146-47; *Sef* 24 (1964) 364-65; *ZAW* 77 (1965) 121; *CBQ* 27 (1965) 430-31; *BO* 25 (1968) 26-34.

CHAPTER X

Concordances

Serious study of the Bible inevitably calls for the use of good concordances, either for the original texts or ancient versions or modern translations. They enable one to study the use of words in a given biblical writer or group of writers and to trace themes for more synthetic study. Listed below are the best concordances for such work, under the following headings: (A) Hebrew and Aramaic biblical concordances: (B) Greek biblical concordances; (C) Latin biblical concordances; (D) Concordances in other languages.

A. Hebrew and Aramaic Biblical Concordances

Mandelkern   **297.**   ****Mandelkern, S.,** *Veteris Testamenti concordantiae hebraicae atque chaldaicae* (2d ed. Berlin: Margolin, 1925; repr., Berlin: Schocken, 1937; Graz: Akademischer Druck, 1955). The work first appeared in 1896 (Leipzig: Veit) under a Hebrew title; and the title has varied at times in the different printings. A reprint with corrections and additions was issued in New York (Schulsinger, 1955). A third, corrected and supplemented edition was put out by M. H. Gottstein (Jerusalem/Tel Aviv: Schocken, 1959). No better concordance to the Hebrew and Aramaic text of the OT exists. The concordance has been photographically reduced in size and printed on thin paper to make one manageable volume (9th ed.; Jerusalem/Tel Aviv: Schocken, 1971).

See *JQR* 40 (1949-50) 173-88; *JJS* 8 (1957) 5-12.

298.   **Lisowsky, G.,** *Konkordanz zum hebräischen Alten Testament* (2d ed.; Stuttgart: Württembergische Bibelanstalt, 1958). A handy concordance to BHK, reproduced from a handwritten copy not always easy to read. Only nouns and verbs are given full coverage, though all the words in the Biblical Hebrew dictionaries are mentioned, and proper names are given with mere references to where they appear. The words are translated into German, English (following BDB), and Latin (classical, not Vulgate). Though useful as a handy reference book, it cannot supplant Mandelkern's concordance (§ 297).

See *BT* 9 (1958) 189-91; *BO* 16 (1959) 41-42; *JSS* 1 (1956) 403; 4 (1959) 71-21; *NRT* 80 (1958) 986-87; *ZAW* 71 (1959) 254; *CBQ* 19 (1957) 391-92.

299.   **Loewenstamm, S. E.** (ed., with the cooperation of J. Blau), *Thesaurus of the Language of the Bible: Complete Concordance,*

Hebrew Bible Dictionary, Hebrew–English Bible Dictionary (Jerusalem: Bible Concordance Press). So far 3 vols. of this detailed combination concordance–lexicon of the Hebrew text of the OT have appeared (1957, 1959, 1968). It covers the letters of the alphabet from *aleph* to *ṭerēpāhî*. Useful.

300. Even-Shoshan, A., *Qônqôrdanṣyāh hǎdāšāh lětôrāh něbî'îm ûkětûbîm: A New Concordance of the Bible: Thesaurus of the Language of the Bible: Hebrew and Aramaic Roots, Words, Proper Names, Phrases and Synonyms* (Jerusalem: Kiryat Sepher Publishing House, 1981). All the words in the Hebrew Scriptures are listed in single alphabetical order according to the form in which they appear in a modern dictionary, not by their roots. Entries of words occurring hundreds or thousands of times are "condensed." This concordance, composed all in Hebrew, appears in a one-volume form, but also in three-volume and four-volume forms (with larger print). There is a four-page English preface.

See *TQ* 162 (1982) 263-64; *JETS* 26 (1983) 482-83.

B. Greek Biblical Concordances

Hatch–
Redpath

301. **Hatch, E. and H. A. Redpath, *A Concordance to the Septuagint and the Other Greek Versions of the Old Testament (Including the Apocryphal Books)* (2 vols.; Oxford: Clarendon, 1897; vol. 3 [Supplement], 1906; repr. in 2 vols., Graz: Akademischer Druck, 1954; repr. as *Tameion tēs hagias graphēs, Palaia diathēkē* [2 vols.; Athens: Beneficial Book Publishers, 1977]). The aim of this work was to present a complete concordance to the Greek OT, the LXX, including its text of deuterocanonical and apocryphal books, and to other Greek versions contained in the Hexapla. The work is based on the uncial mss. A, B, S, and the Sixtine edition of R (1587 [with corrections of its obvious mistakes and blunders]). The Hebrew equivalents of the Greek word are numbered and each entry is followed by a number, in an attempt to indicate the relation. Proper names are separately presented, and a reverse index gives the Greek equivalents of Hebrew words. This work is indispensable for the study of the Bible, but it must be used with caution. The evidence is limited to four mss.; the Hebrew–Greek equivalences must always be checked. Once the references are found, they should then be checked in the critical editions of the LXX (§ 123, 124) for possible variants. An important tool for the use of this concordance is found in E. Camilo dos Santos, *An Expanded Hebrew Index for the Hatch–Redpath Concordance to the Septuagint* (Jerusalem: Dugith, 1973). This index places all the Greek equivalents alongside the Semitic words that are listed in alphabetical order.

See *RB* 2 (1893) 154, 638; 4 (1895) 458-59; 6 (1897) 627-28; 10 (1901) 324; *JBL* 94 (1975) 297-98, 477-79.

VKGNT   **302.**   **Aland, K., *Vollständige Konkordanz zum griechischen Neuen Testament: Unter Zugrundelegung aller kritischen Textausgaben und des Textus Receptus* (2 vols.; Berlin/New York: de Gruyter, 1975-83, 1978). Produced with the aid of a computer and with the collaboration of H. Riesenfeld, H.-U. Rosenbaum, C. Hannick, this long-awaited complete concordance to the Greek NT is the last word in NT reference tools. It not only gives all the Greek words (even *de* and *kai*) and their contexts, but is based on N–A[26] (§ 131), supplying all the variants listed in the modern critical editions of the NT (Bover, Westcott–Hort, Merk, Nestle[25], Vogels, von Soden, Tischendorf, and the *Textus Receptus*). Superscript letters prefixed to the entries analyze categories of the uses of each word. Volume 2 (produced with the aid of H. Bachmann and W. A. Slaby) presents a specific survey of NT data: *Wortstatistik*, giving the frequency of each NT word, book by book; alphabetical listing of all NT Greek words, with the forms of each that actually occur and their frequency; survey of NT Greek vocabulary according to the frequency of occurrence, from the most frequent (*ho*, the definite article, 19904 times) to the *hapax legomena* (listed alphabetically); *hapax legomena* in the canonical order of NT books, a reverse index of the inflected forms of NT Greek words. Now that *VKGNT* is completed, this concordance is the only one to use for serious work.

See *JBL* 95 (1976) 679-81; 97 (1978) 604-6; 100 (1981) 147-49; 102 (1983) 639-40; 104 (1985) 360-62; *TRu* 41 (1976) 94-95; *ETL* 52 (1976) 134-42; 54 (1978) 323-45; 55 (1979) 152-55 [the last three reviews of F. Neirynck are reprinted in *ALBO* 5/36]; 56 (1980) 132-38; 57 (1981) 360-62; *CBQ* 41 (1979) 148-51; 42 (1980) 258-61; 46 (1984) 778-80; *RB* 90 (1983) 619-21.

303.   Bachmann, H. and W. A. Slaby, *Computer-Konkordanz zum Novum Testamentum graece von Nestle–Aland, 26. Auflage und zum Greek New Testament, 3rd Edition* (Berlin/New York: de Gruyter, 1980). An abridged form of *VKGNT*, which omits 29 words that occur very frequently (e.g., *alla, apo, autos, gar, de, dia*), but which gives a list of the relevant passages for these words in an appendix (pp. 1*-64*).

See *RB* 88 (1981) 621-22; *ETL* 56 (1980) 438-42; *NRT* 103 (1981) 767-68; *Bijdragen* 42 (1981) 314-15.

304.   Bruder, C. H., *Tamieion tōn tēs kainēs diathēkēs lexeōn sive concordantiae omnium vocum Novi Testamenti graeci* (Leipzig: E. Bredt, 1842; 4th ed., 1888). This long-used concordance recorded every word in the Greek NT in every instance of its use. It was originally based on the Textus Receptus, but was gradually fitted out with important variant readings from Greek NT mss. in subsequent editions (1853, 1867, 1888 [the last enriched with readings from Tregelles and Westcott–Hort]).

305. *Moulton, W. F. and A. S. Geden, *A Concordance to the Greek Testament according to the Texts of Westcott and Hort, Tischendorf and the English Revisers* (Edinburgh: Clark, 1897; 5th ed., rev. H. K. Moulton, with a supplement, 1978). Because the older concordance of C. H. Bruder (§ 304) became hard to find, this concordance became the indispensable tool for NT study. However, it has its problems: the particles *de* and *kai* were completely omitted and for 21 other words it gives merely the numbers of chapters and verses (in one instance incompletely), without lemmata, and sometimes with a mixture of both systems. Being based on older critical editions of the NT Greek text, it did not keep pace with the 20th-century progress in textual criticism. The one advantage that it still has over the new *VKGNT* (§ 302) is that it cites the OT passage, when the word analyzed is part of an OT quotation. But its references must always be checked. Because of its relatively cheap price and general good quality, it will undoubtedly be used by many NT students, who will not be able to afford the expensive *VKGNT*. The 5th ed. has a supplement of 76 pages, which now supply the references for seven more words (*apo, eis, ek, en, hoti, oun, syn*). These are based on *UBSGNT*[3] (= N–A[26]). It also adds the numbers of J. Strong's *The Exhaustive Concordance of the Bible* (§ 317e), which facilitates the use of this concordance for those who know little Greek.

See *NRT* 101 (1979) 884-85; *NovT* 23 (1981) 91-92; *TS* 41 (1980) 767-69.

306. Edwards, R. A., *A Concordance to Q* (SBLSBS 7; Missoula, MT [now Atlanta, GA]; Scholars, 1975). A key-word-in-context concordance to the Greek text of the Double Tradition in Matthew and Luke. The key word appears in the middle of the page separated on either side from the preceding words and those following. Three unnumbered pages of the preface give the list of passages recognized by Edwards as "Q." The concordance has two parts: (a) all words in "Q" passaages in alphabetical order; and (b) "all words in *each* pericope in alphabetical order." Useful.

See *CBQ* 39 (1977) 147-48; *ETR* 51 (1976) 234; *RSR* 64 (1976) 428; *CurTM* 3 (1976) 188; *RB* 83 (1976) 633-34.

307. Yoder, J. D., *Concordance to the Distinctive Greek Text of Codex Bezae* (NTTS 2; Leiden: Brill, 1961). A useful tool for the study of ms. D. But the data on the definite article have been omitted and also those "instances of *kai* and *de* which occur in supplementary clauses and sentences" (p. v). Being based on one NT ms., its usefulness is not outstripped by *VKGNT* (§ 302).

See *TS* 23 (1962) 341-42; *JBL* 81 (1962) 97-98.

308. Morgenthaler, R., *Statistik des neutestamentlichen Wortschatzes* (Zürich/Frankfurt am M.: Gotthelf, 1958). This is not a con-

cordance, but it contains tables of different sorts: (1) Statistics of
the NT vocabulary: an alphabetical listing of all NT words
according to their frequency in books or groups of books; (2)
statistics for special words (pronouns, prepositions, verbs com-
pounded with single and double prepositions, prefixes, foreign
words; (3) total word count and vocabulary count in each book;
(4) statistics of parts of speech in the NT books; (5) numeric
frequency of words in the NT. A lengthy introduction explains
the tables.

See *JBL* 78 (1959) 351; *Bib* 40 (1959) 109-10; *SJT* 12 (1959) 438-39;
TRu 24 (1958) 363-64.

C. Latin Biblical Concordances

309. *Fischer, B., *Novae concordantiae bibliorum sacrorum iuxta Vulgatam versionem critice editam* (5 vols.; Stuttgart/Bad Cannstatt:
Fromann–Holzboog, 1977). This is not a reworking of any earlier
concordance to the Latin Vulgate, but is "a completely new and
independent work, produced directly from the texts." It has been
computer-produced (at the Centre for Data-Processing of the
University of Tübingen). It is based on the Stuttgart critical
edition of the Vulgate, edited by R. Weber et al. (§ 162). To keep
the concordance within bounds, 22 of the words that occur most
frequently have been omitted (e.g., *ad, de, ego, et, hic*).

See *JTS* 29 (1978) 186-92; *NRT* 99 (1977) 743-44; *JBL* 97 (1978) 577.

310. **Dutripon, F. P.,** *Concordantiae bibliorum sacrorum vulgatae editio-
nis* (Paris: E. Belin, 1853; repr., 1861; 2d ed., Bar-le-Duc: L.
Guérin, 1868; 8th ed., Paris: Bloud et Barral, 1880; repr., Hil-
desheim/New York: Olms, 1980). The best of the older one-volume
concordances to the Latin Vulgate: "in primo genere" (A. Vaccari).

See *VD* 4 (1924) 247-48.

D. Concordances in Other Languages

311. Benedictine Monks of Maredsous, *Concordantia polyglotta: La
concordance de la Bible* (5 vols.; Turnhout: Brepols, 1980). A
computer-generated comparative tabulation of biblical words and
expressions in the books of the Roman Catholic canon as related
to each other and across languages in the following editions and
versions: French (*SBJ*, Bible de Segond, Bible de Maredsous,
Traduction œcuménique de la Bible), Hebrew (*BHS*, ben Sira),
Greek (LXX [Rahlfs], *UBSGNT*[3]), Latin (Vulgate, Weber [§ 162]),
English (*RSVWA*). Extremely common particles are not included.
The main text is French, ingeniously keyed to reveal equivalences
in other languages. It is a tour de force, the utility of which is still
to be assessed.

312. Morrison, C., *An Analytical Concordance to the Revised Standard Version of the New Testament* (Philadelphia, PA: Westminster, 1979). This analytical concordance not only lists the English words in alphabetical order together with a brief context, but also groups them according to the original Greek word(s) that they translate. Thus, "branch" not only lists the 17 instances of the word in the *RSV*, but also groups them as translations of *baion*, *klados*, and *klēma* and even lists one passage (Rom 11:24), where it is absent in the Greek but demanded by the context. An index-lexicon lists the Greek words alphabetically in transcription, telling in how many ways it has been translated in the *RSV*. Two appendices include notes on the analysis of the *RSV* NT and former readings of the *RSV*; the concordance is based on the 2d ed. of *RSV* NT (§ 182).

See *TS* 40 (1979) 572; *JBL* 100 (1981) 312-14; *CBQ* 42 (1980) 415-16.

313. Aufrecht, W. E. and J. C. Hurd, *A Synoptic Concordance of Aramaic Inscriptions* (International Concordance Library 1; Atlanta, GA: Scholars, 1975). This is a key-word-in-context concordance to the Canaanite and Aramaic inscriptions in *KAI* (§ 664). The texts are cited in roman transcription.

See *JBL* 96 (1977) 575-76.

314. Kasovsky (Kasowski), C. Y. *'ôṣar hat-targûm: Qônqordanṣiyā' lĕtargûm 'ônqĕlôs* (Jerusalem: Mosad Harab Kook, 1940). This is a more modern concordance to the official Aramaic translation of the Pentateuch.

315. Dietrich, M. and O. Loretz, *Konkordanz der ugaritischen Text-zählungen* (AOAT 19; Kevelaer: Butzon & Bercker; Neukirchen-Vluyn: Neukirchener-V., 1972). This is a concordance that lists in comparative fashion the various modes of numbering Ugaritic texts, which have been used by various editors of the texts.

See *CBQ* 36 (1974) 100-101; *ZAW* 84 (1972) 382; *ZA* 63 (1973-74) 110-12.

316. Whitaker, R. E., *A Concordance of the Ugaritic Literature* (Cambridge, MA: Harvard University, 1972). This concordance supplies an index to all the words in Herdner's *Corpus* (§ 666), Gordon's *UT* (§ 288), *PRU* 2 and 5, and *Ugaritica* 5 and 6 (§ 667-68).

See *CBQ* 35 (1973) 421; *BO* 36 (1979) 89-90.

317. Biblical Concordances of lesser moment: (a) Darton, M. (ed.), *Modern Concordance to the New Testament* (Garden City, NY: Doubleday, 1976). This is based on the French *Concordance de la Bible: Nouveau Testament* (Paris: Cerf/Desclée de Brouwer, 1970)

and uses all current English translations of the NT. (b) Elder, E., *Concordance to the New English Bible: New Testament* (Grand Rapids, MI: Zondervan, 1964). (c) Ellison, J. W., *Nelson's Complete Concordance of the Revised Standard Version Bible* (New York: Nelson, 1957; 2d rev. ed., 1972). (d) Hartdegen, S. J., *Nelson's Complete New American Bible Concordance* (Nashville, TN: Nelson; Collegeville, MN: Liturgical Press, 1977). This does not include the revision of the NT of 1987 (§ 183). (e) Strong, J., *The Exhaustive Concordance of the Bible* (New York: Hunt Eaton; Cincinnati: Cranston Curts, 1894; often reprinted [even by other publishers]). It is based on the *KJV*, with all entries numbered; these numbers have often been reproduced in other concordances and dictionaries. (f) *A Concordance to the Apocrypha/Deuterocanonical Books of the Revised Standard Version* (Cleveland, OH: Collins; Grand Rapids, MI: Eerdmans, 1983). This concordance is derived from the Bible Data Bank of Maredsous (§ 311). (g) Poswick, R.-F. (ed.), *Concordance de la Bible de Jérusalem, réalisée à partir de la banque des données bibliques de l'abbaye de Maredsous* (Paris: Cerf; Turnhout: Brepols, 1982). (h) Schierse, F., *Konkordanz zur Einheitsübersetzung der Bibel* (Düsseldorf: Patmos; Stuttgart: Katholisches Bibelwerk, 1985). (i) Luján, J., *Concordancias del Nuevo Testamento* (Biblioteca Herder 135; Barcelona: Herder, 1975). (j) Ghiberti, G. and L. Pacomio, *Le concordanze del Nuovo Testamento* (Genoa: Marietti, 1978). This is based on the French concordance: Sr. Jeanne d'Arc, *Concordance de la Bible* (Paris: Cerf, 1970).

See *RB* 89 (1982) 277-78.

CHAPTER XI

Dictionaries

In this chapter an effort is made to list the best dictionaries for the study of the books of the Bible, their theology, realia, and historical or archaeological backgrounds. "Dictionary" is being used here not in the sense of "lexicon" (i.e., a dictionary of the meaning of words in various biblical languages [for which see Chapter VIII], even though "dictionary" sometimes appears in the title of such lexica). The dictionaries that are listed here are grouped under the following headings: (A) General biblical dictionaries (treating matters in both Testaments); (B) OT dictionaries; (C) NT dictionaries; and (D) general theological or classical dictionaries which contain precious material on biblical subjects.

A. General Biblical Dictionaries

DBSup
or *VDBS*
318. ****Cazelles, H. and A. Feuillet (eds.), *Supplément au Dictionnaire de la Bible* (Paris: Letouzey et Ané, 1928-   ). The *Dictionnaire de la Bible* (ed. F. Vigouroux; 5 vols: Paris: Letouzey et Ané, 1895-1912) was long out of date. Instead of attempting a revision, L. Pirot began the work of issuing supplementary volumes in 1928; after his death A. Robert became the editor, and in 1956 he was succeeded by H. Cazelles; since 1966 A. Feuillet's name appears as a coeditor. So far 10 volumes have been published, and the eleventh is appearing in fascicles. Many of the articles are as long as monographs, and some are of book size; references to secondary literature are abundant. Though some of the earlier articles need to be updated, this monumental work of French biblical scholarship is indispensable.

IDB
IDBSup
319. ****Buttrick, G. A. (ed.), *The Interpreter's Dictionary of the Bible: An Illustrated Encyclopedia Identifying and Explaining All Proper Names and Significant Terms and Subjects in the Holy Scriptures, Including the Apocrypha, with Attention to Archaeological Discoveries and Researches into the Life and Faith of Ancient Times* (4 vols.; Nashville, TN/New York: Abingdon, 1962). The subtitle more adequately describes the contents of this valuable dictionary, which is not only devoted to *realia* but also to the teaching and theology of the various biblical writers. Now that a *Supplementary Volume* (ed. K. Crim; Nashville, TN: Abingdon, 1976) has been added to update or add new materials, this dictionary is a "must" for English-speaking students of the Bible.

See *JBL* 82 (1963) 102-4; 97 (1978) 105-6; *CBQ* 25 (1963) 150-51; 39 (1977) 555-57.

BHH   **320.** *Reicke, B. and L. Rost (eds.), *Biblisch-historisches Handwörter-buch: Landeskunde, Geschichte, Religion, Kultur, Literatur* (4 vols.; Göttingen: Vandenhoeck & Ruprecht, 1962, 1964, 1966, 1979). An excellent reference work, containing succinct articles written by many OT and NT scholars on the topics mentioned in the title, and fitted out with good bibliographies. The last volume contains indices and maps of Palestine. The articles are abundantly illustrated. This work is the German equivalent of *IDB* (§ 319).

See *JBL* 86 (1967) 454-57; *Bib* 45 (1964) 276-77; 47 (1966) 304-5; *TLZ* 89 (1964) 825-26; *TRu* 29 (1963) 294; 30 (1964-65) 359-60; 32 (1967) 163-64; *TZ* 19 (1963) 363; 21 (1965) 210; 23 (1967) 353-54.

HBD   **321.** Achtemeier, P. J. (ed.), *Harper's Bible Dictionary* (San Francisco, CA: Harper & Row, 1985). A modern one-volume, well illustrated dictionary of the Bible, composed by members of the Society of Biblical Literature. It is a summary of the best of what is known about the Bible and the world from which it emerged. It includes information about the apocrypha and pseudepigrapha of the OT and the NT and even about early patristic writings. But it emphasizes too much the sociological interpretation of the Bible.

See *JBL* 105 (1986) 699-700; *CurTM* 13 (1986) 122; *ExpTim* 98 (1986-87) 51; *JSJ* 17 (1986) 251-52; *TS* 47 (1986) 300-301.

322. Galling, K., *Biblisches Reallexikon* (HAT 1; Tübingen: Mohr [Siebeck], 1937; 2d ed. completely revised, 1977). The *realia* of the Bible are handled adequately; there are 135 illustrations, and each article is supplied with references to secondary literature.

See *ZDPV* 60 (1937) 246-48; *OLZ* 41 (1938) 538-40; *JBL* 57 (1938) 234; *TLZ* 63 (1938) 355-56; *JPOS* 18 (1938) 133-35; *TRu* 43 (1978) 90-91.

NBL   **323.** *Görg, M. and B. Lang (eds.), *Neues Bibel-Lexikon* (Zürich: Benziger, 1988). This new biblical dictionary is intended as the successor to the well-regarded *Bibel-Lexikon* of H. Haag (same publisher, 1951-56; 2d ed., 1968). It is being issued in fascicles; *Lief.* 1 has 176 cols., covering "Aaron" to "Artemis." It is an interconfessional project with over 200 contributors. The first German edition of this dictionary (1951) was based on a Dutch work by A. van den Born, *Bijbels Woordenboek* (Roermond: Romen en Zonen, 1941; 3d ed., 1966-69), but it was extensively revised by German Catholic scholars. The second Dutch edition (1954-57) was translated into English and freely adapted and expanded: L. F. Hartman (ed.), *Encyclopedic Dictionary of the Bible* (New York: McGraw–Hill, 1963), but it is in need of revision.

See *ZAW* 68 (1956) 261-63; *CBQ* 19 (1957) 132-33; 31 (1969) 95-96; *RB* 64 (1957) 115; 76 (1969) 279; *TS* 25 (1964) 75-77; *JBL* 88 (1969) 108-10; *TLZ* 94 (1969) 656-59.

324. McKenzie, J. L., *Dictionary of the Bible* (Milwaukee, WI: Bruce, 1965). This is a dictionary of the Bible written by one person, and it is a "monumental work," "eminently worthwhile" (J. Swetnam), even though it is *haute vulgarisation*, "a synthesis of the common conclusions of scholarship" (J. L. McK.). There are almost 2000 entries that supply reliable information.

See *Bib* 47 (1966) 290-91; *JBL* 85 (1966) 256-58.

BTW

325. *Bauer, J. B. (ed.), *Bibeltheologisches Wörterbuch* (2 vols.; Graz: Styria, 1958, 1962; 3d ed., 1967). An excellent biblical-theological dictionary in which many European Catholic exegetes collaborated. It is intended for theologians and those in pastoral ministry. Signed articles end with a short bibliography and give an adequate treatment of the most important OT and NT ideas. The 3d ed. has been translated into English under the title, *Sacramentum Verbi: An Encyclopedia of Biblical Theology* (3 vols.; New York: Herder and Herder, 1970).

See *CBQ* 33 (1971) 237-38; *TTZ* 68 (1959) 186-87; *ZKT* 81 (1959) 249.

326. Léon-Dufour, X., *Vocabulaire de théologie biblique* (Paris: Cerf, 1962). This is an analytic dictionary of key biblical terms, treated from a theological perspective. A form of it exists in English, *Dictionary of Biblical Theology* (New York: Desclée, 1967). Though its analysis is generally good, it is completely devoid of any bibliographical information and cannot be compared with J. B. Bauer's *BTW* (§ 325).

See *CBQ* 24 (1962) 443-44; 30 (1968) 457-58; *ExpTim* 74 (1962-63) 180; *Greg* 44 (1963) 582-84; *RTP* 13 (1963) 65-66; *TQ* 143 (1963) 351-52.

327. Müller, P.-G., *Lexikon exegetischer Fachbegriffe* (Biblische Basis Bücher 1; Stuttgart: Katholisches Bibelwerk; Kevelaer: Butzon & Bercker, 1985). This is a dictionary that explains the specific terminology, methods, and research techniques of biblical interpretation, which have developed in 19th and 20th centuries.

See *TRev* 83 (1987) 19-21.

328. Soulen, R. N., *Handbook of Biblical Criticism* (2d ed.; Atlanta, GA: John Knox, 1981). This is actually a dictionary of technical terms and usages of biblical scholarship, which first appeared in 1976.

See *Int* 32 (1978) 108; *CTJ* 46 (1982) 245.

329. Odelain, O. & R. Seguineau, *Dictionnaire des noms propres de la Bible* (Paris: Cerf and Desclée de Brouwer, 1978). In English: *Dictionary of Proper Names and Places in the Bible* (Garden City, NY: Doubleday, 1981). A list of almost 4000 entries, mentioning the names of persons and places in the Bible and gathering the information that locates each name in its proper historical and geographical context. Very useful. In German: *Lexikon der biblischen Eigennamen* (Düsseldorf: Patmos, 1978).

See *NRT* 101 (1979) 273-74; *ETR* 53 (1978) 575-76; *RevThom* 79 (1979) 139-40.

B. OT Dictionaries

TWAT   **330.**   **Botterweck, J. and H. Ringgren (eds.), *Theologisches Wörterbuch zum Alten Testament* (Stuttgart: Kohlhammer, 1970-   ). This multivolume dictionary is being published in collaboration with a number of OT scholars (G.W. Anderson, H. Cazelles, D.N. Freedman, S. Talmon, and G. Wallis); it is international and interconfessional in its approach. Though of smaller scope than Kittel–Friedrich, *TWNT*, it is similar in its treatment of OT words, supplying not only the ancient Near Eastern background (Sumerian, Akkadian, Egyptian, Ugaritic, etc.) of the Hebrew and Aramaic words of the OT but also their theological meaning in the OT itself. Occasionally, paragraphs press on to postbiblical (e.g., Qumran) meanings or rabbinical usage. So far five volumes have been completed, and the sixth is being issued in fascicles. An

TDOT   English translation of this dictionary has been begun: *Theological Dictionary of the Old Testament* (Grand Rapids, MI: Eerdmans, [1974], 1977-   ). After a poor start (see "An Announcement from the Publishers of *TDOT*," *JBL* 94 [1975] 546) and a reissue of the first volume (1977), this dictionary is now appearing regularly in English. Its volumes, however, do not correspond to the German volumes; though use is being made of a bigger format easier to read, the price of two of the volumes of *TDOT* is actually less than that of one of *TWAT*. This is a welcome addition to the study of the OT and will clearly become as much of a household word in exegetical circles as is Kittel–Friedrich. There is also a Spanish form: *Diccionario teológico del Antiguo Testamento* (Madrid: Cristiandad, 1973-   ); also an Italian form: *Grande lessico dell'Antico Testamento* (ed. F. Montagnini; Brescia: Paideia, 1982-   ).

See *Bib* 60 (1979) 128-29; *CBQ* 40 (1978) 231; *TS* 36 (1975) 510-13; 39 (1978) 154-56; *TTZ* 81 (1972) 50-53; *Bijdragen* 32 (1971) 321-22; *TRev* 83 (1987) 188; *Razon y Fe* 199 (1979) 329.

THAT   **331.**   *Jenni, E. and C. Westermann (eds.), *Theologisches Handwörterbuch zum Alten Testament* (2 vols.; Munich: Kaiser; Zürich: Theologischer Verlag 1971, 1976). This two-volume theological dictionary of the OT is no substitute for a Hebrew–Aramaic lexicon (to which one must still go for philological answers to questions), but it is intended to supplement its use by concentrating on semantics, form-criticism, and tradition-history to present the meanings of OT words in their historical and theological OT contexts. Forty scholars from around the world have contributed to this dictionary, which should not be confused with the multi-volume *TWAT/TDOT* (§ 330). In Italian translation: *Dizionario teologico dell'Antico Testamento* (ed. G. L. Prato; Turin: Marietti, 1978, 1982).

See *BO* 30 (1973) 88-89; *TQ* 153 (1973) 290-91.

TWOT **332.** Harris, R. L., G. L. Archer, Jr., and B. K. Waltke, *Theological Wordbook of the Old Testament* (2 vols.; Chicago, IL: Moody, 1980). Forty-six evangelical scholars have written "essay definitions of the important theological terms in the Old Testament" for "the busy pastor or earnest Christian worker who has neither the time nor the background for detailed technical study" such as one might find in standard dictionaries such as *TWAT, TDOT, THAT*. Words are listed in Hebrew according to their roots, as in BDB, but derivatives are also listed in alphabetical order with cross-references to the numbered entries. Bibliographies at the end of articles often (but not always) give leads to further study. Useful, but not to be used as a sole guide for study.

See *CTQ* 47 (1983) 287-88.

333. **Sukenik, E. L. et al., *'Enṣîqlôpēdyāh miqrā'ît: 'ôṣar hayyĕdî'ôt 'al hammiqrā' ûtĕqûpātô: Encyclopaedia biblica: Thesaurus rerum biblicarum alphabetico ordine digestus* (Jerusalem: Bialik Institute, 1950-). Seven volumes have appeared so far, covering up to *Šĕlîšiyāh* (1976). A thorough, detailed encyclopedia of the OT, prepared by top-notch Israeli scholars. Each entry is fitted with a good modern bibliography. As the title implies, the dictionary is written in modern Hebrew.

C. NT Dictionaries

TWNT **334.** **Kittel, G. (ed.), *Theologisches Worterbuch zum Neuen Testament* (10 vols.; Stuttgart: Kohlhammer, 1933-1979). This monumental work of German Protestant NT scholarship, begun under the editorship of G. Kittel and continued under that of G. Friedrich, is the greatest tool that students have for the interpretation of the NT. It is a gold mine of information, in which the most important words of the NT are studied in their historical backgrounds: after a discussion of the etymology of a word, its usage in classical Greek, Hellenistic Greek, the Greek of the LXX, and of Jewish writers is sketched as a background for the treatment of its use in the NT. When a word has a Hebrew counterpart in the OT, an adequate discussion of that is also given. Stress is put on the semantic and theological development in the history of the word. The dictionary has been criticized by J. Barr (*The Semantics of Biblical Language* [New York: Oxford University, 1961]; *Biblical Words for Time* [SBT 33; rev. ed.; London: SCM, 1969]), who found fault with its heavily etymological approach and principle of organization. In a sense, Barr's criticism is merited; but this monument to NT scholarship will still be in use long after Barr and his criticism are forgotten. It should be realized that the first four volumes of this *Wörterbuch* were completed before or during the Second World War (1933, 1935, 1938, 1942). Volume 5 did not appear until 1954. Consequently the material in vols. 1-4 is more in need of updating than the rest. An English translation has been made of this valuable tool: G.W. Bromiley

TDNT

(tr. and ed.), *Theological Dictionary of the New Testament* (10 vols.; Grand Rapids, MI: Eerdmans, 1964-76). Volume 10 in both the German and English is an index volume, but the German vol. 10 also contains updated secondary literature. Hence one must consult it in the original. There is also a "little Kittel": G.W. Bromiley,

TDNTA

Theological Dictionary of the New Testament Abridged in One Volume (Exeter, Devon, UK: Paternoster; Grand Rapids, MI: Eerdmans, 1985). It equals about 1/6 of *TDNT*. All Greek words have been transliterated, but the order is the same as in *TDNT* (hence not strictly alphabetical in English). English meanings have been added to the running headers and in the Table of English keywords. Philological, archaeological, and other supporting matters have been drastically reduced. Relevant numbers of volumes and pages in *TDNT* are appended at the end of the abridged

GLNT

articles. An Italian translation of *TWNT* exists: *Grande Lessico del Nuovo Testamento* (15 vols.; ed. F. Montagnini et al.; Brescia: Paideia, 1963-88).

See *TS* 25 (1964) 424-27; 38 (1977) 402-3; *CBQ* 26 (1964) 490-92; *NRT* 103 (1981) 768-69; 104 (1982) 759.

EWNT   **335.**   **Balz, H. and G. Schneider (eds.), *Exegetisches Wörterbuch zum Neuen Testament* (3 vols.; Stuttgart: Kohlhammer, 1978, 1981, 1983). Similar in format to *TWAT* (§ 330), this dictionary does not aim to update or replace *TWNT/TDNT*, which it still presupposes for the history and background of NT vocabulary. Rather, it aims at covering the meaning(s) of Greek words in their context(s) in the NT writings themselves; in a sense it presents more modern discussions of the meanings of the vocabulary of the Greek NT than certain parts of the articles in *TWNT/TDNT*. But it also covers words that are not treated in the latter (e.g., *monos*). It intends to be what its title implies, an exegetical dictionary. It too is international and interconfessional in its approach. An English version is being prepared: *Exegetical Dictionary of the New Testament* (Grand Rapids, MI: Eerdmans' 1990-   ).

See *BLit* 53 (1980) 246-47; *TLZ* 106 (1981) 415-17; *TTZ* 90 (1981) 74-76; *ETL* 58 (1982) 386-88; 60 (1984) 155-56.

TBLNT   **336.**   *Coenen, L., E. Beyreuther, and H. Bietenhard (eds.), *Theologisches Begriffslexikon zum Neuen Testament* (Vols. I, II/1-2; Wuppertal: Brockhaus, 1967, 1969, 1971). Whereas Kittel–Friedrich, *TWNT/TDNT* (§ 334) orders its articles according to the Greek words of the NT, along with their verbal cognates (e.g., *theos, theotēs, atheos, theodidaktos, theios, theiotēs*), following the order of the Greek alphabet, the *Begriffslexikon* groups words expressing related ideas (e.g., baptism, wash [Greek *baptizō, louō, niptō*]; or bishop, presbyter, elder [Greek *episkopos, episkeptomai*, etc., *presbyteros, presbeuō, proistēmi, kybernēsis*]). This dictionary offsets some of the criticism of J. Barr (§ 334). It was mainly put together to aid theologians, pastors, and ministers of conservative Protestant backgrounds, and many of the articles have been written by them, with a more pastoral tone. The historical, archaeological, and geographical aspects are not in the forefront of the discussion. It concentrates on the theological meaning of the words so grouped. An English form of this dictionary has *NIDNTT*   been published: C. Brown, *The New International Dictionary of New Testament Theology* (3 vols.; Grand Rapids, MI: Zondervan, 1975, 1976, 1978). It is not, however, a simple translation, since it contains many additions and revisions (usually signed) by the editor and his collaborators. The appendix to vol. 3 has an interesting discussion of "prepositions and theology in the Greek New Testament" (pp. 1171-1215). This dictionary has made use of much modern material, which makes some of its articles even better than those in *TWNT/TDNT* vols. 1-4. There is also an Italian form: *Dizionario dei concetti biblici del Nuovo Testamento* (ed. A. Tessarolo; Bologna: Dehoniane, 1976).

See *TS* 38 (1977) 560-63; 40 (1979) 347-49; *RSR* 67 (1979) 624-27; *BeO* 8 (1966) 48; 14 (1972) 226; *BTB* 3 (1973) 98-99; *BL* (1976) 10; *EvQ* 48 (1976) 105-8; 49 (1977) 117-19; 51 (1979) 171-73.

D. General Theological or Classical Dictionaries

TRE   **337.**   **Krause, G. and G. Müller (eds.), *Theologische Realenzyklopädie* (30 vols.; Berlin/New York: de Gruyter, 1976-   ). This is the successor to the old, renowned *Realencyklopädie für protestantische Theologie und Kirche* (ed. A. Hauck; 3d ed.; Leipzig: Hinrichs, 1896-1913); in English, *The New Schaff–Herzog Encyclopedia of Religious Knowledge* (13 vols.; London/New York: Funk and Wagnalls, 1908-14). However, *TRE* has adopted an ecumenical perspective and surveys the entire Christian faith with all the advances of modern modes of study and research. The various theological disciplines are all covered. To date 17 vols. have appeared (from Aaron to Katechismuspredigt); and also a volume devoted to a list of abbreviations.

See *TRev* 83 (1987) 369-70; *TRu* 52 (1987) 432-36.

LTK   **338.** **Höfer, J. and K. Rahner (eds.), *Lexikon für Theologie und Kirche* (11 vols.; 2d ed.; Freiburg im B: Herder, 1957-67). This is the Roman Catholic counterpart to *RGG* (§ 339). Though it is explicitly destined for use by pastors, theologians, and church historians, it contains many excellent articles, succinctly written, on NT and OT topics.

        See *TS* 19 (1958) 572-85.

RGG   **339.** **Galling, K. (ed.), *Die Religion in Geschichte und Gegenwart* (3d ed.: 7 vols.; Tübingen: Mohr [Siebeck], 1957-65). Even though this dictionary covers more than biblical topics, its seven volumes contain many valuable articles on both the OT and the NT, written by top-notch Protestant Scripture scholars.

RAC   **340.** **Klauser, T. (ed.), *Reallexikon für Antike und Christentum: Sachwörterbuch zur Auseinandersetzung des Christentums mit der antiken Welt* (Stuttgart: Hiersemann, 1950-   ). This important dictionary began to appear during the Second World War (1941), but vol. 1 was not completed until 1950. Since then 14 volumes have been published. As the subtitle indicates, the work is a survey of pre-Christian and Christian antiquity, with recognition of their continuity and their difference. Many well-known scholars have contributed masterly articles to it, and many of them are of great value for the student of the OT or the NT. Volume 14 (1988) covers "Heilig" to "Hexe." A second edition began to appear in 1970 (Stuttgart: Hiersemann).

        See *JBL* 67 (1948) 251-60; 71 (1952) 62-63; 73 (1954) 43-44; 74 (1955) 199-200; 75 (1956) 236-37; 77 (1958) 285-86; 78 (1959) 281; 80 (1961) 286.

EKL   **341.** Fahlbusch, E. et al., *Evangelisches Kirchenlexikon: Internationale theologische Enzyklopädie* (Göttingen: Vandenhoeck & Ruprecht) Band 1 (A und O — Futurologie, 1986); two fascicles of Band 2 have been issued. This is the successor to *EKL* (4 vols.; ed. H. Brunotte and O. Weber; same publisher, 1956-61).

        See *TRev* 83 (1987) 95-97.

PW or RE   **342.** ***Paulys Real-Encyclopädie der classischen Altertumswissenschaft* (Neue Bearbeitung, ed. G. Wissowa; Stuttgart: J. B. Metzler, 1905-1978). Commonly referred to as Pauly–Wissowa, this massive dictionary of classical antiquity is now complete. It was started in 1893, but has been published since 1949 by A. Drukkenmüller (Stuttgart). The publication of this encyclopedia has been irregular and the numbering system somewhat confusing. The first series contains articles on subjects A-Q (vol. 1-24/1); the second series began in 1914 and covers R-Z (vols. 1-10). From

PWSup   time to time *Supplementbände* (15 vols.) have appeared (since

1903), giving additional or new material in the letters of the alphabet already published. One should consult J. P. Murphy, *Index to the Supplements and Supplementary Volumes of Pauly–Wissowa's R. E.: Index to the Nachträge and Berichtigungen in vols. I-XXIV of the First Series, vols. I-X of the Second Series, and Supplementary Vols. I-XIV of Paul–Wissowa–Kroll's Realenzyklopädie* (Chicago: Ares, 1976). Also H. Gärtner and A. Wünsch, *Register der Nachträge und Supplemente* (Munich: Druckenmüller, 1980). Biblical students who neglect this encyclopedia do so at their own peril, since there are many well-written and highly-informative articles on matters pertaining to the two Testaments and the intertestamental period.

See *Historia* 1 (1950) 171-72.

DKP **343.** *Ziegler, K. and W. Sontheimer (eds.), *Der Kleine Pauly: Lexikon der Antike von Pauly's Realencyclopädie der classischen Altertumswissenschaft* (5 vols.; Stuttgart: A. Druckenmüller, 1964, 1967, 1969, 1972, 1975). An abridgement of PW in 5 stout vols., welcomed because no individual scholar can afford the more than 80 vols. of "der grosse Pauly." They constitute an excellent handy dictionary to classical antiquity, giving up-to-date information on matters of the Graeco-Roman world that bear on the OT and NT.

See *Gnomon* 37 (1965) 740-42; 47 (1975) 1-5; *Augustinianum* 5 (1965) 444-45; 6 (1966) 350-51; 7 (1967) 391-92; 9 (1969) 187-88; 14 (1974) 379; 15 (1975) 249-50; *EtClass* 44 (1976) 84, 179.

OCD **344.** Hammond, N. G. L. and H. H. Scullard (eds.), *The Oxford Classical Dictionary* (2d ed.; Oxford: Clarendon, 1970). This is the best handy one-volume dictionary on Graeco-Roman antiquity, thoroughly reliable and succinctly composed.

See *CRev* 21 (1971) 124-25; *JBL* 90 (1971) 252; *Greece & Rome* 18 (1971) 110-11; *JRS* 61 (1971) 269-71; *Times Literary Supplement* 69 (1970) 1203.

CHAPTER XII

Introductions to the Bible

As used in this chapter, "introduction" is a translation of the German word *Einleitung* or *Einführung*, that part of biblical studies that seeks to relate the various books of the OT and NT to their historical backgrounds, supply guidance for the comprehension of them as wholes, and tell what each book's message is for readers of today. Normally, they treat of such questions as the date and place of composition, the authenticity or the attribution to traditional authors and the integrity of the work, the occasion and purpose of the writings, the contents and outline of the various books. Often they include a rich select bibliography on the different books of the Bible. These "introductions" should not be confused with the introductions to the biblical text and ancient versions (Chapter IV). They will be listed under three headings: (A) Introductions to the whole Bible; (B) Introductions to the OT; and (C) Introductions to the NT.

A. Introductions to the Whole Bible

345. *Introduction à la Bible: Edition nouvelle* (10 vols.; Paris: Desclée, 1976-   ). This is an expanded and thoroughly revised edition, directed by A. George and P. Grelot, of a two-volume series begun by A. Robert and A. Feuillet under the same main title (1957-59). Tomes 1-5 introduce the various parts of the OT and the NT. Tomes 6-10 treat of specific problems; so far three of them have appeared: tome 6, P. Grelot, *Evangiles et histoire* (1986); tome 7, P. Grelot, *Les paroles de Jésus Christ* (1986); tome 8, P. Grelot and M. Dumais, *Homélies sur l'Ecriture* (1989). What has appeared so far is a great improvement of the older volumes of this, in many respects excellent, introduction to the whole Bible.

See *RB* 95 (1988) 147; *CBQ* 41 (1979) 335-37; 49 (1987) 502-4; 50 (1988) 319-21; *ETL* 55 (1979) 404-9.

B. Introductions to the OT

346. Anderson, B.W., *Understanding the Old Testament* (4th ed.; Englewood Cliffs, NJ: Prentice Hall, 1986). This survey of the OT, highlighting the history and religion of Israel, has proved its worth over the years since it was first published in 1957. It sets the biblical writings in their historical background. Archaeological data and the best of modern secondary literature have been excellently used; maps, chronological charts, illustrations,

and a bibliography of supplementary readings (limited to English titles) make this the best introductory textbook for college-students and seminarians. The British title of the same book is *The Living World of the Old Testament* (London: Longman Group Ltd.).

> See *JSS* 3 (1958) 83; *Int* 12 (1958) 244-48; *CBQ* 38 (1976) 75-76; 49 (1987) 295-96.

347. Bentzen, A., *Introduction to the Old Testament* (2 vols.; Copenhagen: Gad, 1952). This Danish introduction appeared first in 1941; a revised and rewritten English translation was issued in 1948. The second edition (1952) incorporated additional material in appendices. The deuterocanonical/apocryphal books are included. The work is particularly valuable for the presentation of Scandinavian views on the forms of OT literature.

> See *JBL* 67 (1948) 399-402; *TLZ* 75 (1950) 541-45; *BO* 7 (1950) 183-85; *Bib* 32 (1951) 276-80; *Eleven Years* (§ 7), 23, 195, 495.

IOTS   **348.** Childs, B.S., *Introduction to the Old Testament as Scripture* (Philadelphia, PA: Fortress, 1979). This approach to the OT does not wholly dispense with the historical-critical method of interpretation, but it adds a dimension not often found in introductions, viz., the consideration of the OT books as part of the Christian canon.

> See *TToday* 37 (1980) 100-108; *RL* 49 (1980) 245-47; *JBL* 100 (1981) 99-103; *CBQ* 42 (1980) 535-37; *RB* 88 (1981) 437-38; *JSOT* 16 (1980) [seven reviews and a reply of Childs].

349. **Eissfeldt, O., *Einleitung in das Alte Testament unter Einschluss der Apokryphen und Pseudepigraphen sowie der apokryphen- und pseudepigraphenartigen Qumrānschriften* (Neue theologische Grundrisse; Tübingen: Mohr [Siebeck], 1964). This is a revised and greatly expanded form of earlier editions (1934, 1956). It is the best introduction to the OT available. Nearly one quarter of the book is devoted to the preliterary materials (i.e., forms, speeches, records, narratives, poetry) and to the prehistory of the OT books. There are detailed introductions to each of the OT books, including the deuterocanonical/apocryphal writings, as well as to various pseudepigrapha of the OT and Qumran texts. An English translation exists: *The Old Testament: An Introduction Including the Apocrypha and Pseudepigrapha, and also the Works of Similar Type from Qumran* (tr. P.R. Ackroyd; Oxford: Blackwell; New York/Evanston, IL: Harper & Row, 1965).

350. *Fohrer, G., *Einleitung in das Alte Testament* (10th ed.; Heidelberg: Quelle & Meyer, 1965). This introduction was begun by E. Sellin in 1910 and saw seven editions before he died; eds. 8 and 9 were prepared by L. Rost; and now the 10th by G. Fohrer.

Though this introduction started out to be a handbook for students, with this 10th ed. it has reached the status of a comprehensive, technical introduction almost on a par with Eissfeldt's *Introduction* (§ 349). Fohrer espouses a coordinated use of form-critical, traditio-historical, and literary-critical methods in approaching the biblical writings. The discussion is limited to the books of the Hebrew canon. A slightly revised English translation of this work exists, *Introduction to the Old Testament* (tr. D. E. Green; Nashville, TN: Abingdon, 1968).

See *BZ* 12 (1968) 131-33; *ExpTim* 81 (1969-70) 301; *RB* 78 (1971) 475; *JTS* 22 (1971) 171-73; *JBL* 91 (1972) 93-94.

351. Harrison, R. K., *Introduction to the Old Testament: With a Comprehensive Review of Old Testament Studies and a Special Supplement on the Apocrypha* (Grand Rapids, MI: Eerdmans, 1969). This is an introduction to the OT in more than the usual sense, since it touches OT history, archaeology, chronology, and historiography as well. Though a vast and comprehensive coverage is presented, the author writes from a conservative (i.e., evangelical) viewpoint; opposing views are branded as "liberal," and scholars are told that they must "submit to the authority of the Old Testament Scriptures" (p. 491). If one can prescind from such preachments, one can otherwise learn much from this stout tome.

See *JBL* 89 (1970) 227-28; *CBQ* 32 (1970) 608-9.

352. Humphreys, W. L., *Crisis and Story: Introduction to the Old Testament* (Palo Alto, CA: Mayfield, 1979). This is an introduction to the OT that seeks to show that stories about Israel arose in that community at major turning-points or crises in the life of Israel. It follows a historical order of literary production of the books, and not the canonical order. The book contains photos, maps, drawings, charts, and a useful glossary.

See *CBQ* 45 (1983) 457-58.

353. Kaiser, O., *Einleitung in das Alte Testament: Eine Einführung in ihre Ergebnisse und Probleme* (3d ed.; Gütersloh: Mohn, 1975). This book is destined for students, teachers, and pastors as an introduction to the books of the Hebrew canon of the OT. It is not as comprehensive as the introductions of either Eissfeldt or Fohrer (§ 349, 350), but more like that of A. Weiser (§ 358). There exists an English form, *Introduction to the Old Testament: A Presentation of Its Results and Problems* (Minneapolis, MN: Augsburg, 1973). It is a translation of the 2d ed. (1970), but has incorporated further revisions of the author up to 1973.

See *CBQ* 38 (1976) 565-66; *JBL* 97 (1978) 443-44.

354. *Rost, L., *Einleitung in die alttestamentlichen Apokryphen und Pseudepigraphen einschliesslich der grossen Qumran-Handschriften* (Heidelberg: Quelle & Meyer, 1971). The appendices of the older editions of Sellin's *Einleitung* were omitted in G. Fohrer's 10th ed. of 1965 (§ 350). These have now become a book apart, an introduction to the deuterocanonical/apocryphal literature of the OT and to the major Qumran texts. Paragraphs discuss the transmission of the text, content, problems of literary criticism, historicity, literary genre, date of composition, authorship, and religious meaning. An English translation exists under the title, *Judaism outside the Hebrew Canon* (Nashville, TN: Abingdon, 1976).

See *JBL* 90 (1971) 346-47; *CBQ* 39 (1977) 572-73.

355. Sandmel, S., *The Hebrew Scriptures: An Introduction to Their Literature and Religious Ideas* (New York: Knopf, 1963). Written by a prominent Jewish scholar of the U.S.A., "this book is addressed to the beginner, not the scholar. It is a non-technical introduction ...." But it aims "to acquaint the reader who goes no on to become a biblical scholar in the fullest technical sense with basic material that he will not have to unlearn" (p. vii). "In sum, I would place this work high among nontechnical biblical introductions and literary histories" (N. K. Gottwald).

See *JBL* 82 (1963) 441-43; *JQR* 54 (1963-64) 258-65; *JR* 44 (1964) 76-78; *ScEccl* 16 (1964) 187-88.

356. Schmidt, W. H., *Einführung in das Alte Testament* (New York/ Berlin: de Gruyter, 1979). This is an excellent modern German introduction to the OT, written by a well-known OT interpreter. It is a successor to J. Meinhold's *Einführung in das Alte Testament* (same publisher, 1919; 3d ed., 1932). It is limited to the books of the Hebrew canon. An English form exists: *Old Testament Introduction* (tr. M. J. O'Connell; New York: Crossroad, 1984).

See *CBQ* 42 (1980) 390; 48 (1986) 316-18; *RB* 88 (1981) 438-39.

357. *Soggin, J. A., *Introduzione all'antico Testamento: Dalle origini alla chiusura del canone alessandrino: Con appendici sulle iscrizioni palestinesi della prima metà del I millennio a.C. e sui reperti manoscritti dei primi secoli dopo l'esilio* (4th ed.; Biblioteca di cultura religiosa 14; Brescia: Paideia, 1987). This work first appeared in 1967, treating the OT "from the beginnings to the Exile"; the second edition extended the treatment to the closing of the Alexandrian canon. It is an enlightened introduction, written by an Italian professor of the Waldensian Faculty of Theology in Rome, and has been highly praised. Various appendices discuss Semitic inscriptions from the first half of the first millennium B.C., from the first centuries after the Exile, or give a chronological table of biblical dates. The 2d ed. appeared in English translation, *Introduction to the Old Testament: From Its Origins to the Closing of the Alexandrian Canon* (OTL; Philadelphia, PA: Westminster, 1976).

See *RB* 76 (1969) 437-39; 82 (1975) 625-26; *JBL* 96 (1977) 105; *CBQ* 40 (1978) 106.

358. *Weiser, A., *Einleitung in das Alte Testament* (5th ed.; Göttingen: Vandenhoeck & Ruprecht, 1963). It originally appeared in 1939 and was issued in a revised second edition in 1949; the fourth edition was an extensive revision, and the fifth differs little from it, but the bibliographies have been updated. From the second edition on, it has included sections on the deuterocanonical/apocryphal books, as well as on certain pseudepigrapha. It has become in Germany the standard introduction for university students. An English translation exists of its 4th ed.: *The Old Testament: Its Formation and Development* (New York: Association Press, 1961).

See *BZ* 3 (1959) 112-17; *Eleven Years* (§ 7), 30; *BL* (1958) 30; *ExpTim* 74 (1962-63) 46-47; *RB* 71 (1964) 425.

C. Introductions to the NT

359. Davies, W. D., *Invitation to the New Testament: A Guide to Its Main Witnesses* (Garden City, NY: Doubleday, 1966). "... not written for scholars, and not primarily for students of the Bible," but "for those, in schools, colleges, churches, adult classes, and every walk of life, who have neither the time nor the guidance for detailed study of the New Testament, but who yet desire to grasp the central thrust of the foundation document of Christianity" (p. vii).

See *ATR* 48 (1966) 310-12; *JAAR* 35 (1967) 305-6; *CJT* 12 (1966) 287-88; *CBQ* 29 (1967) 610-12.

360. Guthrie, D., *New Testament Introduction* (3 vols.; London: Tyndale, 1961, 1962, 1965; later combined into one volume, 3d ed., Downers Grove, IL: Inter-Varsity, 1970). The first volume was devoted to "The Pauline Epistles," the second to "Hebrews to Revelation," and the third to "the Gospels and Acts." The stance taken is conservative, hypercritical of much solid NT scholarship, and reluctant to admit pseudepigraphical writings in the NT. There is too much preoccupation with historicity in the gospel introductions.

See *CBQ* 33 (1971) 582-84.

361. Harrington, D. J., *Interpreting the New Testament: A Practical Guide* (New Testament Message 1; Wilmington, DE: Glazier,

1979). "It is a beginner's book," says the preface (p. vii), but it is an excellent short introduction for persons who have no technical training and would like to find out something about "formal exegetical training." It gives a concise explanation of literary criticism, textual criticism, translations of the Bible, words and motifs, source criticism, form criticism, historical criticism, redaction criticism, parallels, and the meaning of the text.

See *America* 143 (1980) 373; *CBQ* 43 (1981) 129-30.

362. Köster, H., *Einführung in das Neue Testament im Rahmen der Religionsgeschichte und Kulturgeschichte der hellenistischen und römischen Zeit* (de Gruyter Lehrbuch; Berlin/New York: de Gruyter, 1980). This book is the companion to the introduction of P. Vielhauer (§ 369). The two of them replace the *Einführung* of R. Knopf (Sammlung Töpelmann), which was first published in 1919, then revised by H. Weinel and H. Lietzmann in 1930 and 1949. The latter part of Köster's title emphasizes the thrust of his introduction; it seeks to treat the NT as an integral part of early Christian literature considered in its historical religious and cultural context. Much of the work is devoted to the history of the Greek world, beginning with Alexander the Great, and to the Roman world, beginning with the principate. It also treats the Apostolic Fathers, the Apologetes (Aristides and Justin), and NT apocrypha. The problem that this book raises is that it is not per se an introduction *in das Neue Testament*; it is rather a work that propounds certain theses about the NT by means of hypothetical reconstructions, which are rarely explained or defended as they should be (e.g., his reliance on Nag Hammadi texts as reflecting early Christianity [of the first century]). Köster's treatment of the bearing of the Qumran scrolls on the NT is woefully inadequate. The bibliographies in the book are constructed mostly from German publications; French NT scholarship is ignored. An English translation of the work exists: *Introduction to the New Testament* (Hermeneia: Foundations and Facets; 2 vols.; Berlin/New York: de Gruyter; Philadelphia, PA: Fortress, 1982). Some English versions of German contributions are cited, but not all that should be.

See *JBL* 101 (1982) 445-48; *CBQ* 45 (1983) 141-43; *RB* 90 (1983) 462-64; *ETL* 57 (1981) 357-58; *TS* 44 (1983) 693-95.

363. **Kümmel, W. G., *Einleitung in das Neue Testament* (20th ed.; Heidelberg: Quelle & Meyer, 1980). This is the most widely used introduction to the NT among serious students thereof. Begun by P. Feine in 1913, it was continued by J. Behm (8th ed., 1936). The 9th ed. (1950) made it a classic, even though little use was made of Roman Catholic contributions. The 12th ed. came out in 1963, completely reworked by W. G. Kümmel, who changed much. The contribution of Roman Catholic scholarship was finally recognized and has been since. The 14th ed. of 1965 was translated into English, *Introduction to the New Testament* (Nashville, TN: Abingdon, 1966). The 17th ed. was the first to bear Kümmel's name alone (1973) and was translated into English (under the same title) by H. C. Kee (1975). The 18th and 19th eds. have bibliographical supplements following the index.

See *TPQ* 121 (1973) 363-68; *CBQ* 38 (1976) 245-46; *RB* 46 (1937) 453-54; 74 (1967) 132; *TS* 37 (1976) 134-36; *RHPR* 55 (1975) 312-14; *NRT* 101 (1979) 884.

364. Martin, R. P. *New Testament Foundations: A Guide for Christian Students* (2 vols.; Grand Rapids, MI: Eerdmans, 1975, 1978; rev. ed., 1986). This guide is conservative and seeks to show how the NT books fit into the life, problems, and opportunities of the early Christian communities. Volume 1 treats of the four Gospels; vol. 2, Acts, the Letters, and the Apocalypse.

See *CBQ* 38 (1976) 406-7.

365. Marxsen, W., *Einleitung in das Neue Testament: Eine Einführung in ihre Probleme* (Gütersloh: Mohn, 1978). This book first appeared in 1963; the 4th ed. is a complete reworking of it. This relatively brief introduction, in which Marxsen treats of some of the usual introductory problems, tries to cut through details; stress must be put on the subtitle of the book. For the questions are treated from a definite "theological approach," which is explained at the outset. The order of NT books introduced is as follows: (1) Pauline Epistles (1-2 Thessalonians, Galatians, Philippians, Philemon, 1-2 Corinthians, Romans); (2) Synoptic Gospels and Acts; (3) Pseudo-Pauline Epistles (Colossians, Ephesians, Pastorals, Hebrews); (4) Church Epistles (James, 1 Peter, Jude, 2 Peter); (5) Johannine Writings (John, 1 John, 2-3 John); (6) Apocalyptic literature (Revelation). The student should beware of the author's exaggerated preoccupation with Gnosticism. A English translation was made of the third edition: *Introduction to the New Testament: An Approach to Its Problems* (Philadelphia, PA: Fortress, 1968).

See *TQ* 144 (1964) 1-11; *JBL* 88 (1969) 122; *CBQ* 32 (1970) 140-42; *NRT* 101 (1979) 882-83 (4th Germ. ed.).

366. Michaelis, W., *Einleitung in das Neue Testament: Die Entstehung, Sammlung und Überlieferung der Schriften des Neuen Testaments* (2d ed.; Bern: Haller, 1954; repr., 1961, with an *Ergänzungsheft*). A good, thorough NT introduction, written by a reputable German NT scholar, who taught in Switzerland. Though he expresses rather personal views on certain problems, he is careful to give an accurate résumé of the opinions of others and a searching analysis of them.

See *ZNW* 45 (1954) 275-76; *RB* 63 (1956) 138-39.

367. Robinson, J. A. T., *Redating the New Testament* (London: SCM; Philadelphia, PA: Westminster, 1976). This book handles only some of the usual introductory problems of NT writings, concentrating mainly on an attempt to date them all before A.D. 70. This book is to be used with great caution. The author admits his hypothesis that the whole of the NT was written before 70 started out as "a theological joke" (p. 10).

See *Int* 32 (1978) 309-13; *Duke Divinity School Review* 2 (1977) 193-205; *JBL* 97 (1978) 294-96; *CBQ* 40 (1978) 134-36; *NRT* 101 (1979) 890-92; *JTS* 30 (1979) 255-62.

368. Schierse, F. J., *Einleitung in das Neue Testament* (Leitfaden Theologie 1; Düsseldorf: Patmos, 1978). The book is destined for students of theology or religious education. The first part treats of general questions (text, canon, methods of interpretation); the second is devoted to analysis of NT books, not in their canonical order, but in a chronological order that the author favors (1 Thessalonians, Galatians, 1-2 Corinthians, Philippians, Philemon, Romans; then the Synoptics: Mark, Matthew, Luke; then Acts and the Deuteropaulines: Colossians, Ephesians, 2 Thessalonians, the Pastorals; then Hebrews and Johannine literature: John, 1-3 John, Revelation; finally the Catholic epistles, 1 Peter, James, Jude, 2 Peter).

See *NRT* 101 (1979) 883-84.

369. Vielhauer, P., *Geschichte der urchristlichen Literatur: Einleitung in das Neue Testament, die Apokryphen und die apostolischen Väter* (Berlin/New York: de Gruyter, 1975). An introduction to the NT, following the models of A. von Harnack, H. von Soden, and M. Dibelius. It strives to situate the NT books in the context of the early Christian literature, apocryphal and patristic. An excellent survey, but one not meant for beginners. See § 362.

See *BZ* 21 (1977) 299-302; *JBL* 96 (1977) 595-98; *CBQ* 38 (1976) 603-5.

370. **Wikenhauser, A. and J. Schmid, *Einleitung in das Neue Testament* (6th ed.; Freiburg im B: Herder, 1973; repr., 1977). This German Roman Catholic introduction to the NT first appeared in 1952; an improved second edition of it was issued in 1956 and was eventually translated into English, *New Testament Introduction* (New York: Herder and Herder, 1958). Subsequent editions of the German were published by A. Vögtle (4th ed., 1961; 5th ed., 1963). The 6th ed., completely revised and rewritten by Professor Emeritus J. Schmid, is now the best introduction to the

NT in any language. One will detect in it an affinity to the work of Feine–Behm–Kümmel (§ 363), which inspired it; but there is also an independence of spirit from that tradition. The convergence of treatment in these two introductions speaks eloquently for the achievement of interconfessional historical-critical interpretation of the NT, which has won its place in the sun, despite Cassandra-like cries about the state of the discipline that are heard at times. The *Einleitung* is not free of "typos" and wrong references. There exists a Spanish translation, *Introducción al Nuevo Testamento* (Biblioteca Herder 56; Barcelona: Herder, 1978); also an Italian translation, *Introduzione al Nuovo Testamento* (Biblioteca teologica 9; Brescia: Paideia, 1981).

See *TS* 14 (1953) 602-6; 20 (1959) 114-16; *RB* 61 (1954) 274-76; *JBL* 93 (1974) 305-6; *CBQ* 36 (1974) 147-49; *BZ* 19 (1975) 260-63; *TPQ* 121 (1973) 363-68; *TRu* 42 (1977) 177-83; *Greg* 59 (1978) 753; *Antonianum* 54 (1979) 535-36.

CHAPTER XIII

Commentaries

No attempt will be made in this chapter to list commentaries on individual books of the Bible. There are, of course, some excellent commentaries on individual books of both the OT and the NT, which do not form part of series. Some guidance to such commentaries can be found in the bibliographic aids of B. S. Childs (§ 8), E. Hort (§ 11). The aim here is to list works of a multiple character, whether in one volume or many that comment on the Bible. They will be gathered under the following headings: (A) Commentaries on the whole Bible: (a) in one volume; (b) in many volumes; (B) Commentaries on the OT; and (C) Commentaries on the NT.

A. Commentaries on the Whole Bible

a. In One Volume

PCB　　　**371.** **Black, M. and H. H. Rowley (eds.), *Peake's Commentary on the Bible* (London: Nelson, 1962). This one-volume commentary on the Bible is named after A. S. Peake, who first published a *Commentary on the Bible* in 1919; in 1936, a *Supplement to Peake's Commentary* was edited by A. J. Grieve. The 1962 edition is a completely new work. The contributors to it have been drawn from the best Protestant OT and NT scholars in Great Britain and America, and it has been justly praised for its accurate and reliable popular scholarship, even though this has had to be confined to a short compass.

　　　　　See *JBL* 82 (1963) 454-55; *Bib* 44 (1963) 371-72; *NTS* 9 (1962-63) 399-400; *HeyJ* 4 (1963) 287-89; *RB* 70 (1963) 442-43.

NJBC　　　**372.** **Brown, R. E., J. A. Fitzmyer, and R. E. Murphy (eds.), *The New Jerome Biblical Commentary* (Englewood Cliffs, NJ: Prentice Hall; London: Chapman, 1990). This is the successor to the *Jerome Biblical Commentary*, first issued in 1968. Of the latter it was said, "In content and coverage, *JBC* frequently parallels its 'Protestant counterpart' and recent predecessor, *Peake's Commentary on the Bible* (1962). In a general comparison, *PCB* manifests a more historical and *JBC* a more thematic orientation. Valuable additions in *JBC* include the historical surveys of the OT and NT Criticism ..., and several essays on Hermeneutics ..., Pauline ... and Johannine theology" (J. H. Elliott). "Peake's and the Jerome Commentary remain the two best options for one-volume commentaries, with my personal preference going to the latter" (R. W. Klein, *CTM* 43 [1972] 461). The *JBC* was translated into Spanish: *Comentario Bíblico "San Jeronimo"* (5 vols.; Madrid: Cristiandad, 1972), and into Italian: *Grande Commentario Biblico* (Brescia: Queriniana, 1973). The *NJBC* is not a mere revision of the *JBC*, but, as the title suggests, a widespread reworking of it, being almost two-thirds new. Two articles have been added, "Jesus" and "Early Church"; the commentary on 2 Thessalonians has been separated from that on 1 Thessalonians.

See *RB* 77 (1970) 417-21; *CBQ* 31 (1969) 405-14; *Int* 23 (1969) 468-73; *Bib* 50 (1969) 543-47; *The Tablet* 2 Dec. 1989, 1406-7; *Church Times*, 1 Dec. 1989, 11; *ExpTim* 100 (1989-90) 225-27.

NCCHS **373.** Fuller, R. C., L. Johnston, and C. Kearns (eds.), *A New Catholic Commentary on Holy Scripture* (London: Nelson, 1969). This is a
CCHS revision of *A Catholic Commentary on Holy Scripture* (ed. E. F. Sutcliffe and B. Orchard, 1953), which was supposed to be a Roman Catholic counterpart of *PCB* (§ 371), but which was characterized by what P. Benoit called a "prudence très conservatrice" (*RB* 64 [1957] 600). The new edition has improved this situation in many ways, but it is scarcely representative of modern Catholic biblical interpretation. Some articles in it, however, have only been slightly reworked from *CCHS*; others are completely rewritten, of which some are excellent. The difference in tone in the two editions says much.

See *JBL* 89 (1970) 222-26; *RB* 77 (1970) 607-10; *CBQ* 33 (1971) 112-14; *NRT* 92 (1970) 674-75.

IOVCB **374.** Laymon, C. M. (ed.), *The Interpreter's One-Volume Commentary on the Bible: Introduction and Commentary for Each Book of the Bible Including the Apocrypha* (Nashville, TN: Abingdon, 1971). The emphasis in this commentary was supposed to be "pastoral," but it has not survived serious criticism: "... in terms of general quality of scholarship, ... it is to be feared that, on the whole, *IOVC* tends to come off second best" (H. Hummel); "... a disappointment" (R. W. Klein).

See *Int* 26 (1972) 341-45; *CTM* 43 (1972) 460-61; *ExpTim* 84 (1972-73) 184; *TToday* 29 (1972-73) 207-10.

HBC **375.** Mays, J. L. (ed.), *Harper's Bible Commentary* (San Francisco, CA: Harper & Row, 1988). Eighty-two members of the Society of Biblical Literature have contributed to this popular one-volume commentary on the Bible (the Hebrew Scriptures, the OT apocrypha, and the NT). It follows the order of the *RSV* (Common Bible), putting the deuterocanonical/apocryphal books between the OT and the NT. The commentary on a given book interprets it according to its structure and language, and not merely its prehistory. There are also general topical articles. Each commentary article includes a very brief bibliography, and the comments tend to be essay-like, rather than explanations of excerpted phrases or words.

b. In Many Volumes

376. Anchor Bible (Garden City, NY: Doubleday). Begun in 1964, under the general editorship of W. F. Albright and D. N. Freedman, this multivolume commentary on the Bible now counts 26 volumes on OT books, 15 on NT books, and 7 on the Apocrypha. The format has varied over the years, from short commentaries to extensive ones. The quality has varied even more; in general, the OT commentaries have been less controversial than those of the NT. But there are some noteworthy volumes in the series. Contributors to the series have been Jews, Protestants, and Roman Catholics.

   See *ZAW* 86 (1974) 391-92.

377. The Broadman Bible Commentary (Nashville, TN: Broadman). This series of 12 vols. contains commentaries on books of the both Testaments (but without the deuterocanonical books or the apocrypha). It has been prepared by scholars of the Southern Baptist Convention in the U.S.A. It presents a modern compact commentary (1969-72), "current biblical study within the context of strong faith in the authority, adequacy, and reliability of the Bible as the Word of God" (1. ix).

378. Cambridge Bible Commentary, NEB (Cambridge, UK: University Press, 1963-79). This series of brief, modern, well-written commentaries on books of the two Testaments (including the apocrypha and deuterocanonicals) has been edited by P. R. Ackroyd, A. R. C. Leaney, and J W Packer. It is intended for "the general reader," with teachers and young people especially in mind, persons without expertise in theology or biblical languages. The NT section was completed in 1967, and the sections on the OT and the Apocrypha were well under way.

EBib 379. *Etudes bibliques (Paris: Gabalda). A series begun by M.-J. Lagrange, which is continued under the direction of the Dominicans of the Ecole Biblique of Jerusalem. It contains not only commentaries on books of both Testaments but also many learned monographs on Palestinian history, geography, and archaeology. Though some of the commentaries are outdated today, they still retain their value because of their thoroughness and solid French combination of theological viewpoint and scientific rigor.

380. The Expositor's Bible Commentary with the New International Version of the Holy Bible (Grand Rapids, MI: Zondervan, 1976-   ). Edited by F. Gaebelein, this series is to be completed in 12 volumes. Its stance is that of "a scholarly evangelicalism committed to the divine inspiration, complete

trustworthiness, and full authority of the Bible." So far 4 vols. have been issued: 7 (Daniel and the Minor Prophets, 1985); 10 (Romans to Galatians, 1976); 11 (Ephesians to Philemon, 1978); 12 (Hebrews to Revelation, 1981).

See *JETS* 21 (1978) 173-79.

Hermeneia   **381.**   **Hermeneia — A Critical and Historical Commentary on the Bible (Philadelphia, PA: Fortress). This excellent modern series of commentaries on the two Testaments was begun in 1972. It is edited by F. M. Cross and H. Koester, making available to English-speaking readers solid and detailed commentaries from the viewpoint of the historical-critical method. Many of the volumes issued so far are translations of German commentaries, written by renowned Protestant scholars. The English version is often revised and updated, and quotations in ancient foreign languages are translated into English. So far 11 volumes have appeared in the NT section (John [2 vols.], Acts, 1 Corinthians, 2 Corinthian 8–9, Galatians, Colossians and Philemon, Pastorals, Hebrews, 1-3 John, James, and a volume on the Letters of Ignatius of Antioch; in the OT section six volumes have been issued (Jeremiah [2 parts], Ezekiel [2 parts], Hosea, Joel–Amos, Micah, Song of Songs).

IB   **382.**   The Interpreter's Bible (Nashville, TN, Abingdon). This series began to appear in 1952, with G. A. Buttrick as the editor. It covers both Testaments and is complete in 12 volumes. For each biblical book the *KJV* and the *RSV* are printed in parallel columns; there are extensive introductions and exegetical commentaries, not to mention sections of homiletic exposition. Over half of vols. 1 and 7 is devoted to essays on OT and NT background, which still retain their value. Though the commentaries vary in quality, one will still find a good deal of excellent material in these volumes; in general, the serious student will profitably ignore the homiletic expositions.

ICC   **383.**   *The International Critical Commentary (Edinburgh: Clark). Begun in 1895 under the direction of C. A. Briggs, S. R. Driver, and A. Plummer, this series was intended to provide the English reader with an interpretation of both Testaments that would be comparable to German critical works of the time. The latest published volume was that by J. A. Montgomery and H. Gehman on Kings (1951), and the series was far from complete. The emphasis has been critical and philological, using the latest historical and archaeological data for interpretation. Many of the volumes, however, are now dated. A new series has been begun, edited by J. A. Emerton and C. E. B. Cranfield. So far only the commentaries on Romans (1975, 1977) and Matthew (1st vol., 1988) have appeared in this new series.

LSS   **384.** Los libros sagrados (18 vols.; Madrid: Ediciones Cristiandad,
           1966-77). Edited by L. Alonso Schökel, J. Mateos, and J.M.
           Valverde, this series makes use of a modern Spanish translation
           of the Bible (§ 207), mingling exegetical rigor and literary
           qualities. The translation is accompanied by succinct explanatory
           notes.
           See *BT* 22 (1971) 38-44; *CulB* 23 (1967) 83-90; *EstBib* 28 (1969) 181;
           BL (1977) 47-49; *CBQ* 41 (1979) 122-23; *OrAnt* 18 (1979) 365-67.

NEchtB   **385.** Die Neue Echter Bibel (Würzburg: Echter V., 1980-   ). This is
           a Roman Catholic German commentary series, using the
           Einheitsübersetzung (§ 196). The series is edited by J.G. Plöger
           and J. Schreiner. Its purpose is a succinct and precise summation
           of modern exegesis of OT and NT books. The first fascicle to
           appear was *Kohelet* (N. Lohfink); several others have been
           published on both OT and NT writings.
           See *CBQ* 43 (1981) 624-26; *JBL* 102 (1983) 322; *RB* 96 (1989) 452-54,
           461-62.

NCB   **386.** New Century Bible: Based on the Revised Standard Version
           (London: Oliphants; Greenwood, SC: Attic, 1966-   ). This is a
           series of commentaries of moderate length on both Testaments.
           They avoid foreign words, but seek to explain the Hebrew,
           Aramaic, and Greek text literally. The introductions vary in
           quality. A new form of this series has already undergone revision
           in several of the volumes.

NClarB   **387.** New Clarendon Bible (Oxford: Clarendon). This series exists in
           two forms: one based on the *RSV* (1967-   ), of which 6 vols.
           [Matthew, Luke, John, Acts, Thessalonians, Letters from Prison]
           have appeared; the other based on the *NEB* (1963-   ), of which
           only one volume [Pastorals] has appeared.

           388. La sacra Bibbia (Turin: Marietti). Begun by S. Garofalo in 1948,
           this series of commentaries and monographs on OT and NT
           books is very uneven. The editorship in more recent times has
           been taken over by G. Rinaldi for the OT. Originally, comments
           were made on the Latin Vulgate and an Italian translation; but in
           more recent volumes the Vulgate has been omitted. These are
           usually detailed commentaries written by competent Italian
           scholars.

           389. La sagrada escritura (BAC 207, 211, 214 [NT]; 267, 281, 287, 293,
           312, 323 [OT]; Madrid: Edica). Up-to-date, critical, but somewhat
           conservative commentaries on the two Testaments, published
           under the editorship of Spanish Jesuit biblical scholars. The three
           volumes dedicated to the NT were originally published in
           1961-62; the six on the OT in 1967-71.

SBJ   **390.** La sainte Bible (Paris: Cerf). This is the fascicle edition of *La Bible de Jérusalem*, which began to appear in 1948, under the direction of the Dominicans of the Ecole Biblique in Jerusalem. Covering both Testaments, the series of fascicles was completed in 1954. It contains a critical translation from the original languages, introductions of moderate length, and brief notes. It has undergone several revisions. In 1956 a single-volume edition was issued, in which the notes were shortened and the introductions abbreviated (for a revised form of this one-volume edition, see § 189). Though the contributions differ somewhat in quality, this publication represents the best of modern Roman Catholic scholarship in the French-speaking area. In general, it is highly recommended, despite its brevity.

SB   **391.** Sources bibliques (Paris: Gabalda). Published under the general direction of P. Benoit, J. Guillet, and J. Trinquet, this excellent series was begun in 1963. It contains single-volume commentaries on both Testaments, and is, in effect, a worthy successor to the commentaries in EBib (§ 379), but these volumes do not contain the Greek text of the NT books. In general, they are highly recommended; 16 vols. have appeared to date.

TBC   **392.** Torch Bible Commentaries (London: SCM; New York: Macmillan, 1951-   ). This series has been under the editorship of J. Marsh and A. Richardson. The commentaries on both Testaments are brief and compact, but usually have good introductions and emphasize the religious significance of the biblical books. They are clearly influenced by the historical- critical method (devoting a volume to Genesis 1–11, and another to Genesis 12–50; and three to Isaiah). Being authored by many different persons, they are obviously uneven in value.

WBC   **393.** *Word Biblical Commentary (Waco, TX: Word Books, 1982-   ). Under the general editorship of D. A. Hubbard, this multivolume commentary series on both testaments was first launched in 1977. Its aim is "to make the technical and scholarly approach to a theological understanding of Scripture understandable by... the fledgling student, the working minister, and colleagues in the guild ..." (1. xi). More than half of the series has already appeared. In some instances there is more than one volume in the commentary on a given book.

B. Commentaries on the OT

394. Goldingay, J., *Old Testament Commentary Survey* (2d ed.; Madison, WI: Theological Students Fellowship, 1981).

ATD   **395.**   *Das Alte Testament Deutsch (Göttingen: Vandenhoeck & Ruprecht). This series began to appear in 1949, under the editorship of V. Herntrich and A. Weiser. It consists of 25 vols., of which the first is Weiser's *Einleitung* (§ 358). Several of the volumes have been revised and some even translated into English (e.g., M. Noth on Lev and Num in the OTL). The commentary is presented in running, almost essay-form, with a minimum of philology and great emphasis on theology. Some of the best German Protestant biblical scholars have contributed to it. Though not intended for specialists, this is a very useful commentary series. There is a NT counterpart, NTD (§ 413).

BKAT   **396.**   **Biblischer Kommentar: Altes Testament (Neukirchen-Vluyn: Neukirchener V.). This series began to appear in 1955 under the editorship of M. Noth and has been continued under the direction of S. Herrmann and H. W. Wolff. About half of the volumes have appeared, and some are presently being issued in fascicles. The editors and their collaborators are among the best in German Protestant OT scholarship. The series is intended to be a great technical commentary on the OT of critical, philological, and theological quality; form-criticism and tradition-history play a great part in the discussion of OT passages. The volumes have been highly praised. Some of the volumes have been translated in Hermeneia (§ 381).

CAT   **397.**   *Commentaire de l'Ancien Testament (Neuchâtel: Delachaux et Niestlé). This series, written by French-speaking Protestant interpreters (from France, Belgium, Switzerland, and Italy) and begun in 1963, is the counterpart of CNT (§ 407). The series aims at providing a commentary on various books of the OT that is at once historical-critical and theological, respective of the Christian canon, and intended for "l'Eglise chrétienne." The commentary is based on *BHS* (§ 117). The main editor of the series is R. Martin-Achard. Nine volumes or parts of volumes have appeared to date.

HAT   **398.**   *Handbuch zum Alten Testament (Tübingen: Mohr [Siebeck]). This series of compact commentaries was begun under the editorship of O. Eissfeldt, first appearing in 1937. The emphasis is put on the philological, historical, and archaeological; a good deal of the best of modern German Protestant scholarship can be found in it. Though it is far from complete, several volumes in the series have already been revised. It has a NT counterpart, HNT (§ 409).

HSAT   **399.**   Die heilige Schrift des Alten Testaments (Bonn: P. Hanstein).
or BB   Sometimes called Die Bonnerbibel. It was begun in 1923, under the editorship of F. Feldmann and H. Herkenne; it numbers

31 vols., with commentaries on every book of the OT except Ezra–Nehemiah (vol. 11) and a few supplementary volumes. The quality of the commentaries varies, and it must be remembered that they were all written by German Roman Catholic scholars in pre-Divino–afflante–Spiritu days. Some parts of the series are still worth consulting.

KAT   **400.** Kommentar zum Alten Testament (Gütersloh: Mohn). This new series, begun in 1962 and edited by W. Rudolph, K. Elliger, and F. Hesse, is the successor to an older series, founded by E. Sellin in 1913 (Leipzig: Deichert) and continued by J. Herrmann, which numbered eventually 24 vols. The new series, which has a different numbering, is only about a quarter published. It is a technical commentary-series, not the rival of BKAT (§ 396), but one that will be neglected only with loss.

NICOT   **401.** The New International Commentary on the Old Testament (Grand Rapids, MI: Eerdmans). Begun in 1965 under the editorship of F. J. Young, it is directed today by R. K. Harrison. Conservative in thrust, the commentaries contain much that is useful. To date only eleven volumes have been issued (Lev, Deut, Ezra–Neh, Isa [4 vols.], Jer, Joel–Obad–Jonah–Mic, Hag–Mal). The series has a NT counterpart, NICNT (§ 414).

OTL   **402.** *Old Testament Library (Philadelphia, PA: Westminster, 1962-   ). This is a valuable collection of commentaries on OT books and monographs on special topics of OT theology, history, and interpretation. Many good German commentaries, which have appeared in other series listed above, have been translated into English and made part of this series. Over 30 vols. have already appeared in it.

TynOTC **403.** Tyndale Old Testament Commentaries (London: Tyndale; Downers Grove, IL: Inter-Varsity). Begun in 1964, this series of brief, readable commentaries is edited by D. J. Wiseman. Its aim is to "provide the student of the Bible with a handy, up-to-date commentary on each book, with the primary emphasis on exegesis" (*Genesis*, p. 5). The commentaries represent the conservative thrust of evangelical Christianity. The series has a NT counterpart, TynNTC (§ 419). To date 15 vols. have appeared in the OT series.

C. Commentaries on the NT

404. Carson, D. A., *New Testament Commentary Survey* (3d ed.; Grand Rapids, MI: Baker, 1988).

BNTC   **405.**   Black's New Testament Commentaries (London: A. and C.
or HNTC   Black, 1957). In the U.S.A. this series is known as Harper's New
Testament Commentaries. It was begun under the editorship of
H. Chadwick of Oxford. The purpose of the series is not a
detailed critical or textual discussion of the NT text, but an
understanding of it for the reader who does not know Greek. The
list of contributors has included many of the best-known British
and American non-Roman-Catholic scholars.

CGTC   **406.**   Cambridge Greek Testament Commentary (Cambridge, UK:
University Press, 1955-   ). Begun under the editorship of
C. F. D. Moule of Cambridge University, this series was intended
to replace the old Cambridge Bible for Schools as well as the
Cambridge Greek Testament for Schools and Colleges. Whereas
the old series emphasized questions of authenticity, history, and
philology, the aim of the new series is a theological commentary
based on the foundation of sane historical and philological study.
Knowledge of Greek is presupposed. Space is given in the
introduction of the volumes to religious ideas in the NT books.
To date only two volumes have appeared: *The Gospel according to
St Mark* (C. E. B. Cranfield, 1959); *The Epistles of Paul the
Apostle to the Colossians and to Philemon* (C. F. D. Moule, 1957).

CNT   **407.**   Commentaire du Nouveau Testament (Neuchâtel/Paris: Delachaux
et Niestlé, 1949-   ). This series was begun under the direction of
P. Bonnard and O. Cullmann; others have been added to the staff.
Though 15 volumes were originally projected, only eight appeared
in the "première série" (Matt, Rom, 1 Cor, 2 Cor, Gal–Eph,
Phil–Col, 1-2 Thess, Heb). A "deuxième série" has been begun, in
which two volumes of the first series appear in revised form (Matt,
Gal), and ten fresh volumes have appeared (Rom, 1 Cor, 2 Cor,
Gal, Phil, Phlm, Jas, 2 Pet–Jude, 1-3 John, Apoc). This is an
up-to-date, independent, and often excellent commentary-series,
written by French-speaking Protestants of Switzerland and France.
The series has an OT counterpart, CAT (§ 397)

EKKNT   **408.**   **Evangelisch-katholischer Kommentar zum Neuen Testament
(Einsiedeln: Benziger; Neukirchen-Vluyn: Neukirchener V.,
1969-   ). This NT series of commentaries is born of the ecu-
menical movement in German-speaking lands; both Lutheran-
Evangelical and Roman Catholic scholars are contributing to it.
The editors for the Lutheran side are E. Schweizer and U.
Wilckens; for the Catholic side, R. Schnackenburg and J. Blank.
To date there have appeared four volumes of *Vorarbeiten* and ten
of commentaries: *Der Brief an Philemon* (P. Stuhlmacher, 1975);
Der Brief an die Kolosser (E. Schweizer, 1976); *Der erste Petrusbrief*
(N. Brox, 1979); *Das Evangelium nach Markus* (J. Gnilka, 1978,

1979); *Der Brief an die Römer* (U. Wilckens, 1978, 1980, 1982); *Der Brief an die Thessaloniker* (W. Trilling, 1980); *Der Brief an die Epheser* (R. Schnackenburg, 1982). The manuscript is always reviewed by a Lutheran or Catholic colleague. The series makes use of the historical-critical method, but is also theological in its thrust.

See *CBQ* 40 (1978) 448-50.

HNT   **409.**   *Handbuch zum Neuen Testament (Tübingen: Mohr [Siebeck], 1906-   ). Founded by H. Lietzmann, it has been more recently under the editorship of G. Bornkamm. For the most part, it has been noted for short, compact comments (often very good) of a critical, philological nature, which supply copious material for the interpretation of the books from the viewpoint of the comparative study of religions. They are, in general, highly recommended. The commentary of E. Käsemann, *An die Römer* (vol. 8a, 1973), departed considerably from the older format and is much more theological in character. The series has an OT counterpart, HAT (§ 398).

HTKNT   **410.**   **Herders theologischer Kommentar zum Neuen Testament (Freiburg im B.: Herder, 1953-   ). This series of 14 volumes (often subdivided) was begun under the direction of A. Wikenhauser and is being continued under that of A. Vögtle and R. Schnackenburg. It is a detailed, technical commentary on the books of the NT, representing the best of German Roman Catholic critical scholarship. Many of the volumes that have appeared so far are of multiple parts. As the title implies, the emphasis is on the theological content of the NT books, although critical, textual, philological, archaeological, and historical problems are not neglected. To date, 25 volumes or parts of volumes have appeared; and one or other has already undergone revision.

MeyerK   **411.**   **Kritisch-exegetischer Kommentar über das Neue Testament
or KEK   (Göttingen: Vandenhoeck & Ruprecht, 1832-   ). Founded by H. A. W. Meyer, it is popularly named after him, the Meyer-Kommentar. The series of 16 vols. has often been revised and even completely rewritten at times; some of the older volumes were translated into English, but they are quite out of date today. Composed by the best of German Protestant NT scholars over the last century and a half, they offer a thorough and excellent historical-critical approach to the NT. The series ranks today in a class by itself, being the best NT commentary series in any language, even though individual volumes in it might at times be weaker than this over-all view of the series. The commentary on Galatians has been revised several times by H. Schlier, even after his conversion to Roman Catholicism.

MNTC   **412.**   The Moffatt New Testament Commentary (London: Hodder and Stoughton; New York: Harper & Bros., 1928-1950). The aim of this 17-volume commentary is "to bring out the religious meaning and message of the New Testament writings" (p. v.). To achieve this goal, literary and historical criticism is used. A knowledge of Greek is not presupposed, but the thrust of the commentary is clearly toward well-educated readers. The series is somewhat out of date today. Some of the volumes have been often reprinted (without any revision).

NTD   **413.**   *Das Neue Testament Deutsch (Göttingen: Vandenhoeck & Ruprecht, 1932-). Actually this series began earlier under the name Neues Göttinger Bibelwerk. From 1932 it was edited by P. Althaus and J. Behm; later (1949-69) by P. Althaus and G. Friedrich; and since 1969 by G. Friedrich. It has a supplemental series, GNT (§ 91). The 5th edition (1949-50) appeared in 12 vols., which were eventually gathered into four. Enlightened in its approach and aimed at a general readership, the series seeks to bring out the religious meaning of the text and make the NT relevant for Christians of today. It is far less technical than the MeyerK (§ 411). The OT counterpart of this series is ATD (§ 395).

NICNT   **414.**   New International Commentary on the New Testament (Grand Rapids, MI: Eerdmans, 1952-). This is a series of carefully-written detailed commentaries, leaning more to the technical side than to the popular, and composed by interpreters of a conservative evangelical Protestant tradition. Eighteen volumes have appeared to date, and even though some of them are inferior in quality, others are very good. With the publication of W. L. Lane, *The Gospel according to Mark* (London: Morgan & Scott, 1974), the series has apparently changed its name: The New London Commentary on the New Testament. It has an OT counterpart, NICOT (§ 401).

ÖTNT   **415.**   Ökumenischer Taschenbuchkommentar zum Neuen Testament (Gütersloh: Mohn; Würzburg: Echter V., 1984-). Edited by E. Grässer and K. Kertelge, this ecumenical series is an excellent set of NT commentaries of short compass, with good bibliographies and succinct notes. Both Catholic and Protestant commentators contribute to the series. To date four double vols. have appeared (Mark [2d ed., 1986], Luke [2d ed., 1984], John [1st ed., 1984-85], Acts [1981]).

PNTC   **416.**   Pelican New Testament Commentaries (London/Baltimore: Penguin). This series is mentioned here because it appears in inexpensive paperback-form. It is good for beginners. The commentaries are written by reputable scholars and are at times

detailed. The English text is that of the *RSV*. So far there have
appeared commentaries on *Saint Matthew* (J. C. Fenton, 1963);
Saint Mark (D. E. Nineham, 1963); *Saint Luke* (G. B. Caird,
1963); *Saint John* (J. Marsh, 1968); *Paul's Letter to the Romans*
(J. C. O'Neill, 1975); *I Corinthians* (J. Ruef, 1977); *Paul's Letters
from Prison* (J. L. Houlden, 1970); *The Pastoral Epistles* (J. L.
Houlden, 1976); *Revelation* (J. P. M. Sweet, 1979).

RNT   **417.** *Regensburger Neues Testament (Regensburg: Pustet, 1938).
This series originally contained ten volumes, edited by A.
Wikenhauser and O. Kuss. The numbered volumes were often
revised; but in more recent years they are appearing in expanded,
unnumbered volumes (which makes it a bit confusing to use).
Whereas several NT books might have been interpreted in one
volume earlier, now they have been treated separately and at
greater length. The quality of most of the volumes is excellent; it
is more or less of the same character as the German Protestant
NTD (§413). Certainly, it is, as a series, far less technical than
HTKNT (§410). Highly recommended for the Greekless who
may read German. One volume of the original series has been
translated into English: J. Schmid, *The Gospel according to Mark*
(The Regensburg New Testament; Staten Island, NY: Alba
House, 1968).

THKNT   **418.** Theologischer Handkommentar zum Neuen Testament (Leipzig:
Deichert; then Berlin: Evangelische V., 1928-   ). Since 1957,
this commentary has been under the direction of E. Fascher. It
seeks to interpret the NT books in a theological way, as the title
suggests, and is at once conservative in approach but open to
modern critical problems. The older series was never completed;
and the newer one is moving slowly; twelve volumes or parts of
volumes have appeared to date.

TynNTC   **419.** Tyndale New Testament Commentaries (Leicester, UK: Tyndale,
more recently Inter-Varsity, 1956-84). This series has been under
the direction of R. V. G. Tasker. Its aim is the theological interpretation of the NT books, but includes a detailed historical
introduction to them. The series is now complete, and some
volumes are undergoing revision. It is conservative in its
approach and often quite useful. There is an OT counterpart,
TynOTC (§403).

CHAPTER XIV

Biblical Theology

Treatment of biblical-theology topics in dictionaries will be found listed under "dictionaries" (Chapter XI above). Here the purpose is to list the monographs that have discussed in modern times the concept of "biblical theology" (whether it is possible to compose one or not) and the various treatments of OT and NT biblical theology in book-form. The entries will be listed under the following headings: (A) Common discussions (its possibility, the theology of the OT and NT together); (B) OT theologies; and (C) NT theologies.

A. Common Discussions

420. Childs, B. S., *Biblical Theology in Crisis* (Philadelphia, PA: Westminster, 1970). This is not a biblical theology as such, but a discussion of the problems in the approach to biblical theology on the part of various predecessors (e.g., Cullmann's salvation history, Bultmann's existentialist self-understanding, the linguistic approach to being of Ebeling and Fuchs). Instead Childs would use the Christian canon as the context for biblical theology, and examines Psalm 8, Exod 2:11-12, and Proverbs 7 in the light of this context which is normative for Christian faith. Use with discernment.

See *JBL* 90 (1971) 209-10; *CBQ* 33 (1971) 247-48; *RB* 78 (1971) 294-95.

421. García Cordero, M., *Teología de la Biblia* (3 vols.; BAC 307, 335, 336; Madrid: Edica, 1970, 1972, 1972). Though these are written by one person, vol. 1 is dedicated to the themes of the OT, vols. 2 and 3 to those of the NT. No unity is attempted between the Testaments, but the presentation is dominated by aspects that resemble systematic theology. In vol. 1 the themes treated are these: Basic beliefs, the hopes of Israel; obligations; sin. In vols. 2 and 3 the themes presented are handled in the conviction that there is a continuity between the earthly Jesus and the biblical Christ. Eight parts present: Jesus Christ, the kingdom of God and church of Christ, the mystery of God One and Triune, Redemption, Christian hope, Christian vocation, sacraments, and religious and moral obligations.

See *ETL* 47 (1971) 231; *JBL* 91 (1972) 255-56; 94 (1975) 114-17; *NRT* 94 (1972) 965-66; *RivB* 23 (1975) 455-56; *EstEcl* 47 (1972) 126-27; *CB* 30 (1973) 185-86.

422. *Kraus, H.-J., *Die biblische Theologie: Ihre Geschichte und Problematik* (Neukirchen-Vluyn: Neukirchener V., 1970). A sweeping survey of the various studies of OT and NT theology and the relation between the theologies of the two Testaments since the time of the Reformation; most of it, however, is dedicated to studies in the 19th and 20th centuries. This is a good introduction to the problems involved in the study of biblical theology, even though it is largely confined to German treatments. It does not present a biblical theology itself.

See *CBQ* 34 (1972) 367-68; *Int* 26 (1972) 20-29; *TLZ* 96 (1971) 938-40; *TTZ* 80 (1971) 378-79; *TRu* 37 (1972) 80-88.

423. Laurin, R. B. (ed.), *Contemporary Old Testament Theologians* (Valley Forge, PA: Judson, 1970). A collaborative, evaluative study of the OT theologies written by E. Jacob, G. von Rad, W. Eichrodt, O. Procksch, T. C. Vriezen, G. A. F. Knight, and P. van Imschoot.

See *JAAR* 41 (1973) 303-4; *SJT* 27 (1974) 106-7.

424. Smend, R., *Die Mitte des Alten Testaments* (Theologische Studien 101; Zürich: EVZ Verlag, 1970). This is not so much a theology of the OT as a discussion of the problem whether one can organize the OT data around one principle (*die Mitte*, the core or kernel, central concept). Smend disagrees with von Rad and others who deny that one can find such a principle; after discussing various ideas that have been proposed (redemption, monotheism, theocracy, kingdom of God, covenant), Smend prefers to find it in Yahweh himself. The best formulation of it: "Yahweh, the God of Israel; Israel, the people of Yahweh."

See *CBQ* 34 (1972) 116-17; *BL* (1971) 51; *JTS* 22 (1971) 696; *ZAW* 83 (1971) 147; 86 (1974) 65-82.

425. Strecker, G. (ed.), *Das Problem der Theologie des Neuen Testaments* (Wege der Forschung 367; Darmstadt: Wissenschaftliche Buchgesellschaft, 1975). Sixteen essays or parts of books on NT theology and its problems, written by famous Protestant and Catholic NT interpreters of the 18th, 19th, and 20th centuries. The book ends with a very useful bibliography on the subject. Some of the essays exist in an English translation (those of B. Weiss, R. Bultmann, O. Cullmann, and E. Fuchs).

See *JBL* 95 (1976) 324-25; *BZ* 20 (1976) 289-91; *RSR* 64 (1976) 569-72.

B. OT Theologies

426. Deissler, A., *Die Grundbotschaft des Alten Testaments: Ein theologischer Durchblick* (Freiburg: Herder, 1972). This is meant to be a student's introductory handbook for the study of OT theology; its principle of organization is Yahweh himself, who claims undivided allegiance and manifests concern for his people. As *der zugewendete Gott*, his influence is traced through all levels of OT literature.

See *JBL* 92 (1973) 589-92; *TRev* 68 (1972) 367-68; *NRT* 96 (1974) 418; *ZAW* 85 (1973) 119; *TPQ* 121 (1973) 178.

427.   **Eichrodt, W., *Theologie des Alten Testaments* (6th ed.; Göttingen: Vandenhoeck & Ruprecht, 1959). It is the classic OT theology in modern times, which uses a historical approach to the OT books and seeks a unifying theme for the theology of them in the idea of covenant: God and the people, God and the world, God and man. It seeks to give a synthetic picture of the "world of faith" in the OT. It was in reaction to this approach that G. von Rad composed his *Theologie* (§ 433). The 6th ed. was translated into English: *Theology of the Old Testament* (2 vols.; London: SCM; Philadelphia, PA; Westminster, 1961, 1967).

See *RUO* 32 (1962) 105*-16*; *CBQ* 24 (1962) 228; *HeyJ* 3 (1962) 174-75; *Int* 16 (1962) 311-14; *JBL* 86 (1967) 458-60.

428.   Fohrer, G., *Theologische Grundstrukturen des Alten Testaments* (Theologische Bibliothek Töpelmann 24; Berlin/New York: de Gruyter, 1972). A compact existentialist theology of the OT, which gathers the data about two poles, the lordship of Yahweh and the relationship of Yahweh to mankind.

See *Bib* 55 (1974) 100-101; *JBL* 93 (1974) 594-96.

429.   Imschoot, P. van, *Théologie de l'Ancien Testament* (2 vols.; Tournai: Desclée, 1954, 1956). Though three volumes of this work were projected, only two of them appeared. The approach used in it is that of the categories of systematic theology (vol. 1, God and his relation to the world and to human beings; vol. 2, Man; and vol. 3 was to deal with judgment and salvation). However, the author is conscious of a development of ideas within the OT and has gathered and sifted well a vast amount of material on given topics. An English form of the first volume of this work exists, *Theology of the Old Testament: I. God* (New York: Desclée, 1965).

See *TLZ* 80 (1955) 275-76; 82 (1957) 850-51; *RSR* 43 (1955) 402-5; 45 (1957) 100-102; *RB* 63 (1956) 136-37; 65 (1958) 293-94; *Eleven Years* (§ 7), 683-84; *TS* 28 (1967) 178.

430.   *Jacob E., *Théologie de l'Ancien Testament: Revue et augmentée* (Bibliothèque théologique; Neuchâtel/Paris: Delachaux et Niestlé,

1968). The first edition of 1955 was translated into English, *Theology of the Old Testament* (London: Hodder and Stoughton, 1958). The OT data are organized according to the categories of systematic theology (God, man, salvation), but they are not presented on the grand scale of W. Eichrodt or G. von Rad. The compact presentation will be of use to students. The central idea is "God's action in history, the relation between confession and event, between faith and historical fact" (G. E. Wright).

See *VT* 6 (1956) 326-30; *RB* 64 (1957) 424-27; *Eleven Years* (§ 7), 753; *Greg* 49 (1968) 589-90; *ZAW* 80 (1968) 434; *JBL* 79 (1960) 78-81.

431. Knight, G. A. F., *A Christian Theology of the Old Testament* (London: SCM, 1959; 2d ed., 1964). A theology of the OT which ends up exploring the relation of it to that of the NT; an appendix explicitly treats of Jesus Christ as the goal toward which the whole OT has been tending.

See *Int* 14 (1960) 202-4; *SJT* 13 (1960) 90-91; *JBL* 79 (1960) 290-91; *JTS* 11 (1960) 376-77; *RB* 67 (1960) 296; *RSPT* 45 (1961) 88-90.

432. McKenzie J. L., *The Two-edged Sword* (Milwaukee: Bruce, 1956; repr., Garden City, NY: Doubleday, 1966). This is not an OT theology in the usual sense, but an excellent survey of OT books with an emphasis on their theological content. The material is distributed under such headings as "cosmic origins," "human origins," "king and prophet," "wisdom of the Hebrews," "life and death," etc. Intended for the general reader.

See *CBQ* 18 (1956) 429-31; *RB* 64 (1957) 418; *Int* 11 (1957) 343; *Bib* 38 (1957) 76-78; *JBL* 76 (1957) 250-51.

433. **Rad, G. von, *Theologie des Alten Testaments* (2 vols.; Munich: Kaiser, 1957, 1960; 7th ed., 1978). An English version exists: *Old Testament Theology* (2 vols.; Edinburgh/London: Oliver and Boyd; New York: Harper & Row, 1962, 1965). Also a French version: *Théologie de l'Ancien Testament* (2 vols.; Geneva/Paris: Labor & Fides, 1963, 1967). The author, the theologian of the school of A. Alt, rejects the categories of dogmatic theology for this synthesis and attempts to synthesize the various theologies in the OT in biblical categories. But he also denies the viability of the unifying theme such as W. Eichrodt made use of. He prefers to set forth the essential kerygma of the different OT books or groups of books, historical or prophetic. It is a stimulating treatment, rich in detail and based on solid exegesis; but it is not without its own problems. The English translation of vol. 1 was based on the first German edition, but made use of notes for the revision in the second German edition. An important "Postscript" appears in vol. 2 (pp. 410-29) on the question of method, with which the student would do well to begin. One should also consult later German editions for modifications.

See *IDBSup*, 108; *RB* 65 (1958) 424-27; 70 (1963) 291-93; *JBL* 82 (1963) 106-7; 85 (1966) 238-41; *CBQ* 20 (1958) 257-59; 23 (1961) 217-23; 25 (1963) 517-18; 28 (1966) 263-65; *ZAW* 70 (1958) 271; 73 (1961) 256-57; *ExpTim* 73 (1961-62) 142-46; *VF* 17 (1972) 1-25; *SJT* 16 (1963) 89-90.

434. **Rad, G. von, *Weisheit in Israel* (Neukirchen-Vluyn: Neukirchener V., 1970). It is a highly-praised theology of the wisdom literature of the OT, which supplements von Rad's *Theologie* (§ 433). In English: *Wisdom in Israel* (Nashville, TN: Abingdon, 1972). In French: *Israël et la sagesse* (Geneva/Paris: Labor & Fides, 1970).

See *CBQ* 33 (1971) 286-88; 35 (1973) 549-50; *Int* 25 (1971) 347-49; *RB* 80 (1973) 129-31; *TRev* 67 (1971) 18; *ZAW* 83 (1971) 308-9.

435. *Vriezen, T.C., *Hoofdlijnen der Theologie van het Oude Testament* (Wageningen: Veenman & Zonen, 1950). An expanded and revised Dutch second edition (1954) was translated into German and used as the basis of the English translation, *An Outline of Old Testament Theology* (Oxford: Blackwell, 1958; 2d ed., 1970). There are changes in the bibliography, and the text is fuller than the German. This outline purports to be a Christian theology of the OT. After a long introductory prolegomenon, the data of the OT are organized under the headings: God, man, intercourse between God and man, intercourse between man and man; God, man, and the world in the present and future.

See *ZAW* 62 (1949-50) 312-13; *BO* 9 (1952) 191-92; *Int* 13 (1959) 333-36; *RB* 66 (1959) 132-33; *JBL* 78 (1959) 256-58; 79 (1960) 78-81; *Eleven Years* (§ 7), 287, 688.

436. Zimmerli, W., *Grundriss der alttestamentlichen Theologie* (Theologische Wissenschaft 3; Stuttgart: Kohlhammer, 1972). A compact theology of the OT, organizing the data about the perduring identity of God, known by the name of Yahweh revealed to Israel. In English: *Old Testament Theology in Outline* (Edinburgh: Clark; Atlanta, GA: John Knox, 1978). What is presented here in compact form can be supplemented by the many essays on OT theology by Zimmerli that have been gathered in *Studien zur alttestamentlichen Theologie und Prophetie* (2 vols.; Theologische Bücherei; Munich: Kaiser, 1963, 1974).

See *EvT* 34 (1974) 96-112; *CBQ* 36 (1974) 150-51; *NRT* 95 (1973) 828; *JBL* 94 (1975) 113-14.

C. NT Theologies

437. **Bultmann R., *Theologie des Neuen Testaments* (Tübingen: Mohr [Siebeck], 1948-53; 5th ed., 1965; rev. O. Merk; UTB 630; 1980). *Theology of the New Testament* (2 vols.; London: SCM, 1952, 1955) is an English form of the first German edition. This is the most famous theology of the NT in modern times; it should be read by all serious students of the NT, even though there are many aspects of it that need serious modification today (e.g., its philosophical presuppositions, its treatment of Luke–Acts, its neglect of certain aspects of Pauline theology).

> See *RB* 58 (1951) 252-57; 59 (1952) 93-100; 61 (1954) 432-35; *TZ* 11 (1955) 1-27; *CBQ* 21 (1959) 399-400 (3d Germ. ed.); *Gnomon* 23 (1951) 1-17; N. A. Dahl, *The Crucified Messiah and Other Essays* (Minneapolis, MN: Augsburg, 1974) 90-128; *Salesianum* 43 (1981) 443-44.

438. *Conzelmann, H., *Grundriss der Theologie des Neuen Testaments* (2d ed.; Munich: Kaiser, 1968; repr., UTB, 1980). In English: *An Outline of the Theology of the New Testament* (New York/Evanston, IL: Harper & Row, 1969). The first German edition appeared in 1967. It claims to be a textbook for students, introducing them to NT theology, but it is much more than that. Though it stands in the Bultmannian tradition, it clearly updates the treatment in the light of new discoveries affecting the study of the NT; it admits an implicit christology in Jesus' own teaching; and it shifts the emphasis of the Bultmannian treatment. In general, it makes much of the Bultmannian theology more palatable, but it still has problems of its own.

> See *JBL* 87 (1968) 442-44; *CBQ* 32 (1970) 274-76; *ExpTim* 81 (1969-70) 161-62; *NRT* 91 (1969) 697-98; *SJT* 23 (1970) 115-16; *TTKi* 47 (1976) 21-46; *BZ* 19 (1975) 269-70.

439. **Goppelt, L., *Theologie des Neuen Testaments* (2 vols.; Göttingen: Vandenhoeck & Ruprecht 1975, 1976). When Goppelt died in December 1973, he had been at work on this *Theologie* for over ten years; the first volume was practically finished, and the second well under way at the time of his death. It was posthumously published by J. Roloff. Volume 1 is devoted to the theological significance of Jesus' ministry and existence; vol. 2 to the plurality and unity of the apostolic testimony to Christ. It is an excellent, sophisticated study of all the problems of the modern study of NT theology, but it still reflects a Bultmannian background in some respects. An English translation exists, prepared by J. C. Alsup: *Theology of the New Testament* (2 vols.; Grand Rapids, MI: Eerdmans, 1981, 1982). Also an Italian translation: *Teologia del Nuovo Testamento* (2 vols.; Brescia: Morcelliana, 1982, 1983).

> See *TTKi* 47 (1976) 21-46; *NRT* 99 (1977) 764-66; *TRev* 72 (1976) 18-20; 73 (1977) 21-23; 39 (1977) 433-34; *CBQ* 38 (1976) 105-6; 39

(1977) 433-34; *ExpTim* 94 (1982-83) 163; *JSNT* 16 (1982) 125-27; *America* 148 (1983) 343-44.

440. Jeremias, J., *New Testament Theology: The Proclamation of Jesus* (New York: Scribner, 1971). Published simultaneously in German under the title, *Neutestamentliche Theologie: I. Teil: Die Ver-kündigung Jesu* (Gütersloh: Mohn, 1971). Only the first part of this study appeared before Jeremias's death; so it is not really a NT theology in the usual sense. It discusses Jesus' preaching under the following headings: (1) the reliability of the sayings-tradition; the mission of Jesus; the dawn of the time of salvation; the period of grace; the new people of God; Jesus' testimony to his mission; and Easter. The book sums up, in effect, Jeremias's long study of Jesus' words; in it all the sayings are scrutinized for their retrovertibility into Aramaic in an attempt to establish their authenticity. The approach is conservative and will not meet with universal acceptance.

See *BTB* 2 (1972) 87-88; *ExpTim* 83 (1971-72) 33-34; *NRT* 93 (1971) 433; *TS* 33 (1972) 133-34; *EvT* 32 (1972) 92-95; *TTKi* 47 (1976) 21-46; *Int* 26 (1972) 345-48; *BZ* 19 (1975) 272-73.

441. *Kümmel, W. G., *Die Theologie des Neuen Testaments nach seinen Hauptzeugen Jesus, Paulus, Johannes* (GNT 3; Göttingen: Vandenhoeck & Ruprecht, 1969). A translation of the German 3d ed. (1976) represents a thorough revision: *The Theology of the New Testament according to Its Major Witnesses: Jesus — Paul — John* (Nashville, TN: Abingdon, 1973). A presentation of NT doctrine under the following headings: the proclamation of Jesus in the first three Gospels; the faith of the primitive community; the theology of Paul; the Johannine message of Christ in Gospel and Epistles; Jesus Paul John as the heart of the NT. Kümmel omits all treatment of Ephesians, the Pastorals, James, 1-2 Peter, Jude, Hebrews, and Revelation. In effect, this is a presentation of NT theology based on a "canon within the canon," strangely making Jesus out to be one of the "major" witnesses to NT *theology*. There are many excellent things in this study, which counteracts in sane ways the Bultmann–Conzelmann tradition. But its heavily Lutheran background pierces to the fore.

See *CBQ* 37 (1975) 120-22; *JBL* 89 (1970) 255-56; *NRT* 92 (1970) 717-18; *TTZ* 79 (1970) 319; *Bijdragen* 31 (1970) 200-201; *Int* 29 (1975) 297-300; *TTKi* 47 (1976) 21-46; *BZ* 19 (1975) 270-71.

442. Meinertz, M., *Theologie des Neuen Testamentes* (BB Ergänzungs-band 1-2; Bonn: Hanstein, 1950). A thorough and rich coverage of NT theology by a well-known Roman Catholic exegete, which is divided into four parts: (1) Jesus; (2) Primitive Community (Acts, James, Jude); (3) Paul; (4) John. Unfortunately, the OT roots of NT doctrines are not given quite the treatment that they deserve, and the work is in need of revision.

See *Bib* 32 (1951) 120-26; *NRT* 74 (1952) 533-34; *TS* 12 (1951) 112-13; *RB* 58 (1951) 596-600.

443. Richardson, A., *An Introduction to the Theology of the New Testament* (New York: Harper & Bros., 1959). A handy, one-volume presentation of NT teachings from a conservative stand-point. The author frames a hypothesis concerning the content and character of the faith of the apostolic church and tests it in the light of all available techniques of NT scholarship. Jesus himself is regarded as the author of a brilliant reinterpretation of the OT scheme of salvation found in the NT. Though one cannot agree with the author in all points of interpretation, this book has had much influence in the English-speaking world of NT studies. It is quite different from the Bultmannian approach.

See *ExpTim* 70 (1958-59) 167-68; *HibJ* 57 (1958-59) 302-4; *JBL* 78 (1959) 272-77.

444. *Schelkle, K.-H., *Theologie des Neuen Testaments* (4 vols.; Düsseldorf: Patmos, 1968, 1973, 1970, 1974, 1976 [vol. 4 is in two parts]). This is a modern German Roman Catholic presentation of NT Theology. Volume 1 is devoted to creation (world, time, and humanity); vol. 2 to "God was in Christ"; vol. 3 to Christian conduct; vol. 4/1 to the accomplishment of creation and redemption; and vol. 4/2 to the early community and the church. A English translation has been prepared by W. A. Jurgens, *Theology of the New Testament* (4 vols.; Collegeville, MN: Liturgical Press, 1971, 1973, 1976, 1978). Spanish translation: *Teologia del Nuevo Testamento* (Barcelona: Herder, 1975, 1977, 1975, 1978).

See *BZ* 19 (1975) 273-76; *NRT* 94 (1972) 659; 96 (1974) 799-800; 100 (1978) 261-62; *TRev* 70 (1974) 364-68; 73 (1977) 23-26; *TTKi* 47 (1976) 21-46; *CBQ* 35 (1973) 113-14; *EstBib* 36 (1977) 301-3.

445. Stauffer, E., *Die Theologie des Neuen Testaments* (Gütersloh: Bertelsmann, 1941, 4th ed., 1948). An English translation exists: *New Testament Theology* (London: SCM, 1955). It emphasized allegiance to Christ in contrast to worship of a political ruler as the basic theme of NT teaching. Its organizing principle is salvation history, which gives a general view of the whole eschatological process of redemption. A compact, schematic presentation of the main themes of biblical theology from creation to the Second Coming; rich in older bibliography. It is neither in the Bultmannian tradition nor does it exaggerate the Hellenistic element in NT thought; it attempts to give due attention to genuine OT traditions and rabbinical material. However, the discussions are filled with highly personal remarks that will not be acceptable to all.

See *ExpTim* 67 (1955-56) 8-9; *JTS* 7 (1956) 291-93; *ATR* 38 (1956) 248-51; *JBL* 75 (1956) 350-52; *TLZ* 75 (1950) 421-26.

446.   *Schnackenburg, R., *Die sittliche Botschaft des Neuen Testaments* 2 vols.; HTKNTSup 1-2; Freiburg im B.: Herder, 1986, 1988). This is fully revised edition of a work that first appeared in 1954. Volume 1 treats of the ethical teaching "from Jesus to the church"; vol. 2, early Christian preachers.

      See *TRev* 84 (1988) 195-98; *EstEcl* 63 (1988) 372-73.

447.   *Schrage, W., *Ethik des Neuen Testaments* (GNT 4; Göttingen: Vandenhoeck & Ruprecht, 1982). In English form: *The Ethics of the New Testament* (Philadelphia, PA: Fortress, 1988). Schrage discusses NT ethical teaching under nine headings: (1) Jesus' eschatological ethics; (2) ethical beginnings in the earliest congregations; (3) ethical accents in the Synoptics; (4) the christological ethics of Paul; (5) the ethics of responsibility in the deutero-Paulines; (6) parenesis in James; (7) the command of brotherly love in Johannine writings; (8) exhortations addressed to the pilgrim people in Hebrews; (9) eschatological exhortation in the Apocalypse.

      See *TRev* 79 (1983) 203-5.

448.   Wendland, H.-D., *Ethik des Neuen Testaments* (GNT 4; Göttingen: Vandenhoeck & Ruprecht, 1970). Wendland denies that there is anything like philosophical or systematic ethics in the NT. He seeks rather to cull from various parts of the NT the ethics of Jesus, of the earliest church, of Paul, of deutero-Pauline teaching, of James, John, and the Apocalypse. A French translation exists: *Ethique du Nouveau Testament: Introduction aux problèmes* (Geneva: Labor et Fides, Paris: Librairie Protestante, 1972). Also an Italian, *Etica del Nuovo Testamento* (Brescia: Paideia, 1975).

      See *BLeb* 12 (1971) 133-34; *TP* 46 (1971) 314; *TRev* 67 (1971) 556; *CTM* 43 (1972) 639; *RTP* 22 (1972) 276-77; *NRT* 98 (1976) 691; *TLZ* 100 (1975) 423-24.

CHAPTER XV

Archaeology

In the listings in this chapter no attempt is made to take sides in the debate about the concept of "biblical archaeology" or to distinguish the entries in categories. They are simply listed alphabetically.

449. Aharoni, Y., *The Archaeology of the Land of Israel: From the Prehistoric Beginnings to the End of the First Temple Period* (tr. A. F. Rainey; London: SCM; Philadelphia, PA: Westminster, 1982). A documented survey of results of archaeological excavations in Israel from the palaeolithic period to the end of the First Temple period.

See *AUSS* 21 (1983) 173-75; *BTB* 13 (1983) 67-68; *PSB* 4 (1983) 127-28.

ARI **450.** Albright, W. F., *Archaeology and the Religion of Israel* (5th ed.; Baltimore: Johns Hopkins University, 1968; repr., Garden City, NY: Doubleday, 1969). This work was first published in 1942; the 3d ed. was improved by the addition of eight closely-printed pages. It sketches the archaeological and historical background of premonarchic and monarchic religion in Israel and of religion at Elephantine. It is still of value, even though it is in need of revision.

See *OLZ* 52 (1956) 522-23; *TLZ* 83 (1958) 261-64; *RB* 55 (1948) 283-87.

451. *Albright, W. F., *The Archaeology of Palestine* (new ed., rev. by W. G. Dever; Magnolia/Gloucester, MA: Peter Smith, 1976). This remarkable survey of archaeology in Palestine was first published in 1949 and revised in 1960 (especially to include the excavations at Qumran). It surveys archaeological technique and work done on Palestinian sites; its organization is according to periods (from the Old Stone Age to NT times). The last third of the book is devoted to peoples, languages, writing in Palestine, daily life, etc. An excellent small book, packed with information.

See *RB* 57 (1950) 310-12; *Eleven Years* (§ 7), 230; *Syria* 27 (1950) 150-52; *JAOS* 70 (1950) 114-15.

452. Amiran, R., P. Beck, and H. Zevulun, *Ancient Pottery of the Holy Land* (New Brunswick, NJ: Rutgers University: Jerusalem/ Ramat Gan: Massada, 1969). This is a survey of ancient pottery, so important for archaeological dating, from the beginnings in the Neolithic period to the end of the Iron Age. It is a translation from modern Hebrew, *ḥqyr'myqh ḥqdwmh šl 'rṣ yśr'l*. See §465.

See *CTM* 41 (1970) 737; *AJA* 75 (1971) 333-34; *IEJ* 21 (1971) 69-72; *ZDPV* 87 (1971) 209-10.

453. Avigad, N., *Discovering Jerusalem* (Nashville, TN: Nelson, 1983). This is an authoritative English report on the first excavation of the Jewish Quarter in the Upper City of Jerusalem by the excavator himself. The story is well told and amply illustrated in color and black-and-white photographs.

See *JBL* 104 (1985) 742-44; *CBQ* 47 (1985) 505-6.

454. **Avi-Yonah, M. (ed.), *Encyclopedia of Archaeological Excavations in the Holy Land* (4 vols.; Englewood Cliffs, NJ: Prentice Hall, 1975; 2 vols.; London: Oxford University, 1975; Jerusalem: Israel Exploration Society and Massada Press, 1976). An English edition of B. Mazar et al. (eds.), *'nṣyqlwpdyh lḥpyrwt 'rky'wlwgywt b'rṣ yśr'l* (2 vols.; Jerusalem: Israel Exploration Society and Massada Ltd., 1970). A comprehensive survey of archaeology in Palestine, culled from the contributions of 68 authors, many of whom were the chief excavators of the sites. There are many beautiful photographs, diagrams, and maps. Each article ends with a bibliographical note. 155 sites or archaeological topics are covered in the two (or four) volumes.

See *JBL* 90 (1971) 349-50; *Ariel* 31 (1972) 119-20; *CBQ* 42 (1980) 528-31; *RB* 85 (1978) 153-55.

455. Dever, W. G. and H. D. Lance (eds.), *A Manual of Field Excavation: Handbook for Field Archaeologists* (Cincinnati, OH: Hebrew Union College; Jerusalem: Israel Exploration Society, 1978). This manual is a revised handbook prepared by the staffs of the Gezer Project. It describes excavation and recording procedures, applicable to planned excavations of multiperiod mounds in the Levant. It deals with principles of excavation, archaeological tools, balks, field recording system, surveying and drafting, archaeological photography, geology. It is considered a "must" for all modern archaeological work.

See *JBL* 99 (1980) 295-96; *BASOR* 242 (1981) 83-86.

456. Dothan, T., *The Philistines and Their Material Culture* (New Haven, CT: Yale University, 1982). This is a comprehensive study of the Philistines on the basis of textual and archaeological evidence by one who has spent two decades investigating the culture of these Sea Peoples.

See *BARev* 8/4 (1982) 12-13; *AJA* 87 (1983) 559-61; *Syria* 60 (1983) 195-96.

457. Ehrich, R. W., *Chronologies in Old World Archaeology* (Chicago/ London: University of Chicago, 1965). This is the successor to the earlier *Relative Chronologies in Old World Archaeology* (Chicago: University of Chicago, 1954). It is well illustrated and documented, presenting a massive amount of material that bears on dating eras between 5000-1400 B.C. It is a basic reference work.

See *CBQ* 28 (1966) 350-51.

458. *Finegan, J., *The Archaeology of the New Testament: The Life of Jesus and the Beginning of the Early Church* (Princeton, NJ: Princeton University, 1969; paperback repr., 1978). Despite the broad title, this is an excellent survey of the sites connected with the story of John the Baptist, Jesus, and the early Christian community in Palestine. It includes a discussion of Palestinian tombs, catacombs, sarcophagi, ossuaries, and the history of the cross mark. A second part is found in *The Archeology of the New Testament: The Mediterranean World of the Early Christian Apostles* (Boulder, CO: Westview; London: Croom Helm, 1981). These two volumes are highly recommended; the author knows how to amass and use good information. Bibliographies appear periodically throughout the volume.

See *RB* 77 (1970) 631-33; *CBQ* 32 (1970) 604-6; *JBL* 89 (1970) 363-66; *Bib* 64 (1983) 571-72; *Church History* 39 (1970) 391-92.

459. *Finegan, J., *Light from the Ancient Past* (2d ed.; Princeton, NJ: Princeton University, 1959; repr., 1969). This work, first published in 1946, is a very broad survey of the archaeological background of Judaism and early Christianity. Though the author is mainly at the mercy of secondary sources, he uses the best of them and his references to such literature are abundant. The book contains good summaries of the history of Egypt and Mesopotamia, of archaeological work in Palestine in the late pre-Christian period, of the beginnings of Christianity and its spread in the Roman empire, and of the subapostolic church. This very readable book will give the beginner an excellent introduction to the background of biblical history.

See *BA* 9 (1946) 43-44; *JNES* 5 (1946) 239-40; *JBL* 65 (1946) 407-11; *Or* 17 (1948) 105-8; *TZ* 4 (1948) 346-47; *CBQ* 22 (1960) 238-39.

460. Geraty, L. T. and L. G. Herr (eds.), *The Archaeology of Jordan and Other Studies* (Berrien Srpings, MI: Andrews University, 1987 [distributed by Eisenbrauns, Winona Lake, IN]). A compilation of 28 articles, presented to S. H. Horn; 11 of them deal with archaeological method, pottery, inscriptions, and sites related to Jordan.

See *BL* (1989) 27.

461. Hadidi, A., *Studies in the History and Archaeology of Jordan I* (Amman: Department of Antiquities; London: Noonan Hurst, 1982). A collection of 49 papers delivered at the first international conference on the history and archaeology of Jordan held at Christchurch, Oxford, March 1980. The 43 papers of the second conference held in Amman (1983) were published under the same title, vol. II (Amman: Department of Antiquities; London: Routledge & Kegan Paul; Boston, MA: Melbourne and Henley, 1985).

See *SBFLA* 33 (1983) 423-24; *Syria* 60 (1983) 190-92; *AJA* 88 (1984) 606-8; *BL* (1984) 31; (1988) 30.

462. Kenyon, K., *The Bible and Recent Archaeology* (rev. P. R. S. Moorey; Atlanta, GA: John Knox, 1987). An updated and expanded version of Kenyon's classic work, first published in 1978. It discusses the relationship between archaeology and the Bible, surveying recent archaeological discoveries touching on the patriarchs, entry into Canaan, Palestine in the time of David and Solomon, the period of the divided monarchy, and NT Palestine.

See *BL* (1988) 31-32.

463. King, P. J., *American Archaeology in the Mideast: A History of the American Schools of Oriental Research* (Philadelphia, PA: ASOR, 1983). A chronicle of archaeological achievements in the Mideast, beginning with E. Robinson in 1838. Primary attention is given to American excavators, but the work of British, French, German, Israeli, and Arab scholars is also described.

See *JBL* 104 (1985) 333-34; *RB* 91 (1984) 476-77; *BL* (1984) 32; *TToday* 41 (1984-85) 138-39.

464. Lance, H. D., *The Old Testament and the Archaeologist* (Guides to Biblical Scholarship; Philadelphia, PA: Fortress, 1981). An introduction by a field archaeologist to the complexities of archaeological method (stratigraphy and typology), as well as a discussion of the relationship between archaeology and biblical studies. The reader will smile at Lance's characterization of the "quasi-sacramental nature of archaeology" (p. 61).

See *JBL* 102 (1983) 291-92; *CBQ* 44 (1982) 482-83; *ETR* 57 (1982) 621-22; *RevExp* 79 (1982) 687-89.

465. Lapp, P. W., *Palestinian Ceramic Chronology 100 B.C. — A.D. 70* (ASOR Publications of the Jerusalem School, Archaeology 3; New Haven, CT: American Schools of Oriental Research, 1961). This is a slightly revised Harvard dissertation (1960), which catalogues and surveys the neglected Hellenistic and Roman periods of Palestinian pottery. Its aim was to relate these periods to the pottery of the Persian and Byzantine periods. See § 452.

See *BASOR* 164 (1961) 28-29; *CBQ* 24 (1962) 309-13; *ZAW* 74 (1962) 240.

466. Matthiae, P., *Ebla: An Empire Rediscovered* (Garden City, NY: Doubleday; London: Hodder & Stoughton, 1980). This is the excavator's account of the extraordinary discovery of the ancient empire of Ebla in northern Syria, dating from 2400 B.C.

See *ExpTim* 92 (1980-81) 120; *RelStRev* 7 (1981) 347; *TToday* 38 (1981-82) 526-27.

467. Moorey, R., *Excavation in Palestine* (Cities of the Biblical World; Guildford, UK: Lutterworth; Grand Rapids, MI: Eerdmans, 1981). This is an illustrated introduction to archaeology, including the history of archaeology, the development of its methods, and its proper relationship to the Bible.

See *CBQ* 47 (1985) 538-39; *JSOT* 24 (1982) 125.

468. *Murphy-O'Connor, J., *The Holy Land: An Archaeological Guide from Earliest Times to 1700* (2d rev. ed.; Oxford: Oxford University, 1986). This guide first appeared in 1980. It is actually much more than a guide-book; it gives the historical and archaeological background of important sites in Israel, with special emphasis on Jerusalem. The section on Jerusalem is one of the best available. It first appeared in 1980 and has been translated into German by U. von Puttkamer, *Das Heilige Land: Ein archäologischer Führer* (Munich/Zürich: Piper, 1981).

See *RB* 89 (1982) 155-56; 94 (1987) 127-29; *ExpTim* 92 (1980-81) 151; *CBQ* 44 (1982) 520-21.

469. Negev, A., *Archaeological Encyclopedia of the Holy Land* (London/Jerusalem: Weidenfeld & Nicolson, 1972). This book lists the majority of the geographical names mentioned in the OT and NT, localizing them, describing the excavations that have been carried out at or near them, and interpreting the significance of the finds that have turned up. A French version of the book exists: *Dictionnaire archéologique de la Bible* (Paris: Hazan, 1970). "Though there are good points in this book it cannot seriously be recommended to the student or general reader. Its errors, combined with too slight coverage of 'popular' themes, make it more of a danger than an aid. It cannot be regarded as the 'indispensable reference book for students of archaeology and the Bible,' which is its claim" (K. Prag).

See *PEQ* 106 (1974) 92-93; *BSOAS* 36 (1973) 642; *Ant* 47 (1973) 246-47; *NRT* 95 (1973) 310-11; *RivB* 21 (1973) 441-42.

470. Parrot, A. (ed.), *Cahiers d'archéologie biblique* (Neuchâtel: Delachaux et Niestlé, 1952-   ). These monographs, now numbering 14, treat of specific subjects on which contemporary archaeology sheds light. An introductory volume (unnumbered) surveys ancient Near Eastern archaeology in general. Parrot himself has written eight of the volumes; many of them have been translated into English (in SBA [§91]). *Découverte des mondes ensevelis*; (1) *Déluge et arche de Noé*; (2) *La tour de Babel*; (3) *Ninivé et l'ancien Testament*; (4) *Les routes de saint Paul dans l'orient grec*; (5) *Le temple de Jérusalem*; (6) *Golgotha et Saint-Sépulchre*; (7) *Samarie, capitale du royaume d'Israël*; (8) *Babylone et l'ancien Testament*; (9) *Le Musée de Louvre et la Bible*; (10) *Sur la pierre et l'argile*; etc. These volumes have been well received and can be warmly recommended.

471. Shiloh, Y., *Excavations at the City of David: I. 1978-1982. Interim Report of the First Five Seasons* (Qedem 19; Jerusalem: Hebrew University, 1984). This interim report on the first five seasons of excavation at the City of David was written by the director of the excavation before his untimely death. The report is written in both Hebrew and English, with 41 plates of photographs, which describe the work in the eleven areas opened. The excavations have been continued.

See *RB* 93 (1986) 142-44.

472. *Wright, G.E., *Biblical Archaeology* (Philadelphia, PA: Westminster, 1957; rev. ed., 1962). This comprehensive survey of archaeological information illustrates well the OT and the NT. The material is arranged in historical sequence from prehistoric times to the NT period. This excellent work is most profitably used with the *Westminster Historical Atlas* (§479).

See *CBQ* 19 (1957) 528-29; *JSS* 2 (1957) 392-93; *AJA* 62 (1958) 112-13; *RB* 65 (1958) 312; *TLZ* 84 (1959) 94-98; *JBL* 77 (1958) 78-80; 83 (1964) 84.

473. Navch, N., "Bibliography of Personal Bibliographies of Scholars of the Archaeology of Palestine," *IEJ* 35 (1984) 284-88. This valued list gives guidance to the bibliographies that have been published.

Chapter XVI

Geography

At some point in biblical study the student will begin to wonder where biblical sites are located and about the extent to which they can be identified today. What is listed in this chapter is an attempt to guide the student to publications that try to answer such questions. The entries will be listed under the following headings: (A) Atlases of the Holy Land; (B) Discussions of the historical and physical geography of the Holy Land; and (C) NT sites.

A. Atlases of the Holy Land

474. *Aharoni, Y. and M. Avi-Yonah, *The Macmillan Bible Atlas* (rev. ed.; New York: Macmillan, 1977). Two distinguished Israeli archaeologists teamed up with cartographers to produce this excellent modern atlas of the Holy Land. The first edition appeared in 1968. Before their deaths, Aharoni supervised the revision of the OT section, and Avi-Yonah that of the rest. Its 264 maps cover every period of the land and are accompanied by well-illustrated explanations. Some minor errors have been detected in the work.

See *CBQ* 40 (1978) 398-99; *Int* 22 (1968) 476; *RevExp* 66 (1969) 75-76; *JAAR* 37 (1969) 297-300; *ZAW* 81 (1969) 270; *TS* 40 (1979) 739-40.

475. **Atlas of Israel: Cartography, Physical Geography, Human and Economic Geography, History* (Jerusalem: Survey of Israel, Ministry of Labour; Amsterdam: Elsevier, 1970). Although this atlas is intended for the study of more modern aspects and periods of Israel than the biblical times, the latter are not neglected. It contains a section on ancient maps, beginning with that of Madaba, and has many maps pertinent to the periods of the OT and the NT. It is an excellent modern tool for biblical study that few other atlases can match.

See *RB* 78 (1971) 442-47.

476. *Grollenberg, L. H., *Atlas of the Bible* (London: Nelson, 1956). This is a translation of *Atlas van de Bijbel* (Amsterdam/Brussels: Elsevier, 1954), which also appeared in French, *Atlas de la Bible* (Brussels/Paris: Elsevir, 1954), and from which the English form is actually derived. Though the text that accompanies the maps, charts, and illustrations is in many ways inferior to that of *WHAB* (§ 479), this is still a very good biblical atlas. It includes

over 400 pictures and illustrative pieces, each adequately identified.
An ingenious use of symbols on the maps incorporates a great deal
of information. It is highly recommended.

See *RB* 62 (1955) 595-97; *Bib* 37 (1956) 84-87; *JSS* 1 (1956) 83; 2
(1957) 281-83; *CBQ* 19 (1957) 270-71; *Eleven Years* (§ 7), 654.

477. May, H.G., *Oxford Bible Atlas* (2d ed.; New York/London:
Oxford University, 1974). This atlas first appeared in 1962. A
small, compact atlas, containing 26 excellent maps, and an accompanying text discussing the history of the Holy Land from the
patriarchs to the time of Paul. Though good, this atlas cannot
compare with those of larger scope. It is available in paperback
form.

See *JBL* 82 (1963) 133; *CBQ* 25 (1963) 206.

478. Monson, J. et al., *Student Map Manual: Historical Geography of
the Bible Lands* (Jerusalem: Pictorial Archive; Grand Rapids, MI:
Zondervan, 1979). "Bible lands" means Israel and parts of Egypt
and Transjordan. This is "a Bible-atlas which accurately reflects
the configuration of the country" (J. Murphy-O'Connor). It has
15 sections: section 1 has 16 regional maps; section 2 has ten
maps summarizing archaeological work in the Holy Land;
sections 3-13 provide historical maps for events from the
Canaanite to the Byzantine periods; section 14 is devoted to the
archaeology of Jerusalem; section 15 has indices to 865 places
that appear in the maps.

See *RB* 89 (1982) 136-39; *CBQ* 42 (1980) 551-52.

WHAB   **479.** *Wright, G.E. and F.V. Filson, *The Westminster Historical
Atlas to the Bible* (rev. ed.; Philadelphia, PA: Westminster, 1956).
The text of this work has undergone considerable revision in
detail; it first appeared in 1946, and new sections have been added
on the rise of Jewish sects and on archaeological progress in
Palestine; some new pictures have been introduced, while others
have been dropped; new identifications have been incorporated
into the maps.

See *Bib* 38 (1957) 357-58; *CBQ* 19 (1957) 390; *JBL* 76 (1957) 256-57;
JSS 2 (1957) 283-84.

B. **Discussions of the Historical and Physical Geography of the Holy Land**

480. *Abel F.-M., *Géographie de la Palestine* (2 vols.; EBib; Paris:
Gabalda, 1933, 1938). Though old, these volumes remain the
standard reference work on Palestinian geography. Volume 1 is
devoted to the physical and historical geography of Palestine; vol.
2 to the political geography; it also gives an extensive list of bibli-

cal and other historical sites with references to ancient sources and modern discussions. See § 485.

See *JPOS* 15 (1935) 185-90; *JBL* 58 (1939) 177-87; *ZDPV* 59 (1936) 246-48; 63 (1940) 229-33.

481. **Aharoni, Y., *The Land of the Bible: A Historical Geography* (London: Burns & Oates; Philadelphia, PA: Westminster, 1967; rev. A. F. Rainey, 1980). This volume is the modern counterpart to G. A. Smith's classic (§ 487). Part I presents the geographical setting of Palestine (the land of many contrasts, its roads and highways, its boundaries and names, historical sources used, and the toponymy). Part II describes Palestine throughout the ages (Canaanite period, Israelite conquest and settlement, united monarchy, kingdoms of Israel and Judah, latter days of the Judean kingdom). The survey does not go beyond the Persian period.

See *JBL* 87 (1968) 229-31; 102 (1983) 119-20; *Int* 22 (1968) 475; *RB* 77 (1970) 91-94; *JAOS* 89 (1969) 172-74; *OLZ* 64 (1969) 464-65; *RevExp* 66 (1969) 322-23; *CBQ* 44 (1982) 287-88.

482. *Avi-Yonah, M., *The Holy Land from the Persian to the Arab Conquests (536 B.C. to A.D. 640): A Historical Geography* (Baker Studies in Biblical Archaeology; rev. ed.; Grand Rapids, MI: Baker, 1977). A translation of the modern Hebrew *Gy'grpyh hs̱twryt šl 'rṣ yśr'l* (3d ed.; Jerusalem: Bialik Institute, 1962). In a way, this book builds on Aharoni's *The Land of the Bible* (§ 481), since it continues the discussion of the land of Palestine according to various periods from the Persian conquest to that of the Arabs. It does not, however, have the detail of the other book.

See *BSac* 124 (1967) 272; *IEJ* 17 (1967) 199; *ZAW* 80 (1968) 121; *AUSS* 6 (1968) 204-7; *Int* 22 (1968) 476-77; *EvQ* 40 (1968) 178.

483. Baly, D., *Geographical Companion to the Bible* (New York: McGraw–Hill, 1963). This volume is really a supplement to Baly's *Geography* (§ 484). Written by a long-time resident of the Holy Land and one trained in scientific geography, this *Companion* stresses those factors which have helped determine the ways of life of the people in biblical times, the main trade routes, and the natural battlefields in the different periods of the history of the land. "Those who have not yet discovered the immense value of geography to the study of the OT could not do better than to study Denis Baly" (S. D. Walters).

See *JBL* 84 (1965) 467; *CBQ* 26 (1964) 140; *BSac* 122 (1965) 184-85; *RHPR* 45 (1965) 162-63; *ZAW* 76 (1964) 225.

484. Baly, D., *The Geography of the Bible* (2d ed.; New York: Harper, 1974). This is a thorough revision of a book that first appeared in

1957. "...every paragraph has been rewritten...on almost every page new information has been added" (p. xi). This is not a historical geography of Palestine, but one devoted to its physical geography (i.e., its geology, meteorology, and ecology). Part 2 describes the physical and geological structure of the land in five main regions or divisions. This is a valuable book, packed with accurate information, but the detail may overwhelm the beginner at times.

See *JBL* 76 (1957) 333-35; 94 (1975) 634-35; *NTA* 18 (1973-74) 398.

485. *Buit, M. du, *Géographie de la Terre Sainte* (2 vols.; Paris: Cerf, 1958). This work is part of the supplementary volumes of the fascicle edition of *SBJ* (§ 189). Volume 1 covers the physical and historical geography of the land, giving a topical index with biblical references and brief notes on regions and towns (in part this updates the information in Abel's *Géographie*, vol. 2 [§ 480]). Volume 2 is a collection of 18 maps. It is concise and a very useful tool for biblical study.

See *RB* 66 (1959) 305-6; *JBL* 78 (1959) 265-66; *CBQ* 21 (1959) 385-87; *BL* (1959) 12; *Bib* 41 (1960) 442.

486. Donner, H., *Einführung in die biblische Landes- und Altertumskunde* (Die Theologie; Darmstadt: Wissenschaftliche Buchgesellschaft, 1976). An excellent, modern and brief introduction to the physical and historical geography of the land of Palestine. It is to be used with existing atlases, since it contains no maps of its own.

See *BO* 34 (1977) 203-4; *BZ* 22 (1978) 312-13; *TRev* 74 (1978) 189.

487. Smith, G. A., *Historical Geography of the Holy Land* (4th ed.; London: Hodder and Stoughton, 1896). First published in 1894, it has often been reprinted in this 4th ed. Though outmoded in much of its detail, it has remained over the years the classic work on the historical geography of Palestine. It is still available in paperback (Grand Rapids, MI: Kregel, 1977).

488. Vogel, E. K., "Bibliography of Holy Land Sites," *HUCA* 42 (1971) 1-96. An invaluable bibliography on sites in Palestine (from 'Abdah to Zarethan). This has been continued by E. K. Vogel and B. Holtzclaw, "Bibliography of Holy Land Sites: Part II," *HUCA* 52 (1981) 1-92; "Part III: 1981-1987," *HUCA* 58 (1987) 1-63.

C. NT Sites

ELS **489.** Baldi, D., *Enchiridion locorum sanctorum: Documenta s. evangelii loca respicientia* (2d ed.; Jerusalem: Franciscan Press, 1955).

Ancient descriptions of NT sites, preserved in the NT itself, patristic writers, medieval and Renaissance pilgrims and travellers, have been collected in this handy volume. The original text is usually given together with a Latin translation below it on the same page. It is a very useful tool.

See *Bib* 37 (1956) 93-94; *RB* 45 (1936) 158-59; 63 (1956) 157-58.

490. Kopp, C., *The Holy Places of the Gospels* (New York: Herder and Herder, 1963). This is a translation of *Die heiligen Stätten der Evangelien* (Pustet: Regensburg, 1959). It is a good discussion of the history and archaeological remains of ancient sites connected with gospel history: Bethlehem, Nazareth, John the Baptist (and areas associated with him), Jesus in Cana and at Jacob's Well, the Lake of Gennesareth, sites near the Lake (Caesarea Philippi, Nain, Tabor), sites along the final journey to Jerusalem, and Jerusalem itself and its environs. There is good bibliography and illustrations (gathered at the end of the book); it resembles J. Finegan's *Archeology of the NT* (§ 458), but is more aptly entitled.

See *CBQ* 22 (1960) 231-32; 26 (1964) 146; *RB* 67 (1960) 152-54; *PEQ* 91 (1959) 142-43.

491. Metzger, H., *St. Paul's Journeys in the Greek Orient* (SBA 4; London: SCM, 1959). This is a translation of *Les routes de saint Paul dans l'orient grec* (Cahiers d'archéologie biblique 4; Neuchâtel: Delachaux et Niestlé, 1956 [§ 470]). This is an attempt to trace Paul's movements in his missionary journeys; even though all will not agree with every last detail, it is a good starting-point for the discussion. The original first appeared in 1954.

See *RB* 62 (1955) 291-92; *BO* 12 (1955) 206; *RevScRel* 29 (1955) 81-82.

CHAPTER XVII

History

Invariably the student of the Bible soon begins to ask about the history of the times in which the OT, the intertestamental literature, and the NT took shape. Much is known from extrabiblical sources that can be related to the context of these writings. For this reason the student turns to histories of Israel (or of the religion of Israel, as some prefer to put it), of Judaism in the last centuries prior to the emergence of Christianity, and to the period in which the NT took shape. An even larger or broader historical background can also be studied when one tries to put the OT and NT against the history of the ancient Near East. The items listed here will be grouped under the following headings: (A) Histories of OT times; (B) Histories of Judaism in the intertestamental period; (C) Histories of NT times; and (D) Histories of the ancient Near East (in general).

A. Histories of OT Times

BPAE   **492.**   Albright, W. F., *The Biblical Period from Abraham to Ezra: An Historical Survey* (Torchbooks; New York: Harper & Row, 1963). This short account originally appeared as *The Biblical Period* (Pittsburgh: Biblical Colloquium, 1950), having been composed actually as a chapter in L. Finkelstein, *The Jews: Their History, Culture, and Religion* (New York: Harper, 1949). It traces in broad outlines the history of Israel from the period of Abraham to the restoration; it is packed with information and has had much influence in American OT studies.

      See *JBL* 82 (1963) 362; *RB* 64 (1957) 418-19.

FSAC   **493.**   ****Albright, W. F., *From the Stone Age to Christianity* (2d ed., with a new introduction; Garden City, NY: Doubleday, 1957). This monumental theological-historical synthesis first appeared in 1940 and was revised in 1946; the new introduction provides the author's revised views. The French translation (*De l'age de pierre à la chrétienté: Le monothéisme et son évolution historique* [Paris: Payot, 1951]) also contains an important introduction; but the translation was not carefully produced.

      See *RB* 54 (1947) 435-40; *TS* 3 (1942) 109-36; *Or* 20 (1951) 216-36; *Bib* 32 (1951) 305-11; 39 (1958) 361-62; *JSS* 2 (1957) 427-28; *L'Ami du clergé* 63 (1953) 73-76.

    494.   Anderson, G. W., *The History and Religion of Israel* (NClarB, OT 1; London: Oxford University, 1966). "The history and the religion [of Israel] are treated not separately, but together, so far as may be, in chronological sequence; and the historical narrative ... is here continued as far as the Maccabaean Revolt" (p. vii). This is a succinct, readable account for beginners.

See *TS* 28 (1967) 625; *OLZ* 63 (1968) 565-66; *A Decade* (§ 7), 632.

495. Ben-Sasson, H. H. (ed.), *History of the Jewish People* (Cambridge, MA: Harvard University, 1976). This is a translation of a modern Hebrew history, *Tôlĕdôt 'am Yiśrā'ēl*. Part 1, which covers the period from the beginnings to the 7th century A.D., was written by A. Malamat, H. Tadmor, M. Stern, and S. Safrai; part 2, which covers the period from the 7th century to the 17th, was written by H. H. Ben-Sasson; part 3, which covers the period from the 17th century to the present, was written by S. Ettinger. A German translation exists: *Geschichte des jüdischen Volkes* (3 vols.; Munich: Beck, 1978, 1979, 1980).

See *BL* (1971) 295.

496. Bright, J., *Early Israel in Recent History Writing* (SBT 19; London: SCM, 1956). An exposition and critique of the historical methods of the Alt–Noth school; also a brief summary of the work of Y. Kaufmann, *The Biblical Account of the Conquest of Palestine*. The author draws up an outline of the method to be followed in writing the early history of Israel. A knowledge of this book is requisite for an understanding of Bright's own history of Israel (§ 497).

See *A Decade* (§ 7), 23; *JBL* 76 (1957) 249; *Int* 11 (1957) 461-63; *CBQ* 19 (1957) 392-96; *JSS* 4 (1959) 72-73.

497. *Bright, J., *A History of Israel: Second Edition* (2d ed.; Philadelphia, PA: Westminster, 1972; 3d ed., greatly revised, 1981). This is the systematic presentation of the history of Israel according to the principles of the Albright school. For an explanation of them, see Bright's *Early Israel* (§ 496). This book has been highly praised, even though all will not accept the principles on which the early history of Israel used in it are constructed.

See *RB* 67 (1960) 620-23; 80 (1973) 475; *JBL* 79 (1960) 369-72; 93 (1974) 449; *CBQ* 22 (1960) 330-32; 37 (1975) 378; 44 (1982) 477-78; *JNES* 22 (1963) 279-81; *OLZ* 58 (1963) 259-62; *Int* 28 (1974) 108-10; *JSS* 19 (1974) 287-89.

498. Ehrlich, E. L., *Geschichte Israels von den Anfängen bis zur Zerstörung des Tempels (70 n. Chr.)* (Sammlung Göschen, 231/231a; Berlin: de Gruyter, 1958) This is a brief, but adequate survey of the history of Israel intended for students. An English translation exists, *A Concise History of Israel, from the Earliest Times to the*

Destruction of the Temple in A.D. 70 (Torchbooks; New York: Harper & Row, 1962).

See *BO* 17 (1960) 58; *JSS* 4 (1959) 168; *PEQ* 90 (1958) 149.

499. Freedman, D. N. and F. G. Graf (eds.), *Palestine in Transition: The Emergence of Ancient Israel* (Sheffield, UK: Almond Press, 1983). A collection of essays dealing with the models or hypotheses put forth to explain how Israel gained control over the land of Canaan.

See *CBQ* 47 (1985) 573-75.

500. **Hayes J. H. and J. M. Miller (eds.), *Israelite and Judaean History* (OTL; Philadelphia, PA: Westminster, 1977). This survey of the history of Israel from its beginnings down to the Roman period (A.D. 132) has been written by 14 scholars of international repute. In eleven chapters it presents the sources of historical information currently available, assesses the state of discussion among scholars, and gives a reconstruction of the history of Israel and Judea as this can be done today. Each contributor treats a specific period of history from the patriarchal to the Roman. An appendix supplies a chronology of Israelite and Judean kings. This volume is said to mark "the end of the dominance of the moderately conservative critical school of Albright–Bright–Wright" (*ExpTim* 89 [1977-78] 67), but it is questionable whether the deemphasis found here on the "archaeological approach" will be accepted by all who use this important work.

See *JTS* 29 (1978) 508-11; *Bib* 59 (1978) 423-26; *BZ* 23 (1979) 124-25; *RB* 87 (1980) 131-37; *JBL* 99 (1980) 589-91.

501. Herrmann, S., *Geschichte Israels in alttestamentlicher Zeit* (Munich: Kaiser, 1973). This history was written as an introductory manual for students and surveys the periods of the history of Israel down to Alexander the Great. It has been written in the tradition of A. Alt and M. Noth. Though not as detailed as the history of J. Bright (§ 497), it is a very readable and useful survey. An English translation exists, *A History of Israel in Old Testament Times* (Philadelphia, PA: Fortress, 1975).

See *JBL* 95 (1976) 655-56; *CBQ* 38 (1976) 238-40; *ZAW* 86 (1974) 119-20; *BL* (1974) 19; *EvT* 34 (1974) 304-13; *ETR* 50 (1975) 107-9; *TTZ* 83 (1974) 380.

502. Kaufmann, Y., *History of the Religion of Israel: Volume IV, From the Babylonian Captivity to the End of Prophecy* (New York [now Hoboken, NJ]: Ktav; Jerusalem: Hebrew University; Dallas, TX: Institute for Jewish Studies, 1977). This is the sequel to the abridged translation of vols. 1-3, published by M. Greenberg (§ 503). The translation of vol. 4, part I (part II was never written), done by C. W. Efroymson, makes use of a translation of chaps. 1-2 prepared earlier and published by the Union of American Hebrew Congregations, *The Babylonian Captivity and Deutero-Isaiah* (New York, 1970). This is an important work, despite its repetitious and polemical character.

See *CBQ* 40 (1978) 243-44; *JBL* 98 (1979) 292-93.

503. **Kaufmann, Y.,** *The Religion of Israel: From Its Beginnings to the Babylonian Exile* (Chicago: University of Chicago, 1960). This is a translation and abridgment of Kaufmann's modern Hebrew history, *Twldwt h'mwnh hyśr'lyt: Mymy qdm 'd swp byt šny* (4 vols.; Tel Aviv: Bialik Institute-Dvir, 1937-56), prepared by M. Greenberg. The abridgement is limited to vols. 1-3, to those treating the preexilic age, "a self-contained unit ... within which Professor Kaufmann places the bulk of ancient Hebrew literature and religious creativity" (p. v). Part I of the abridgment treats of the character of Israelite religion; part II of the history of Israelite religion prior to classical prophecy; and part III, classical prophecy. See further § 502.

See *Bib* 42 (1961) 367-69; *CBQ* 23 (1961) 68-69; *JBL* 81 (1962) 185-90; *JBR* 29 (1961) 52-57; *JNES* 21 (1962) 158-60; *ZRGG* 13 (1961) 279-80.

504. ****Noth, M.,** *Geschichte Israels* (2d ed.; Göttingen: Vandenhoeck & Ruprecht, 1954). This is the classic formulation of the history of Israel according to the Alt–Noth school. It differs considerably from that of J. Bright (§ 497), especially in the treatment of Israel's early history. An English translation exists: *The History of Israel* (rev. tr. by P. R. Ackroyd; New York: Harper, 1960). The original translation of the 2d German ed. was quite defective (see *JSS* 4 [1959] 151-64); the revised translation is not without its problems.

See *RB* 58 (1951) 474-76; 62 (1955) 280-81; *TLZ* 76 (1951) 335-40; 77 (1952) 677-84; *VT* 1 (1951) 72-74; *JBL* 73 (1954) 106-8; J. Bright, *Early Israel* (§ 496).

505. ****Vaux, R. de,** *Histoire ancienne d'Israël* (2 vols.; EBib; Paris: Gabalda, 1971, 1973). De Vaux died before he could finish this work. Volume 1 ("Des origines à l'installation en Canaan") appeared before he died; only a part of vol. 2 ("La période des Juges") was published posthumously under the care of R. Tournay. It was to be a comprehensive three-volume history. What de Vaux left behind is the work of a master. His study fits, as he himself says, "halfway between" Noth and Bright. An English translation exists: *The Early History of Israel* (2 vols.; London: Darton, Longman & Todd; Philadelphia, PA: Westminster, 1978).

See *RB* 80 (1973) 82-92; *JBL* 92 (1973) 285-87; 98 (1979) 422-23; *CBQ* 35 (1973) 417-20; 38 (1976) 423-25; 41 (1979) 638-39; *Bib* 53 (1972) 565-75; 56 (1975) 426-29.

B. Histories of Judaism in the Intertestamental Period

506. Abel, F.-M., *Histoire de la Palestine depuis la conquête d'Alexandre jusqu'à l'invasion arabe* (EBib; 2d ed.; 2 vols.; Paris: Gabalda, 1952). Volume 1 covers the political history of Palestine from the conquest of Alexander to the first revolt of the Jews against Rome; vol. 2 continues the history up to the Arab conquest. The two volumes are a remarkable synthesis of a thousand years of history, which has become a fundamental work for the study of late pre-Christian Judaism in Palestine and of Jewish history in that country in Christian times.

See *Eleven Years* (§ 7), 392; *RB* 60 (1953) 631-32; *JBL* 73 (1954) 108-9; *Bib* 35 (1954) 246-49; *OLZ* 49 (1954) 43-46.

507. **Hengel, M., *Judentum und Hellenismus: Studien zu ihrer Begegnung unter besonderer Berücksichtigung Palästinas bis zur Mitte des 2. Jh.s v. Chr.* (WUNT 10; 2d ed.; Tübingen: Mohr [Siebeck], 1973). "... all students of the intertestamental period and of the NT will find that it provides an unequalled view of the political and religious sources of this time" (R. E. Murphy). However, though it does not really cover the NT period, it provides a mass of material for the proper understanding of Judaism and Hellenism just prior to this period. An English translation exists: *Judaism and Hellenism: Studies in Their Encounter in Palestine during the Early Hellenistic Period, I-II* (2 vols.; Philadelphia, PA: Fortress, 1974).

See *CBQ* 36 (1974) 407-9; 37 (1975) 579-80; *RB* 80 (1973) 423-26; 84 (1977) 142; *JBL* 90 (1971) 228-31; 94 (1975) 637; *JSS* 17 (1972) 269-71; *ZAW* 85 (1973) 388; *IRev* 68 (1972) 107-11.

508. Tcherikover, V., *Hellenistic Civilization and the Jews* (Philadelphia, PA: Jewish Publication Society of America, 1959). This work, by the professor of classical history in the Hebrew University, appeared posthumously; it provides a good background for the history and culture of the Jews between the conquest of Alexander and the Roman period. Today it is overshadowed by M. Hengel's *Judentum* (§ 507), but it still has merit.

See *BO* 17 (1960) 193-94; *JJS* 10 (1959) 75-78.

C. Histories of NT Times

509. *Bruce, F. F., *New Testament History* (London: Nelson, 1969; Garden City, NY: Doubleday, 1972). After a rapid survey, entitled "From Cyrus to Augustus," the book concentrates on the period from the Herodian succession to the time of Hadrian, describing the situation of Palestinian Judaism and the emergence of John the Baptist, Jesus, and the primitive church. In many ways this is the most readable, modern history of NT times available to students.

See *JTS* 21 (1970) 466-69; *JEH* 22 (1971) 57-58; *Scr* 2 (1970) 51-52; *TToday* 29 (1972-73) 203-4; *Int* 26 (1972) 236-37.

510. Conzelmann, H., *Geschichte des Urchristentums* (GNT 5; Göttingen: Vandenhoeck & Ruprecht, 1969). In English: *History of Primitive Christianity* (Nashville, TN: Abingdon, 1973). "This brief survey examines the origins and early development of the Christian religion from the time following the life and ministry of Jesus up to approximately A.D. 100" (cover). It explains the emergence of the Christian church from the viewpoint of modern German critical scholarship. To be read with discernment.

See *CBQ* 32 (1970) 442-43; 37 (1975) 107; *JBL* 91 (1972) 119-20; *NRT* 92 (1970) 722-23; *TTZ* 79 (1970) 318; *TQ* 150 (1970) 276-77; *TZ* 26 (1970) 358-59.

511. Foerster, W., *Neutestamentliche Zeitgeschichte* (Die urchristliche Botschaft 26; 2 vols.; Hamburg: Furche, 1955, 1956). Part 1 treats of Palestinian Judaism in the time of Jesus and the Apostles; part 2, the Roman empire in NT times. Volume 1 actually appeared in 1940 (during World War II) and was reissued in 1955. This is a good account of the history of NT times, even taking into account the data from the discovery of the Dead Sea Scrolls. The first volume exists in English translation: *From the Exile to Christ: A Historical Introduction to Palestinian Judaism* (Philadelphia, PA: Fortress, 1964).

See *JBL* 75 (1956) 58-59; 76 (1957) 62-64; 84 (1965) 131-32; *TQ* 137 (1957) 87-88; *CBQ* 27 (1965) 189-90.

512. **Reicke, B., *Neutestamentliche Zeitgeschichte: Die biblische Welt 500 v. — 100 n. Chr.* (Sammlung Töpelmann 2/2; Berlin: Töpelmann, 1965). An excellent sketch of the political, social, and economic conditions of the centuries that preceded and coincided with the emergence of the primitive Christian church; it treats of Judaism, Hellenism, and the Roman empire. The author adopts generally conservative positions on NT chronology. There is a good bibliography and good maps, but the index is lean. The reader will prescind from the anachronistic use of modern labels for groups and movements. An English version exists: *The New Testament Era: The World of the Bible from 500 B.C. to A.D. 100* Philadelphia, PA: Fortress; London: Black, 1968). The translator (D. E. Green) has incorporated a number of corrections supplied by the author.

See *CBQ* 27 (1965) 176-77; 31 (1969) 124-25; *RB* 73 (1966) 292-93; *JBL* 84 (1965) 466-67; 89 (1970) 112-14.

513. Compendia rerum iudaicarum ad Novum Testamentum (Assen: Van Gorcum; Philadelphia, PA: Fortress). This is projected as a monumental, ten-volume series written by Christian and Jewish scholars in cooperation and "designed as a historic work on the relationship of Judaism and Christianity" throughout the centuries (I/1. ix). So far five volumes of the first two sections have appeared: (I/1-2) Safrai, S. and M. Stern (eds.), *The Jewish People in the First Christian Century* (1974, 1976). (II) *The Literature of the Jewish People in the Period of the Second Temple and the Talmud*: (1) M. J. Mulder (ed.), *Mikra: Text, Translation, Reading and Interpretation of the Hebrew Bible in Ancient Judaism and Early Christianity* (1988); (2) M. E. Stone (ed.), *Jewish Writings of the Second Temple Period: Apocrypha, Pseudepigrapha, Qumran, Sectarian Writings, Philo, Josephus* (1984). (3a) S. Safrai (ed.), *The Literature of the Sages: Oral Tora, Halakha, Mishna, Tosefta, Talmud, External Tractates* (1988). Though packed with information, the various contributions, which deal with the legal, political, social, and economic aspects of Palestinian Jewish life, are unequal. In the first volumes (I/1-2) most of the contributions have been written by Jewish scholars who uncritically use materials of a much later date and predicate such evidence of "the first century." "Severely criticized by some distinguished scholars," these volumes are to be used with caution. This criticism, however, is not necessarily true of all volumes in the series.

See *TS* 36 (1975) 335-38; 39 (1978) 769-71; *CBQ* 37 (1975) 291-92; 40 (1978) 282; 48 (1986) 160-61; *JBL* 93 (1974) 608-10; 97 (1978) 456-57; 105 (1986) 720-22; *RB* 81 (1974) 296-97.

514. **Schürer, E., *The History of the Jewish People in the Age of Jesus Christ (175 B.C. — A.D. 135): A New English Version Revised and Edited* (ed. G. Vermes, F. Millar et al.; 3 vols. [the 3d in two parts]; Edinburgh: Clark, 1973, 1979, 1986, 1987). This is a translation and modern adaptation of *Geschichte des jüdischen Volkes im Zeitalter Jesu Christi* (Leipzig: Hinrichs), which saw its fourth German edition in 1910-11. The second German edition had been translated into English, *A History of the Jewish People in the Time of Jesus Christ* (3 vols.; Edinburgh: Clark, 1898-1905). It is a massive account that is packed with information and good bibliographies, even though some of the new material in the modern adaptation may not always be rightly interpreted. It "will be of great benefit to those who use it critically, but students should be warned that it is not representative of contemporary scholarship" (J. J. Collins). An Italian translation of this revision has been begun, of which two vols. have appeared, *Storia del popolo giudaico al tempo di Gesù Cristo (175 a.C. — 135 d.C.)* (ed. O. Soffritti; Brescia: Paideia, 1985, 1987).

See *JBL* 94 (1975) 150-52; 100 (1981) 120; *CBQ* 36 (1974) 432-33; 42 (1980) 391-92; 50 (1988) 336-38, 730-32; *RB* 81 (1974) 296; 88 (1981) 298; 95 (1988) 142-44, 625-26.

D. Histories of the Ancient Near East

CAH   **515.** *The Cambridge Ancient History* (3d ed.; ed. I. E. S. Edwards et al.; Cambridge, UK: University Press, 1970-   ). Of the third edition five volumes, often in two or more parts, have appeared so far. Volume 1/1 (prolegomena and prehistory, 1970); 1/2 (early history of the Middle East, 1971); 2/1 (history of the Middle East and the Aegean region [1800-1380 B.C.], 1973); 2/2 (same [1380-1000 B.C.], 1975); pls. to vols 1-2 (1977); 3/1 (pre-history of the Balkans, Middle East and Aegean World [10th-8th c. B.C.], 2d ed., 1982); 3/3 (expansion of the Greek world [8th-6th c. B.C.], 2d ed., 1982); pls. to vol. 3 (1984); 4 (Persia, Greece and Western Mediterranean area, 2d ed., 1988); pls. to vol. 4 (1988); 7/1 (Hellenistic world, 2d ed., 1984); pls. to vol. 7/1 (1984). Then one has to use the older edition of vols. 3-12 (ed. J. B. Bury et al., 1925-1939, repr. 1965), which cover the periods of the Assyrian empire (vol. 3) to the (Roman) imperial crisis and recovery (A.D. 193-324). This is a remarkable, well-written survey that explains well the political, social, and economic world into which the OT and NT fit. Highly recommended.

See *HZ* 241 (1985) 659-61; *BL* (1985) 33.

AOR   **516.** Cassin, E., J. Bottéro, and J. Vercoutter, *Die altorientalischen Reiche* (3 vols.; Fischer Weltgeschichte 2-4; Frankfurt am M.: Fischer Bücherei, 1965, 1966, 1967). These three volumes offer a good, succinct account of the history of the ancient Near East prior to and during which the books of the OT came into being. Volume 1 treats of the period from the paleolithic age to the middle of the second millennium B.C.; vol. 2 covers the time the end of the second millennium B.C.; and vol. 3 deals with the first half of the first millennium B.C. In broad strokes the history of ancient Egypt, Mesopotamia, Syria, and Palestine is drawn.

See *WZKM* 61 (1967) 175-77; *Stimmen der Zeit* 178 (1966) 69; *HZ* 206 (1968) 752-53; *OLZ* 63 (1968) 455-56.

517. Hallo, W. W. and W. K. Simpson, *The Ancient Near East: A History* (New York: Harcourt, Brace, Jovanovich, 1971). This historical survey is intended for graduate students who are beginning their study of the ancient Near East. The authors are an Assyriologist and an Egyptologist at Yale University. The survey begins at the end of the fourth millennium B.C. and reaches to the end of the Neo-Babylonian period in Mesopotamia or to the conquest of Alexander in Egypt. It concentrates on Mesopotamia and Egypt and gives a good background for the understanding of the OT or Israelite history. But certain parts and periods of the ancient Near East are not treated (Iran, Anatolia, Arabia; Achaemenid, Hellenistic, and Roman periods).

See *JNES* 32 (1973) 252-53; *JAOS* 93 (1973) 575-76.

HM   **518.**   *Historia mundi: Ein Handbuch der Weltgeschichte* (10 vols.; ed. F. Valjavec; Bern: Francke, 1952-61). The first four volumes of this series are a German counterpart to *CAH* (§ 515), though all of the material in them is not as authoritatively written as in the latter.

See *HZ* 177 (1954) 90-95; 179 (1955) 110-12; 182 (1956) 83-88.

RRAM   **519.**   Magie, D., *Roman Rule in Asia Minor to the End of the Third Century after Christ* (2 vols.; Princeton, NJ: Princeton University, 1950). The author's purpose was "to present what is known of the expansion of Rome's Empire in Asia Minor and the lands adjacent on the east and of her rule over the Asianic provinces ... to the end of the third century after Christ." Volume 1 contains the text of Magie's study; vol. 2 his abundant notes. The two volumes provide an excellent background study of the cities mentioned in Acts and the Pauline letters.

See *CHR* 38 (1952-53) 342-43; *CP* 47 (1952) 235-38.

520.   Jones, A. H. M., *The Cities of the Eastern Roman Provinces* (Oxford: Clarendon, 1937; 2d ed., 1971). The author's purpose was "to trace the diffusion of the Greek city as a political institution through the lands bordering on the eastern Mediterranean which were included within the Roman empire." It deals mainly with the period after Alexander in the time of the Hellenistic kings; it tries to show the effect that incorporation into Roman provinces had on the cities of that area. A very useful book for the understanding of the hellenization and romanization of the world in which the NT grew up.

See *JPOS* 18 (1938) 139-40; *CRev* 52 (1938) 141-42.

521.   Rostovtzeff, M., *A History of the Ancient World* (2 vols.; 2d ed.; Oxford: Clarendon, 1930, repr., 1936). This is a translation of a history written in Russian. Volume 1 treats the Orient and Greece; vol. 2, Rome and the Roman provinces (down to the decline of ancient civilization).

522.   Rostovtzeff, M. I., *The Social and Economic History of the Hellenistic World* (3 vols.; Oxford: Clarendon, 1941; 2d ed., 1952). A study of the period from Alexander to Augustus, especially of the world created by Alexander's conquest of the East and of the states into which it disintegrated, for as long as they retained political independence and the Greeks in those states held the leading role in spheres of life.

See *Historia* 1 (1950) 116-28; *Gnomon* 30 (1958) 314-15.

523.   Rostovtzeff, M., *The Social and Economic History of the Roman Empire* (2 vols.; 2d ed.; rev. by P. M. Fraser; Oxford: Clarendon, 1957). This sweeping work was first published in 1926. Rostovtzeff has a thesis that the Roman empire and its civilization were built on an urban middle class, a bourgeoisie (*honestiores*) reluctant to open its way of life to lower types (*humiliores*); so country areas and cities came into conflict. If one prescinds from such ideological interpretations, there is much to be learned from this history of the Roman world in the period in which the NT took shape. In a sense it is a classic. The bibliography in it, however, was antiquated even in 1957.

See *CJ* 22 (1926-27) 307-13; *Times Literary Supplement* 57 (#2917, 24 January 1958) 6.

524. Finegan, J., *Handbook of Biblical Chronology: Principles of Time Reckoning in the Ancient World and Problems of Chronology in the Bible* (Princeton, NJ: Princeton University, 1964). This book has grown out of an appendix in the author's *Light from the Ancient Past* (§ 459). It sets forth in part I the principles of chronology in the ancient world (numbers, reckoning of time, official and regnal years, eras, early Christian chronographers). In part II it deals with problems of chronology in the Bible. Though praised for the clarity of the treatment of the principles and problems of NT dating, it has been criticized for its scanty treatment of the notoriously difficult chronological problems of the OT (only a score of pages is devoted to them).

See *RB* 73 (1966) 146-47; *CQR* 166 (1965) 234-35; *CBQ* 27 (1965) 59-61; *JBL* 84 (1965) 76-80.

525. Bickerman, E. J., *Chronology of the Ancient World: Revised Edition* (Aspects of Greek and Roman Life; ed. H. H. Scullard; London: Thames and Hudson; Ithaca, NY; Cornell University, 1980). A thorough study of the calendar systems used by the ancients and of their modes of reckoning time. The book appeared earlier in German, Italian, and Russian, and in 1968 in its first English form. But in this edition a valuable supplement with various chronological tables of Greek and Roman history is added to a "completely revised and often changed" text. This book covers much of the same ground as does that of J. Finegan (§ 524), but in a more complete way and written with a master's hand.

See *JRS* 58 (1968) 251; *Phoenix* 22 (Toronto 1968) 280-81.

ANRW   **526.** **Temporini, H. (ed.), *Aufstieg und Niedergang der römischen Welt: Geschichte und Kultur Roms im Spiegel der neueren Forschung* (Berlin/New York: de Gruyter, 1972-   ). This multivolume history of Rome is mammoth in its conception, treatment, and coverage. Volume I (from the beginnings of Rome to the end of the Republic) has four subvolumes and a volume of plates; vol. II (the Principate) presently has 36 subvolumes (often in two or more parts). II/25.1-6 (ed. W. Haase, 1982-88) treats Religion, especially pre-Constantinian Christianity. Though most of the contributions are written in German, many are in English. The authors are scholars from all over the world.

See *RHPR* 65 (1985) 486-87; *TLZ* 110 (1985) 110-11; *TQ* 165 (1985) 245-48; *EtClass* 53 (1985) 511-13.

CHAPTER XVIII

Literature of the Intertestamental Period

The literature of the Jews stemming from the period between the closing of the OT books and the emergence of the NT writings has often been described, somewhat infelicitously, as "intertestamental literature." The term is problematic because it is sometimes used to include the deuterocanonical/apocryphal writings. We are using it here to group together the writings of Philo Alexandrinus, Flavius Josephus, the pseudepigrapha of the OT, and other Jewish writings that emerged in the last centuries prior to Christianity. The items listed below will be grouped under the following headings: (A) Bibliographical data; (B) Main primary texts (for more detailed listing, see A); (C) Collections of translations; and (D) Studies and tools.

A. Bibliographical Data

PMR   **527.** *Charlesworth, J. H., *The Pseudepigrapha and Modern Research with a Supplement* (SBLSCS 7; Chico, CA [now Atlanta, GA]: Scholars, 1981). This work first appeared in 1976. Assisted by P. Dykers, Charlesworth has amassed here a tremendous amount of information and bibliographical data for the study of intertestamental pseudepigrapha, often calling attention to writings little known. The bibliography itself is prefixed with a state-of-the-question survey and is preparatory to his edition of the pseudepigrapha in English translation (§ 556). The supplement incorporates 750 new titles.

> See *JBL* 97 (1978) 614; *CBQ* 39 (1977) 587-88; 42 (1980) 147-59; 45 (1983) 452-53; *RB* 86 (1979) 624-25; 89 (1982) 141-42; *JTS* 29 (1978) 515-16; *TLZ* 105 (1980) 832-33.

BJHIL   **528.** Delling, G., *Bibliographie zur jüdisch-hellenistischen und intertestamentarischen Literatur: 1900-1970* (2d ed.; TU 106; Berlin: Akademie, 1975). This valuable bibliographical survey first appeared in 1969, covering the period from 1900-1965. It is a necessary complement to Charlesworth's book (§ 527), since the latter almost always omits what Delling had in his first edition. It has now 3650 entries under 45 headings. Indispensable.

> See *Muséon* 89 (1975) 257; *NTA* 22 (1978) 232.

529. Schreckenberg, H., *Bibliographie zu Flavius Josephus* (ALGHJ 1; Leiden: Brill, 1968). A *Supplementband mit Gesamtregister* (ALGHJ 14) was published in 1979. It was pioneer work, with many lacunae and mistakes; see L. H. Feldman (§ 531).

> See *ZAW* 81 (1969) 430; *BO* 26 (1969) 457; *RSR* 58 (1970) 119-20; *REG* 83 (1970) 263-64.

530. Feldman, L. H., *Studies in Judaica: Scholarship on Philo and Josephus (1937-1962)* (New York: Yeshiva University [distributor: Bloch Publ. Co.], 1963). This topically arranged, critical bibliography on the writings of Philo and Josephus appeared earlier in *CWorld* 54 (1960-61) 281-91; 55 (1961-62) 36-49, 236-44, 252-55, 278-92, 299-301.

See *RB* 73 (1966) 294-95; *Bib* 45 (1964) 461-62; *ZAW* 76 (1964) 229.

531. Feldman, L. H., *Josephus: A Supplementary Bibliography* (New York/London: Garland, 1986). This bibliography is supplementary to that of H. Schreckenberg (§ 529); it not only adds material but corrects many of the errors in the latter. It also supplies corrigenda to Feldman's *Josephus and Modern Scholarship (1937-1980)* (Berlin/New York: de Gruyter, 1984).

DSSMPTS 532. **Fitzmyer, J. A., *The Dead Sea Scrolls: Major Publications and Tools for Study* (3d ed.; SBLSBS 8; Atlanta, GA: Scholars, 1990). First published in 1975, and with an addendum in 1977, this is an attempt to keep abreast of the publication of texts and fragments from the caves of the wadies Qumran (1-11), Murabba'at, Khabra, Seiyal, and Mahras, and from Masada, Khirbet Mird, and (in part) the Cairo Genizah. Record is made of the *editiones principes* and of the provisional publication of fragments (often in out-of-the-way books or periodicals). In addition to the major publications, it gives guidance to translations, studies, tools for all sorts of research on the scrolls. It also lists further bibliographies (pp. 95-98), making the repetition of them unnecessary here. The first section of the book explains the conventional sigla and the mode of referring to the scrolls and fragments (pp. 3-8). "Qumran scholars, particularly those who are just getting started in this fascinating field, will greatly profit by making much use of it [= *DSSMPTS*]" (W. S. LaSor).

See *JBL* 95 (1976) 681-82; *JSS* 21 (1976) 185-86; *JSJ* 7 (1976) 61; *RB* 83 (1976) 295-96; *Muséon* 89 (1976) 477; *CBQ* 38 (1976) 379-80; *ZAW* 91 (1979) 464; *RelStRev* 5 (1979) 61.

B. Main Primary Texts

533. **Niese B., *Flavii Iosephi opera* (7 vols.; Berlin: Weidmann, 1888-1897; repr., 1955). This is the critical edition of the works of Josephus. Volumes 1-4 contain the *Antiquities of the Jews* and his *Life*; vol. 5, the treatise *Against Apion*; vol. 6, the *Jewish War*, and vol. 7, an index to the works. From this edition are derived the section numbers that are often used. The latter, however, should always be added to the more commonly used older system of reference, which still persists in many publications; thus *Ant.* 18.3.3 § 63-64.

534. Michel, O. and O. Bauernfeind, *De bello judaico — Der jüdische Krieg: Griechisch und deutsch* (3 vols.; Munich: Kösel; Darmstadt: Wissenschaftliche Buchgesellschaft, 1959-69). A modern German critical edition of Josephus' *Jewish War* with a fresh translation and commentary.

See *Bible Bibliography* (§ 7), 268; *Erbe und Auftrag* 46 (1970) 157-58; *HZ* 200 (1965) 688-89; 210 (1970) 676-77.

535. Pelletier, A., *Flavius Josèphe: Guerre des Juifs* (Paris: Editions Les Belles-Lettres, 1975, 1980, 1980, 1982). *Flavius Josèphe: Autobiographie* (Paris: Belles-Lettres, 1959; 2d ed., 1983). A new French translation of Josephus' works.

See *ETR* 52 (1977) 563-64; *REG* 90 (1977) 177-78; *RSR* 66 (1978) 353-54; *Gnomon* 53 (1981) 312-15.

536. *Thackeray, H. St. J. et al., *Josephus with an English Translation* (9 vols.; LCL; Cambridge, MA: Harvard University; London: W. Heinemann, 1926-1965). After the 5th vol., Thackeray was succeeded by R. Marcus; and after he died, A. Wikgren completed the 8th vol. L. H. Feldman was responsible for the 9th, with its important index to the whole. This edition not only supplies a good Greek text of Josephus, but an English translation, and brief critical notes.

See *JBL* 85 (1966) 263-64; *Bib* 47 (1966) 306; *VD* 44 (1966) 63-64; *RB* 73 (1966) 295-96; *REG* 79 (1966) 555-56.

537. *Arnaldez, R. et al. (eds.), *Les œuvres de Philon d'Alexandrie* (Paris: Cerf, 1961-73). This series of 35 vols. presenting the Greek text of Philo with a facing French translation is the latest treatment of Philonic writings.

See *NRT* 83 (1961) 873-74; *OrChr* 27 (1961) 453-54; *Greg* 43 (1962) 563-64.

538. **Cohn, L. and P. Wendland, *Philonis alexandrini opera quae supersunt (editio maior)* (7 vols.; Berlin: G. Reimer, 1896-1930); *editio minor* [smaller pages] (6 vols. [no indices], 1896-1915). The volumes of the *editio maior* were published thus: 1 (1896), 2 (1897), 3 (1898), 4 (1902), 5 (1906), 6 (1915 [with S. Reiter]), 7/1 (index, 1926 [with J. Leisegang]), 7/2 (index, 1930 [with J. Leisegang]). This is the critical edition of the Greek text of Philo's works; the *editio maior* was reprinted in 1962 (Berlin: de Gruyter). Cohn was also the editor (with others) of a German translation of Philo's writings, *Die Werke Philos von Alexandria in deutscher Übersetzung* (5 vols.; Berlin: de Gruyter, 1909-29, repr., 1962).

See *TRev* 8 (1909) 302-3; 10 (1911) 382; 19 (1920) 48-49; *TLZ* 36 (1911) 713-15; 45 (1920) 30; 49 (1924) 54-55; 55 (1930) 225; *Gnomon* 8 (1932) 155-62.

539. *Colson, F.H. and G.H. Whitaker, *Philo with an English Translation* (10 vols., with two supplementary vols.; LCL; Cambridge, MA: Harvard University; London: W. Heinemann, 1919-62 [suppl., 1953]). Colson was assisted by Whitaker for the first five volumes, and by J.W. Earp for the indices of vol. 10; R. Marcus was responsible for the supplementary volumes. This set supplies ready access to a good Greek text of Philo, and an English translation with brief critical notes.

540. Harrington, D.J. et al., *Pseudo-Philon, Les Antiquités bibliques* (SC 229-30; 2 vols.; Paris: Cerf, 1976). Volume 1 contains a critical introduction and critical text of Pseudo-Philo (prepared by D.J. Harrington), and a French translation (by J. Cazeaux); vol. 2 presents a literary introduction, commentary, and index (by C. Perrot and P.-M. Bogaert, assisted by D.J. Harrington).

See *RB* 84 (1977) 142-43; *CBQ* 39 (1977) 598-600; *JJS* 25 (1974) 305-12; *RTL* 3 (1972) 334-44.

1QapGen   **541.** Avigad, N. and Y. Yadin, *A Genesis Apocryphon: A Scroll from the Wilderness of Judaea, Description and Contents of the Scroll, Facsimiles, Transcription and Translation of Columns II, XIX-XXII* (Jerusalem: Magnes Press, 1956). This was supposed to be a preliminary publication of what could easily be read of the fragmentary columns of 1QapGen, the so-called seventh scroll of Qumran cave 1. Badly preserved, it required delicate treatment to open the scroll, but unfortunately it has been impossible to extract anything more from what remains. So this publication has turned out to be the definitive edition of it. Recently, American scholars have tried to use computers and special photographic techniques to attempt further reading of the fragments; but so far no results have been announced.

See my commentary, *The Genesis Apocryphon of Qumran Cave 1* (BibOr 18A; Rome: Biblical Institute, 1971); also *MPAT* (§ 676), § 29. Cf. *Time*, 14 March, 1988, 80-81.

DSSMM   **542.** Burrows, M. (ed.), *The Dead Sea Scrolls of St. Mark's Monastery* (2 vols.; New Haven, CT: American Schools of Oriental research, 1950-51). Volume 1 contains black-and-white photographs and transcription of the first Isaiah scroll of Cave 1 (1QIsaᵃ) and of the commentary on Habakkuk (1QpHab), published in 1950; a corrected reprint, with considerably poorer photographs, appeared in 1953. Of vol. 2, only fasc. 2 ever appeared, containing the photographs and transcription of the so-called Manual of Discipline (1QS, *Serek hay-yahad*), published in 1951. Fascicle 2 was originally intended to contain the Genesis Apocryphon (§ 541). The black-and-white photographs (without transcription) were later made available in one volume: F.M. Cross et al. (eds.), *Scrolls from Qumran Cave 1: The Great Isaiah Scroll, The Order* *of the Community, The Pesher to Habakkuk: From Photographs by John C. Trever* (Jerusalem: Albright Institute of Archaeological Research and the Shrine of the Book, 1974). In 1972 another publication, bearing the same title as the last mentioned and with the same editorship and publishers, reproduced both color and black-and-white photographs of the same three texts in an expensive volume.

> See *ZAW* 64 (1952) 68; *Bib* 34 (1953) 403-4; *MUSJ* 29 (1951-52) 375-77; *JBL* 92 (1973) 628-30; *CBQ* 36 (1974) 144; *TToday* 30 (1973-74) 316-18; *ZAW* 85 (1973) 395.

DJD   **543.** **Discoveries in the Judaean Desert (of Jordan) (Oxford: Clarendon, 1955-). Started under the general direction of G. Lankester Harding, at the time the head of the department of antiquities in Jordan, the series has been more recently continued by R. de Vaux and P. Benoit, and now by J. Strugnell of Harvard University. Numbering at present eight volumes (some in two parts), it presents the *editio princeps* of texts from Qumran caves 1-11 and from Murabba'at. Transcriptions, translations, brief notes, and excellent photographs mark the publication of texts in this important series. For further details, see § 532, pp. 11-75, 79-84.

CD   **544.** Schechter, S., *Documents of Jewish Sectaries* (2 vols.; Cambridge, UK: University Press, 1910; repr. with a prolegomenon by J. A. Fitzmyer; New York [now Hoboken, NJ]: Ktav, 1970). Volume 1 contains the *editio princeps* of the Damascus Document, often also called the Zadokite Document.

> See *RB* 78 (1971) 298-99; *CBQ* 33 (1971) 608-10; *RevQ* 7 (1969-71) 607-8; *JAOS* 94 (1974) 515-16.

DSSHU   **545.** Sukenik E. L., *The Dead Sea Scrolls of the Hebrew University* (Jerusalem: Magnes Press, 1955). First published in modern Hebrew *'ôṣar hammĕgillôt haggĕnûzôt* (Jerusalem: Bialik Foundation, 1954), this publication presents the black-and-white photographs and transcription of three scrolls of Cave 1: Isaiah scroll B (1QIsaᵇ), the War Scroll (1QM), and the scroll of the Thanksgiving Psalms (1QH).

> See *Bib* 37 (1956) 227-30; *RB* 62 (1955) 597-601; *JBL* 75 (1956) 87-88; *IEJ* 5 (1955) 200-202.

11QtgJob   **546.** Ploeg, J. P. M. van der and A. S. van der Woude (avec la collaboration de B. Jongeling), *Le targum de Job de la grotte xi de Qumrân* (Koninklijke nederlandse Akademie van Wetenschappen; Leiden: Brill, 1971). The *editio princeps* of a first-century B.C. Aramaic translation of Job 17:14–42:11, much of which is preserved only in fragmentary columns.

> See *RevQ* 8 (1972) 105-14; *JBL* 91 (1972) 414-15; *ETR* 47 (1972) 365-66; *RTL* 3 (1972) 86-90; *Bib* 54 (1973) 283-86; *OLZ* 70 (1975) 468-72; *CBQ* 36 (1974) 503-24; *MPAT* § 5 (esp. pp. 194-97).

11QTemple **547.** Yadin Y., *Mĕgillat ham-miqdāš: The Temple Scroll (Hebrew Edition)* (3 vols. with a supplement; Jerusalem: Israel Exploration Society, 1977). The *editio princeps* of the most important scroll to come from Qumran Cave 11, which is longer than the Book of Isaiah. It contains an introduction, transcription, and commentary on the scroll, together with black-and-white photographs of the columns of the scroll and other fragments related to it. An English edition of this work has been published: *The Temple Scroll* (3 vols. with a supplement; Jerusalem: Israel Exploration Society, 1983). The plates in vol. 3 and the supplement remain the same, but there are corrections and additions in vols. 1 and 2, thus making the English edition more important than the Hebrew.

> See *JBL* 97 (1978) 584-89; *RevQ* 12 (1985-87) 425-40; *CBQ* 48 (1986) 547-49.

BE **548.** Milik, J. T., *The Books of Enoch: Aramaic Fragments of Qumrân Cave 4* (Oxford: Clarendon Press, 1976). Milik was aided in the publication of this material by M. Black. It is the *editio princeps* of most of the Enoch texts from Qumran Cave 4, but not of all of them (unfortunately). It is also a massive commentary on the Enochic literature, a book that will be consulted for decades to come. Whether one agrees with every thesis that Milik proposes in it remains to be seen. It must be used in conjunction with the critical edition of Ethiopic Enoch put out by M. A. Knibb (§ 549).

> See *TS* 38 (1977) 332-45; *RB* 83 (1976) 605-18; *Bib* 58 (1977) 432-36; *CBQ* 40 (1978) 411-19; *BZ* 22 (1978) 132-34; *JTS* 29 (1978) 517-30; *Numen* 26 (1979) 89-103; *Maarav* 1 (1979) 197-224; especially *BSOAS* 40 (1977) 601-2.

1 Enoch **549.** Knibb, M. A. (in consulation with E. Ullendorf), *The Ethiopic Book of Enoch: A New Edition in the Light of the Aramaic Dead Sea Fragments* (2 vols.; Oxford: Clarendon, 1978). The first volume supplies the text and the *apparatus criticus* of Ethiopic Enoch, and the second volume an introduction, translation, and commentary on this text. It clearly supersedes all earlier editions of the Ethiopic text of *1 Enoch*.

> See *JBL* 99 (1980) 631-36; *CBQ* 43 (1981) 133-35; *RB* 87 (1980) 312-13.

TQHD **550.** Lohse, E., *Die Texte aus Qumran hebräisch und deutsch* (Munich: Kösel, 1964; 4th ed., 1986). This volume contains a pointed Hebrew text of major Qumran scrolls with a German translation facing it; brief notes are found in an appendix. The texts include the following: 1QS, 1QSa, 1QSb, CD, 1QH, 1QM, 1QpHab, 4QPB, 4QTestim, 4QFlor, 4QpNah, 4QpPs.

> See *Bib* 46 (1965) 257; *ATR* 47 (1965) 335-36; *BLE* 66 (1965) 199; *BZ* 9 (1965) 296-97; *ZAW* 76 (1964) 366.

PVTG   **551.** Pseudepigrapha Veteris Testamenti graece (ed. A. M. Denis and
          M. de Jonge; Leiden: Brill, 1964-   ). This series has been
          making available critical texts of various pseudepigrapha. So far
          the following volumes have appeared: (1/1) *Testamenta XII
          Patriarcharum: Edited according to Cambridge University Library
          MS Ff 1.24 fol. 203a-262b with Short Notes* (M. de Jonge, 1964);
          (1/2) *The Testaments of the Twelve Patriarchs: A Critical Edition
          of the Greek Text* (M. de Jonge, 1978); (2) *Testamentum Iobi*
          (S. P. Brock) and *Apocalypsis Baruchi graece* (J.-C. Picard, 1967);
          (3) *Apocalypsis Henochi graece* (M. Black) and *Fragmenta
          pseudepigraphorum quae supersunt graeca: Una cum historicorum
          et auctorum judaeorum hellenistarum fragmentis* (A.-M. Denis,
          1970). (4) *Apocalypsis Esdrae; Apocalypsis Sedrach; Visio beati
          Esdrae* (O. Wall, 1977).

          See *RB* 77 (1970) 416-17; *RTL* 1 (1970) 203-4.

SBLTT   **552.** Society of Biblical Literature Texts and Translations, Pseude-
          pigrapha Series (Missoula, MT [now Atlanta, GA]: Scholars,
          1972-   ). This series is under the editorship of R. A. Kraft. Of
          the 28 volumes in this series, the following belong to the category
          of pseudepigraphic intertestamental literature: (1) *Paraleipomena
          Jeremiou* (R. A. Kraft and A.-E. Purintun, 1972); (2) *The Testa-
          ment of Abraham: The Greek Recensions* (M. E. Stone, 1972); (3)
          The Hebrew Fragments of Pseudo-Philo's Liber antiquitatum
          biblicarum *Preserved in the Chronicles of Jeraḥmeel* (D. J.
          Harrington, 1974); (5) *The Testament of Job* (R. A. Kraft et al.,
          1974); (6) *The Armenian Version of the Testament of Joseph*
          (M. E. Stone, 1975); (8) *The Book of Baruch: Also Called I Baruch
          (Greek and Hebrew)* (E. Tov, 1975); (13) *The Odes of Solomon*
          (J. H. Charlesworth, 1978 [corrected reprint of Clarendon edition
          of 1973]); (17) *The History of the Rechabites* (J. H. Charlesworth,
          1982); (18) *The Books of Elijah* (M. E. Stone and J. Strugnell,
          1979); (19) *The Apocalypse of Elijah* (A. Pietersma et al., 1981);
          (20) *Fragments from Hellenistic Jewish Authors, Volume I:
          Historians* (C. R. Holladay, 1983): (25) *Sepher Ha-Razim: The
          Book of Mysteries* (M. A. Morgan, 1984).

JAL   **553.** Jewish Apocryphal Literature: Dropsie College Edition (ed. S.
          Zeitlin et al.; New York: Harper & Row, 1950-73). Each volume
          in the series contains an introduction, the original text, a transla-
          tion, and brief notes. So far seven volumes have appeared: (1) *The
          First Book of Maccabees* (S. Tedesche and S. Zeitlin, 1950); (2)
          Aristeas to Philocrates (Letter of Aristeas) (M. Hadas, 1951; re-
          pr., New York [now Hoboken, NJ]: Ktav, 1973); (3) *The Third
          and Fourth Books of Maccabees* (M. Hadas, 1953; repr., New
          York [now Hoboken, NJ]: Ktav, 1976); (4) *The Second Book of
          Maccabees* (S. Tedesche and S. Zeitlin, 1954); (5) *The Book of*

Wisdom (J. Reider, 1957); (6) *The Book of Tobit* (F. Zimmermann, 1958); (7) *The Book of Judith* (M.S. Enslin [Leiden: Brill], 1972).

C. Collections of Translations

554. Bonsirven, J., *La Bible apocryphe* (rev. M. Philonenko; Textes et études pour servir à l'histoire du judaïsme intertestamentaire; Paris: Cerf–Fayard, 1975). This book was first published by Bonsirven in 1953, but the new edition contains an important "avertissement" and bibliographical notes which cover literature up to 1973.

See *ETL* 30 (1954) 466.

APOT **555.** *Charles, R.H. (ed.), *The Apocrypha and Pseudepigrapha of the Old Testament* (2 vols.; Oxford: Clarendon, 1913). This work contains English translations, done by various scholars, of the apocryphal/deuterocanonical and pseudepigraphical literature related to the OT. There are also extensive introductions, critical and explanatory notes, and a detailed topical index. The pseudepigrapha include: *Jubilees, Letter of Aristeas, Books of Adam and Eve, Martyrdom of Isaiah, I Enoch, Testaments of the XII Patriarchs, Sibylline Oracles, Assumption of Moses, 2 Enoch, 2 Baruch, 3 Baruch, 4 Ezra, Psalms of Solomon, 4 Maccabees, Pirqe 'Abot, Ahiqar, Damascus Document*. Though this work has been replaced by the more modern translations edited by J.H. Charlesworth and H.D.F. Sparks, it retains its value because of its introductions, notes, and especially its index.

OTP **556.** **Charlesworth, J.H. (ed.), *The Old Testament Pseudepigrapha* (2 vols.; Garden City, NY: Doubleday, 1983, 1985). A collection of English translations of 65 pseudepigraphical texts related to the OT. Volume 1 contains apocalyptic literature and testaments; vol. 2, OT expansions and legends, wisdom and philosophical literature, prayers, psalms, odes, and fragments of lost Judeo-Hellenistic works. Each text is accompanied by a succinct introduction and brief critical notes. The translations have been freshly made from the best available critical texts of the pseudepigrapha, but they are very uneven in quality. All the texts found in R.H. Charles's *APOT* (§ 555) are included here except the *Zadokite Document* and *Pirqe 'Abot* (which do not belong in such a collection).

See *Bijdragen* 45 (1984) 432; *CurTM* 11 (1984) 336; *JJS* 35 (1984) 200-209; *BL* (1984) 22; *CBQ* 50 (1988) 288-91.

EWQ **557.** Dupont-Sommer, A., *The Essene Writings from Qumran* (Oxford: Blackwell, 1961; repr., Gloucester/Magnolia, MA: Peter Smith,

1973). This is the best translation of the Qumran Scrolls in English, since it supplies column and line numbers so that one can easily find the Qumran text or part of a text that one seeks. But the translation suffers from some of the peculiar interpretations of Dupont-Sommer. It was translated from the French second edition, *Les écrits esséniens découverts près de la Mer morte* (Paris: Payot, 1959) by G. Vermes. One will find here the translation of 1QS, 1QSa, 1QSb, CD, 1QM, 1QH, 1QpHab, 4QpNah, 4QpPs, 4QpIsaᵃ, 4QpHos, 4QpMic, 4QpZeph, 1QapGen, 4QTLevi, 4QDM, 4QFlor, 4QPB, 4QTestim, 4QPrNab, 4QMyst, 4QJN, 4QŠirŠabb. Unfortunately, it does not include the translation of some more recently published texts (e.g., 11QTemple).

See *RB* 68 (1961) 309-10; *Bib* 42 (1961) 121-22; *ZDMG* 110 (1960) 455-57; *ArOr* 29 (1961) 484-86.

JSHRZ   **558.** Jüdische Schriften aus hellenistisch-römischer Zeit (6 vols.; ed. W. G. Kümmel et al.; Gütersloh: Mohn, 1973-   ). This series is currently appearing in fascicles; it is eventually to include 49 apocryphal or deuterocanonical and pseudepigraphical writings. Each will be translated anew from the best modern critical text and commented on in historical-critical fashion. (I/1) H. Bardtke, *Zusätze zu Esther*; O. Plöger, *Zusätze zu Daniel* (1973); (I/2) W. Nikolaus, *Fragmente jüdisch-hellenistischer Historiker* 1976); (I/3) C. Habicht, *2. Makkabäerbuch: Historische und legendarische Erzählungen*, 1976); (II/1) E. Hammershaimb, *Das Martyrium des Jesaja*; N. Meisner, *Der Aristeasbrief* (1973); (III/1) J. Becker, *Die Testamente der zwölf Patriarchen* (1974); (IV/1) E. Osswald, *Das Gebet Manasses*; A. S. van der Woude, *Die fünf syrischen Psalmen* (1974); (IV/2) S. Holm-Nielsen, *Die Psalmen Salomos*, 1977); (V/1) W. Hage, *Die griechische Baruch- Apokalypse*; K. G. Eckart, *Das Apokryphon Ezechiel (1974); (V/2)* E. Branden- burger, *Himmelfahrt Moses*; A. F. J. Klijn, *Die syrische Baruch- Apokalypse*; U. B. Müller, *Die griechische Esra- Apokalypse*, 1976).

See *TRu* 44 (1979) 197-226; *ZAW* 86 (1974) 122-23; 87 (1975) 720; *JSJ* 4 (1973) 194-96; 5 (1974) 209-10; *TLZ* 101 (1976) 115-16, 500-502; *TPQ* 124 (1976) 76-77; *RB* 82 (1975) 313-14.

APAT   **559.** Kautzsch, E. (ed.), *Die Apocryphen und Pseudepigraphen des Alten Testaments* (2 vols.; Tübingen: Mohr, 1900). This is the German counterpart of *APOT* (§ 555). The pseudepigrapha that it includes are: *Letter of Aristeas, Jubilees, Martyrdom of Isaiah, Psalms of Solomon, 4 Maccabees, Sibylline Oracles, 1 Enoch, Assumption of Moses, 4 Ezra, 2 Baruch, 3 Baruch, Testaments of the XII Patriarchs, Life of Adam and Eve*. It is badly in need of revision and is, in fact, being replaced by JSHRZ (§ 558), but because of its introductions and notes, it retains some value.

560. Moraldi, L., *I manoscritti di Qumrān* (Classici delle religioni 13; Turin: Unione Tipografico-editrice, 1971). An excellent annotated Italian translation of most of the Qumran texts published up to 1970. Columns and lines are numbered to facilitate reference to them. The bibliographies need to be updated.

See *CBQ* 34 (1972) 95-97; *BeO* 13 (1971) 238; *Bib* 53 (1972) 575-79.

ASAB   **561.** Riessler, P., *Altjüdisches Schrifttum ausserhalb der Bibel übersetzt und erläutert* (Augsburg: B. Filser, 1928; repr., Heidelberg: F. H. Kerle, 1966). The collection of non-biblical Jewish texts that is here translated into German is much more extensive than those of *APOT* (§ 555) or *APAT* (§ 559). It contains many texts which are ordinarily very difficult to find, and so it serves a purpose, even though it is scarcely a critical translation. Charlesworth's *OTP* (§ 556) has a more modern treatment of most of these texts.

See *Bib* 9 (1928) 473-76; *OLZ* 33 (1930) 295.

AOT   **562.** **Sparks, H. F. D., *The Apocryphal Old Testament* (Oxford: Clarendon, 1984). This work was originally planned as the counterpart of M. R. James, *The Apocryphal New Testament* (§ 578), but it is really the successor of R. H. Charles's *APOT* (§ 555), though of different scope. The collection of texts includes none of the deuterocanonical OT books (in contrast to *APOT* 1), but includes 25 pseudepigraphical writings. The translation of each text has been produced afresh and is fitted out with a brief introduction and a bibliography (that lists the editions of the text, other translations, and general studies). In general, the translations are more carefully done than those in *OTP*.

See *CBQ* 50 (1988) 288-91; *BL* (1985) 143-45; *JTS* 37 (1986) 152-55; *ExpTim* 96 (1984-85) 291-92; *VT* 35 (1985) 506-7.

D. Studies and Tools

563. *Braun H., *Qumran und das Neue Testament* (2 vols.; Tübingen: Mohr [Siebeck], 1966). The first volume is a reprint of articles that originally appeared in *TRu* 28 (1962-63) 97-234; 29 (1963) 142-76, 189-260; 30 (1964) 1-38, 89-137. They surveyed in a remarkable way the relation between Qumran literature and the NT writings as discussed in the years 1950-1959. Comments follow chapters and verses of the NT books from Matthew to Revelation. The second volume is a synthetic treatment of theological subjects and themes in which Qumran parallels bear on those of the NT. The book contains abundant references to secondary literature, usually with an assessment of the contributions. It is an invaluable guide, even if one does not always agree

with Braun's judgments. Unfortunately, there is no counterpart
to it for the years after 1966.

See *RevQ* 6 (1967-69) 573-81; *Greg* 48 (1967) 601-2; *LW* 14 (1967)
216; *RSR* 56 (1968) 110-15; *ZRGG* 19 (1967) 278.

564. Daniélou, J., *Philon d'Alexandrie* (Les temps et les destins; Paris:
A. Fayard, 1958). An introductory survey of Philo's life and
times, his use of the OT, his mode of interpreting the OT, his
theology, and his spirituality.

See *Angelicum* 36 (1959) 247-48; *BLE* 60 (1959) 154-57; *RHE* 54
(1959) 300; *Bijdragen* 19 (1958) 318; *RSPT* 42 (1958) 556-57.

565. Denis, A.-M., *Introduction aux pseudépigraphes grecs d'ancien
Testament* (SVTP 1; Leiden: Brill, 1970). This is an excellent,
thorough introduction to the pseudepigrapha of the OT preserved
in Greek, either in their entirety or only in fragments. But there
are some problems in the presentation of material and in the
overwhelming bibliography.

See *TLZ* 96 (1971) 673-75; *ZAW* 83 (1971) 130; *BO* 28 (1971) 227-28;
ETL 47 (1971) 234-35; *NTS* 16 (1969-70) 348-53.

566. Goodenough, E. R., *An Introduction to Philo Judaeus* (New
Haven, CT: Yale; London: Oxford University, 1940; 2d ed.,
1962). A valuable introduction to Philo's writings, his political
thinking, his Jewishness, his metaphysics, ethics, and mysticism.
This book is written by a person who spent much of his life
studying Philo and who has written many large monographs on
him, but it is a book that students often find difficult. See § 569.

See *CP* 39 (1944) 123-25; *AJP* 64 (1943) 383.

567. Mayer, G., *Index philoneus* (Berlin/New York: de Gruyter, 1974).
This is a very useful index to the Greek vocabulary of Philo's
writings, based on the *editio princeps*. This is different from J. Lei-
segang's *index verborum* in the *editio princeps* of Cohn–Wendland
(§ 538), which did not pretend to be exhaustive, whereas this
index does.

See *EtClass* 43 (1975) 212-13; *Revue philosophique de Louvain* 74
(1976) 458-59.

568. **Rengstorf, K. H. (ed.), *A Complete Concordance to Flavius
Josephus* (4 vols.; Leiden: Brill, 1973, 1975, 1979, 1983). Rengstorf
and his collaborators worked for over 25 years to produce this
valuable concordance. There is nothing better for Josephus studies
in general. It is, however, not without its difficulties. Its exorbitant
price makes it possible only for rich libraries to acquire it.

See *JBL* 94 (1975) 628-31; 96 (1977) 132-34; 100 (1981) 151-54; 104
(1985) 739-42; *RB* 81 (1974) 152-53; 84 (1977) 147; 89 (1982) 148-49;
92 (1985) 581-89.

569. Sandmel, S., *Philo of Alexandria: An Introduction* (New York: Oxford University, 1979). This book has been written for those who are beginning their study of Philo. It has two main parts: the first discussing Philo's thought, and the second his relation to Palestinian Judaism, gnosticism, and Christianity. There is also a chapter on "Goodenough on Philo."

See *JBL* 100 (1981) 138-39.

570. Schalit, A., *Namenwörterbuch zu Flavius Josephus* (Leiden: Brill, 1968). This is actually Supplement I to Rengstorf's *Concordance* (§ 568). It is an index to the proper names in the writings of Josephus.

See *RSR* 58 (1970) 120; *REG* 83 (1970) 264-65; *RSO* 44 (1969) 252; *ZAW* 81 (1969) 429; *RB* 81 (1974) 152-53.

571. Slingerland, H. D., *The Testaments of the Twelve Patriarchs: A Critical History of Research* (SBLMS 21; Missoula, MT [now Atlanta, GA]: Scholars, 1977). After a brief introduction, the author surveys the five main periods of research into this pseudepigraphical writing (A.D. 1242 — 1883; 1884 — 1908; 1908 — 1951; 1952 — 1958; 1958 to the time of writing). The final chapter discusses the presuppositions, methodology, and a new approach to the problem of the origin of the Testaments.

See *JBL* 97 (1978) 594-95).

572. Thackeray, H. St. J. and R. Marcus, *A Lexicon to Josephus* (Paris: Geuthner, 1930, 1934, 1948, 1955). Only four fascicles of this important work have appeared (up to the Greek word *emphilochōrein*). They have been published by the Alexander Kohut Memorial Foundation for the Jewish Institute of Religion in New York. Since Marcus's death (1956), the lexicon had been entrusted to H. R. Mochring of Brown University, but he too has died.

See *RB* 41 (1932) 140-41.

573. Wahl, C. A., *Clavis librorum Veteris Testamenti apocryphorum philologica* (Leipzig: J. A. Barth, 1853). This book has been reissued under the editorship of J. B. Bauer, who has added a new appendix: Indicem verborum in libris pseudepigraphis usurpatorum (Graz: Akademische Druck- und Verlagsanstalt, 1972). This book illustrates the vocabulary of the Greek apocryphal and pseudepigraphical OT writings by comparison with examples drawn from Xenophon, Demosthenes, Lucian, Plutarch, etc. It was an old classic and has been improved by Bauer's appendix.

See *CBQ* 36 (1974) 437-38.

CHAPTER XIX

NT Apocrypha

Just as there grew up apocryphal writings based on the canonical books of the OT, so too there emerged a literature which took off from the NT writings. These writings are Gospels, Acts, Epistles, and Apocalypses, imitating the four main genres of the NT books. Some of these writings are known to stem from gnostic authors of the second century and later, and so the student will have to consult the items listed in Chapter XX as well as those given here. The entries are listed here in alphabetical order, without any attempt to distinguish or group them.

574. Amiot, F., *La Bible apocryphe: Evangiles apocryphes* (Textes pour l'histoire sacrée; Paris: Fayard, 1952). Despite its title, this book contains French translations not only of the apocryphal Gospels, but also of some of the Agrapha, apocryphal Acts, Epistles, and Apocalypses.

See *Bib* 35 (1954) 107.

575. *Charlesworth, J. H. (with J. R. Mueller et al.), *The New Testament Apocrypha and Pseudepigrapha: A Guide to Publications, with Excursuses on Apocalypses* (ATLA Bibliography series 17; London/Metuchen: American Theological Library Association and Scarecrow Press, 1987). This book includes a report on NT Apocrypha research, a survey of the Johannine Apocalypse, and a discussion of the continuum of Jewish and Christian Apocalypses. Then it provides a bibliographic guide to publications of 104 apocrypha and pseudepigrapha.

See *NovT* 31 (1989) 182-85.

CCSA   576. *Corpus Christianorum: Series apocryphorum* (Turnhout: Brepols, 1983). This is an important new series of Christian apocryphal writings. So far four vols. have appeared: 1-2. *Acta Iohannis* (ed. E. Junod and J.-D. Kaestli, 1983); 3. *Ecrits apocryphes sur les apôtres: Traduction de l'édition arménienne de Venise* (ed. L. Leloir, 1986); 5. *Acta Andreae: Praefatio — Commentarius* (ed. J.-M. Prieur, 1989). Several other vols. are in preparation.

See *ETL* 61 (1985) 200-202.

HSNTA   577. **Hennecke, E., *Neutestamentliche Apokryphen* (2 vols.; 3d ed., rev. W. Schneemelcher; Tübingen: Mohr [Siebeck], 1959, 1964). First published by Hennecke in 1904, under the title, *Handbuch zu den neutestamentlichen Apokryphen*, its second edition appeared in

1924 with the present title. The 3d ed. is a full revision, which contains large sections of gnostic texts of Nag Hammadi — those which were published up to that time. This has long been regarded the best text of NT Apocrypha because of its valuable introductions and bibliographies. The first volume of a completely revised 5th ed., bearing the name of W. Schneemelcher only, appeared in 1987. However, *HSNTA* contains none of the original texts (for which one can consult, for the Gospels, A. de Santos Otero [§ 581]). An English translation was prepared by R. M. Wilson, *New Testament Apocrypha* (2 vols.; London: Lutterworth; Philadelphia, PA; Westminster, 1963, 1965).

See *JTS* 25 (1923-24) 184-89, 422-25; *TS* 21 (1960) 292-94; 26 (1965) 116-18; *TQ* 139 (1959) 340-41; 144 (1964) 233-34; *TRu* 6 (1960-61) 84-85; 30 (1964) 278-79; *JBL* 83 (1964) 316-17, 428-31; 85 (1966) 524-25.

JANT **578.** James, M. R., *The Apocryphal New Testament: Being the Apocryphal Gospels, Acts, Epistles and Apocalypses* (Oxford: Clarendon, 1953). An excellent, one-volume collection of English translations of the most important NT Apocrypha; first published in 1924, it is somewhat out of date in its introductions and notes.

See *JTS* 26 (1924-25) 181-85; *RB* 33 (1924) 459-60.

579. *Klostermann, E., Apocrypha, I-IV* (KIT 3, 8, 11, 12; Berlin/New York: de Gruyter, 1921², 1929³, 1911², 1912²). These small manuals supply a form of the original text of various NT Apocrypha: (I) Fragments of the *Gospel of Peter, Apocalypse of Peter*, and *Kerygma Petri*; (II) Fragments of Gospels; (III) Agrapha, Slavonic Josephus, POxy 1911; (IV [ed. A. Harnack]) Apocryphal letters of Paul to the Laodiceans and the Corinthians. The text of other Apocrypha can be found in KIT 10 (*Assumption of Moses*); 31 (Frgs. of Apocryphal Gospels); 64 (*Odes of Solomon*); 152 (*Ep. Apostolorum*).

580. Michaelis, W., *Die apokryphen Schriften zum Neuen Testament übersetzt und erläutert* (Sammlung Dieterich 129; Bremen: Schünemann, 1956; 2d ed., 1958). A handy collection of NT Apocrypha for the general reader, gathered, translated, and commented on.

See *Scholastik* 32 (1957) 619-20; *BenMon* 33 (1957) 325-26.

581. **Santos Otero, A. de, *Los evangelios apócrifos: Colección de textos griegos y latinos, versión crítica, estudios introductorios, comentarios e ilustraciones* (3d ed.; BAC 148; Madrid: Edica, 1975). This is a very important edition of the apocryphal Gospels, supplying not only a Spanish translation of them, but also the original Greek and Latin texts. The introductions, comments, and notes are excellent. The first edition appeared in 1956; the second in 1963; the third was reprinted in 1979.

See *NRT* 85 (1963) 869; *WZKM* 55 (1959) 180-81.

582. Strycker, E. de, *La forme la plus ancienne du Protévangile de Jacques* (Subsidia hagiographica 33; Brussels: Bollandistes, 1961). The *Protevangelium of James* was sometimes called "Birth of Mary: Revelation of James." The form published here is from the 3d or 4th century A.D. It is important for the study of early mariology.

See *JBL* 80 (1961) 399; *RB* 69 (1962) 450-51; *Chronique d'Egypte* 37 (1962) 215-16; *JTS* 13 (1962) 408-12.

Chapter XX

Gnostic Materials

The influence of gnostic writings on those of the NT is a moot question today. Listed below are the main publications of gnostic texts from Nag Hammadi and of other gnostic texts, studies, and tools related to them.

583. Bianchi, U. (ed.), *Le origini dello gnosticismo. Colloquio di Messina* (Studies in the History of Religions — *Numen* Sup. 12; Leiden: Brill, 1967). A collection of important articles, written in English, French, German, and Italian, drawn from a colloquium held on gnosticism in 1966. They debate the idea of gnosticism, its origins, and its relation to the NT.

See *JBL* 89 (1970) 82-84; *Gnomon* 40 (1968) 451-54; *RHR* 173 (1968) 203-7; *ZRGG* 20 (1968) 177-78.

584. *Foerster, W. (ed.), *Die Gnosis* (2 vols.; Bibliothek der Alten Welt: Antike und Christentum; Zürich/Stuttgart: Artemis, 1969, 1971). Aided by E. Haenchen and M. Krause, Foerster has gathered an important collection of gnostic texts in these two volumes. Volume 1 gives the patristic evidence; vol. 2, Coptic and Mandean sources. An English translation has been prepared by R. M. Wilson: *Gnosis: A Selection of Gnostic Texts* (2 vols.; Oxford: Clarendon, 1972, 1974). A note to the English edition explains: "The actual texts, however, have been translated with the original at hand, and revised to ensure that they are really English translations and not merely at third hand through the German" (1.24).

See *CBQ* 36 (1974) 259; 37 (1975) 571-72; *TRev* 67 (1971) 533-34; *NedTTs* 25 (1971) 215-17.

585. Jonas, H., *Gnosis und spätantiker Geist* (2 vols.; FRLANT 51, 63; Göttingen: Vandenhoeck & Ruprecht, 1934, 1954; latest edition, 1966). An introduction to the study of gnosticism, written by a long-time student of it. There is an English translation of the book, *The Gnostic Religion: The Message of the Alien God and the Beginnings of Christianity* (Boston: Beacon, 1958; 2d ed., 1963). Whether all that is discussed in this book pertains to the "beginnings of Christianity" is questionable.

See *RSPT* 42 (1958) 562-63; *RTAM* 26 (1959) 150-51; *TLZ* 84 (1959) 813-20; 86 (1961) 26-31; *Commentary* 27 (1959) 81-82.

586. **Rudolph, K., *Die Gnosis: Wesen und Geschichte einer spätan-tiken Religion* (Leipzig: Koehler & Amelang, 1977). This work deals with the literary sources, the nature and structure of gnosticism, and its history. An important appendix contains a chronological table, notes, and select bibliography. The book has been translated into English by P. W. Coxon and K. H. Kuhn under the editorship of R. M. Wilson, *Gnosis: The Nature and History of Gnosticism* (Edinburgh: Clark, 1984; in paperback, San Francisco, CA: Harper & Row, 1987).

> See *ArOr* 48 (1980) 268-69; *BO* 36 (1979) 109-10; *ETR* 55 (1980) 158-59; *ExpTim* 90 (1978-79) 27; *Greg* 61 (1980) 169-70; *TLZ* 104 (1979) 500-502; *BSOAS* 48 (1985) 544-45; *SJT* 38 (1985) 264-66; *HR* 25 (1985-86) 282-84.

587. Wilson, R. M., *The Gnostic Problem* (London: Mowbrays, 1958). "An admirable survey of a topic which has not hitherto received adequate treatment" (R. A. Markus).

> See *NTS* 6 (1959-60) 99-100; *ExpTim* 70 (1958-59) 203-4; *ZRGG* 12 (1960) 94, 96; *RSR* 48 (1960) 610.

588. Yamauchi, E. M., *Pre-Christian Gnosticism: A Survey of the Proposed Evidences* (Grand Rapids, MI: Eerdmans, 1973). An examination of the patristic, Hermetic, Iranian, Syriac, Coptic, Mandaic, and Jewish evidence for pre-Christian gnosticism; the author criticizes modern scholars, especially Reitzenstein and Bultmann, for the claim of a pre-Christian redeemer myth. This book is not the last word, but it is pointing in a direction that needs serious consideration.

> See *JBL* 93 (1974) 482-84; *RB* 83 (1976) 468-69; *CBQ* 36 (1974) 296-97; *Louvain Studies* 5 (1974-75) 211-12.

FENHC
or
NHC

589. **The Facsimile Edition of the Nag Hammadi Codices (13 vols.; Leiden: Brill, 1972—84). Published under the auspices of the Department of Antiquities of the Arab Republic of Egypt in conjunction with the United Nations Educational, Scientific, and Cultural Organization, this deluxe publication contains excellent photographic reproductions of the various treatises in the thirteen codices retrieved. The thirteen volumes in the series are ordered thus: (1) Codex I (1977); (2) Codex II (1974); (3) Codex III (1976); (4) Codex IV (1975); (5) Codex V (1975); (6) Codex VI (1972); (7) Codex VII (1972); (8) Codex VIII (1976); (9) Cod. IX-X (1977); (10) Cod. XI-XIII (1973); (11) Cartonnage (1979); (12) Introduction (1984). These volumes are to be accompanied by a fifteen-volume series, Coptic Gnostic Library (§ 591), a series of translations and studies of the Coptic treatises. For an important introduction to these codices, see J. M. Robinson, "The Coptic Gnostic Library Today," *NTS* 14 (1967-68) 356-401.

CGL

> See *Bib* 59 (1978) 572-74; 56 (1975) 257-59; *CBQ* 39 (1977) 275-77.

NHS   **590.**   *Nag Hammadi Studies (ed. M. Krause et al.; Leiden: Brill 1971-). This is a series of important studies of the treatises of the Nag Hammadi find. So far 17 vols. have appeared in *NHS*. However, some of the vols. are part of a subseries, CGL, which is listed below: (1) *Nag Hammadi Bibliography 1948-1969* (D. M. Scholer, 1971; § 593); (2) *L'Evangile de Vérité* (J.-E. Ménard, 1972); (3) *Essays on the Nag Hammadi Texts in Honour of Alexander Böhlig* (ed. M. Krause, 1972); (5) *L'Evangile selon Thomas* (J.-E. Ménard, 1975); (6) *Essays on the Nag Hammadi Texts in Honour of Pahor Labib* (ed. M. Krause, 1975); (7) *Les textes de Nag Hammadi: Colloque du centre d'histoire des religions (Strasbourg, 23-25 octobre 1974)* (ed. J.-E. Ménard, 1975); (8) *Gnosis and Gnosticism* (ed. M. Krause, 1977); (10) *The Enthronement of Sabaoth: Jewish Elements in Gnostic Creation Myths* (F. T. Fallon, 1978); (12) *Die Polemik der Gnostiker gegen das kirchliche Christentum: Unter besonderer Berücksichtigung der Nag-Hammadi–Traktate 'Apokalypse des Petrus' (NHC VII,3) und 'Testimonium veritatis' (NHC IX,3)* (K. Koschorke, 1978); (14) *Nag Hammadi and Gnosis* (ed. R. McL. Wilson, 1978). (17) *Gnosis and Gnosticism: Papers Read at the Eighth International Conference on Patristic Studies (Oxford, September 3rd-8th 1979)* (ed. M. Krause, 1981). A preliminary form of the translations to be used in this series has been gathered into one volume (§ 592).

CGL   **591.**   The Coptic Gnostic Library: Edited with English Translation, Introduction and Notes (Leiden: Brill, 1975-). This may seem confusing, but this series is actually a subseries of NHS. The following volumes have appeared: (NHS 4) *Nag Hammadi Codices III,2 and IV,2: The Gospel of the Egyptians* (CGL; A. Böhlig et al., 1975); (NHS 9) *Pistis Sophia* (CGL; ed. C. Schmidt and V. MacDermot, 1978); (NHS 11) *Nag Hammadi Codices V,2-5 and VI with Papyrus Berolinensis 8502,1 and 4* (CGL; ed. D. M. Parrott, 1979); (NHS 13) *The Books of Jeu and the Untitled Text in the Bruce Codex* (CGL; ed. C. Schmidt and V. MacDermot, 1978); (NHS 15) *Nag Hammadi Codices IX and X* (CGL; B. A. Pearson, 1981); (NHS 16) *Nag Hammadi Codices: Greek and Coptic Papyri from the Cartonnage of the Covers* (CGL; J. W. B. Barns et al., 1981).

NHLE   **592.**   Robinson, J. M. (director), *The Nag Hammadi Library in English: Translated by Members of the Coptic Gnostic Library Project of the Institute for Antiquity and Christianity* (San Francisco, CA/New York: Harper & Row; Leiden: Brill, 1977). The editor of this volume was M. W. Meyer. This is the first publication of a full translation of the Nag Hammadi codices, found in Egypt in 1945, into any modern language. Some of the texts of this find had been known for some time previously and well worked over by scholars (e.g., *Gospel of Thomas, Gospel of Truth, Gospel of*

Philip), but for many of the texts this is the first attempt to translate them. The translation has, therefore, all the hazards of pioneer work. Forty-seven gnostic writings are presented here. A third edition, completely revised (ed. R. Smith, who has contributed an afterword, "The Modern Relevance of Gnosticism") appeared in 1988.

See *JBL* 97 (1978) 610-12; *CBQ* 41 (1979) 167-70; *Bib* 59 (1978) 574-76.

593.   *Scholer, D. M., *Nag Hammadi Bibliography 1945-1969* (NHS 1; Leiden: Brill, 1971). This is an invaluable bibliography for gnostic studies in general and for the Nag Hammadi treatises in particular. It treats the material under the following headings: (1) Gnosticism (in general); (2) Gnostic Texts (previously known: Codex Askewianus, Codex Brucianus, Codex Berolinensis, Bala'izah Gnostic Text, Hymn of the Pearl); (3) Gnostic Schools and Leaders; (4) NT and Gnosticism; (5) Qumran and Gnosticism; (6) Coptic Gnostic Library (General matters and specifics on Codices I-XIII). The continuation of this bibliography is found each year in *NovT* ("Bibliographia gnostica: Supplementum"), beginning with vol. 13 (1971). The 18th supplement appeared in *NovT* 31 (1989) 344-78.

See *BO* 29 (1972) 302-4; *RB* 80 (1973) 144-45.

594.   Siegert, F., *Nag-Hammadi–Register: Wörterbuch zur Erfassung der Begriffe in den koptisch-gnostischen Schriften von Nag-Hammadi* (WUNT 26; Tübingen: Mohr [Siebeck], 1982). This book lists all significant words in the Nag Hammadi and related texts, first Coptic, then Greek, and finally a German index.

See *Greg* 65 (1984) 755-56; *Augustinianum* 24 (1984) 581.

CHAPTER XXI

Early Literature of the Rabbinic Period
(A.D. 200-500)

Since the rabbinic writings are an outgrowth of the traditions current among the Pharisees, many scholars have sought to look to this literature to illustrate NT passages or the teaching of Jesus. The Mishnah, the earliest of this body of literature, was compiled ca. A.D. 200 by Rabbi Judah the Prince, and the question of the traditions found in it as pertinent to the NT has always been moot. The student of the NT has to learn to use this material with care. Listed below are: (A) Texts and translations; and (B) Tools and studies.

A. Texts and Translations

595. *Albeck, C. and H. Yalon, *Ššh sdry mšnh mpwršym bydy Ḥ. 'lbq wmnwqdym bydy Ḥ. Ylwn* [The Six Orders of the Mishnah Explained and Pointed] (Jerusalem: Bialik Institute; Tel Aviv: Dvir, 1952-59). A good modern edition of the Mishnah.

See *Eleven Years* (§ 7), 620-21; *KirSeph* 34 (1959) 274-80.

596. *Rengstorf, K.-H. and L. Rost (eds.), *Die Mischna: Text, Übersetzung und ausführliche Erklärung* (Berlin: Töpelmann, 1910-) Interrupted by the two wars, this series is being continued. It is often called the "Giessener Mischna" (having been published originally in Giessen). It gives the vocalized Hebrew text of the Mishnaic tractates, a German translation (facing the Hebrew), and a full commentary at the bottom of the pages. This is the best text for Christian scholars to consult when recourse to the original of the Mishnah is needed.

See *RB* 64 (1957) 148; 65 (1958) 150 51; 66 (1959) 627-28; 73 (1966) 308; *NRT* 80 (1958) 988.

597. *Danby, H., *The Mishnah, Translated from the Hebrew with Introduction and Brief Explanatory Notes* (Oxford: Clarendon, 1933; repr., 1954). This is the standard English translation of the whole Mishnah.

See *PEFQS* 67 (1935) 49-52; *JTS* 35 (1934) 332-33.

598. Neusner, J., *The Mishnah: A New Translation* (New Haven, CT/ London: Yale University, 1988). Aim: "to present the Mishnah in as close to a literal rendition of the Hebrew as is possible in American English" (p. ix). This translation is based on Neusner's

previous publications, *History of the Mishnaic Law of*... [various subjects] (Leiden: Brill, 1974-82). The translation is accompanied by a glossary of Mishnaic terms and an index.

599. *Lieberman, S., *The Tosefta according to Codex Vienna, with Variants from Codex Erfurt, Genizah Mss. and editio princeps (Venice 1521): Together with References to Parallel Passages in Talmudic Literature and a Brief Commentary* (2 vols.; New York: Jewish Theological Seminary, 1955, 1962). Volume 1 contains the order of Zera'im; vol. 2, the order of Mo'ed. The title of vol. 2 changed slightly. Lieberman has also published a more elaborate commentary on the Tosephta: *Tosefta kifshuṭah: A Comprehensive Commentary on the Tosefta* (5 vols.; New York: Jewish Theological Seminary, 1955-1962).

See *REJ* 223 (1964) 244-45; *KirSeph* 41 (1965-66) 344-55.

600. Kittel, G. and K. H. Rengstorf (eds.), *Rabbinische Texte* (Stuttgart: Kohlhammer). There are two important series in this collection: The first contains *Die Tosefta*, with the Hebrew text, German translation, and explanatory notes on the tractates; the second contains the *Tannaitische Midraschim* in a German translation, with explanatory notes. The collection was begun in 1930, but was interrupted in Nazi times and has been begun anew.

See *JTS* 34 (1933) 421-22; *RB* 63 (1956) 152-53; 64 (1957) 456; 66 (1959) 628-29; 68 (1961) 624-25; 70 (1963) 159.

601. *Lauterbach, J. Z., *Mkylt' drby Yšm'l: Mekilta de-Rabbi Ishmael: A Critical Edition on the Basis of the Manuscripts and Early Editions with an English Translation, Introduction and Notes* (3 vols.; Schiff Library of Jewish Classics; Philadelphia, PA: Jewish Publication Society of America, 1933-35; repr., 1949; paperback ed., 1976). In a format resembling the LCL, this is a handy critical edition of the Hebrew text and an English translation of an important part of the Tannaitic midrashim, containing haggada and halakha on the Book of Exodus (beginning with 12:1).

602. Neusner, J. (ed.), *The Talmud of the Land of Israel* (Chicago: University of Chicago, 1982-   ). This is a new multivolume translation of the Palestinian Talmud into English. So far there are 22 vols. Coming from a Palestinian tradition, it is naturally more of a reflection of the Judaism associated with the matrix of the Christian movement than the Babylonian Talmud (§ 605-8). This talmud antedates its Babylonian counterpart by about 50 years, roughly A.D. 450. Parts of the translation, especially those done by Neusner himself, have been severely criticized.

See *JAOS* 104 (1984) 315-19; *BARev* 11/2 (1985) 14-16.

603. Hengel, M. et al. (eds.), *Übersetzung des Talmud Jerushalmi* (?
      vols.; Tübingen: Mohr [Siebeck], 1980-   ). A fresh multivolume
      German translation of the Palestinian Talmud. So far 8 vols. have
      appeared: (1/4) Berakot (1980-81); (1/6) Terumot (1985); (2/11)
      Hagiga (1983); (4/4) Sanhedrin (1981); (4/5) Makkot (1983); (4/6)
      Shevuot (1983); (4/7) Aboda Zara (1980); (4/8) Horayot (1984).

      See *NRT* 105 (1983) 615; 106 (1984) 440-41; *JSJ* 15 (1984) 212-14;
      Greg 65 (1984) 731-33 66 (1985) 752-53; *Henoch* 7 (1985) 105-6.

604. Goldschmidt, L., *Der babylonische Talmud* (9 vols. [sometimes
      repr. in 13 vols.]; Berlin: Calvary, 1897-1935). In reality, vols. 1-3
      and 7 were published in Berlin (Calvary, 1897, 1901, 1899, 1903);
      vols. 4-6 and 8 were published in Leipzig (Harrassowitz, 1931,
      1912, 1906, 1909); and vol. 9 in The Hague (M. Nijhoff, 1935).
      This is a good edition of the Babylonian Talmud to consult, since
      it gives the text with a German translation. But it must be
      remembered that this talmud came into its final form ca. A.D.
      500 — and in Babylonia. It is questionable, therefore, to what
      extent one can appeal to what is found about Judaism in this
      talmud to interpret the NT. The date of the material must be kept
      in mind. There is also a concordance to this edition of the
      Babylonian Talmud: L. Goldschmidt, *'znym ltwrh: Subject Con-
      cordance to the Babylonian Talmud* (ed. R. Edelman; Copenhagen:
      Munksgaard, 1959).

605. Epstein, I. (ed.), *The Babylonian Talmud* (35 vols.; London:
      Soncino, 1935-52). A modern translation of the complete Baby-
      lonian Talmud.

      See *RSR* 26 (1936) 229-30.

606. Epstein, I. (ed.), *Hebrew–English Edition of the Babylonian Talmud*
      (London: Soncino, 1960-   ). This is a folio-size publication with
      notes, glossary, and indices. So far 22 vols. have been issued, many
      of them in the 1980s.

607. Neusner, J. (ed.), *The Talmud of Babylonia: An American Trans-
      lation* (Brown Judaic Studies; Atlanta, GA: Scholars, 1984-   ).
      This translation is destined to fill 36 volumes, of which the
      following have already appeared: I (Berakot, 1984); VI (Sukkah,
      1984); VII (Besah, 1986); XVII (Sotah, 1984); XXIIIA (Sanhe-
      drin, chaps. 1-3, 1984); XXIIIB (Sanhedrin, chaps. 4-8, 1984);
      XXIIIC (Sanhedrin, chaps. 9-11, 1984); XXVI (Horayot, 1987);
      XXXII (Arakhin, 1984); XXXV (Meilah and Tamid, 1986).

      See *RB* 93 (1986) 623.

608. Freedman, H. and M. Simon (eds.), *Midrash Rabbah* (10 vols.;
      London–Bournemouth: Soncino, 1951). The first nine volumes

contain a modern English translation of the Great Midrash on Genesis (2 vols.), Exodus, Leviticus, Numbers (2 vols.), Deuteronomy, and Lamentations, Ruth, and Ecclesiastes. Volume 10 contains a useful glossary, general index, and scriptural references.

609. Wünsche, A., *Bibliotheca rabbinica: Eine Sammlung alter Midraschim zum ersten Male ins Deutsche übertragen* (12 vols.; Leipzig, 1880-85; repr. in 5 vols.; Hildesheim: Olms, 1967). A German translation (with notes and emendations) of rabbinic midrashim. The reprinted vol. 1 contains *Der Midrasch Kohelet* and *Bereschit Rabba*; vol. 2, *Schir ha-Schirim, Esther*, and *Echa Rabbati*; vol. 3, *Schemot Rabba, Debarim Rabba*, and *Ruth Rabba*; vol. 4, *Bemidbar Rabba* and *Mischle*; vol. 5, *Wajikra Rabba* and *Pesikta de Rab Kahana*.

B. Studies and Tools

610. *Albeck, C., *Einführung in die Mischna* (SJud 6; Berlin/New York: de Gruyter, 1971). This is a German translation of *Mābô' lammišnāh* (Jerusalem: Bialik Institute; Tel Aviv: Dvir, 1960). This is an indispensable book for an understanding of the Mishnah; it explains all aspects of the writing (its name, oral form, redaction, order, language, and sages quoted).

See *Bible Bibliography* (§ 7), 409; *JSJ* 2 (1971-72) 183-84; *LR* 22 (1972) 235-36; *ZAW* 84 (1972) 118.

611. Bonsirven, J., *Le judaïsme palestinien aux temps de Jésus-Christ: Sa théologie* (2 vols.; Bibliothèque de théologie historique; 2d ed.; Paris: Beauchesne, 1934-35). Though the materials discussed are gathered under headings which are not very appropriate (1. la théologie dogmatique; 2. théologie morale, vie morale et religieuse), one can still find many good things in this synthetic approach to Palestinian Judaism. However, one must realize that Bonsirven tends to date things found in the talmuds and midrashim to the "time of Jesus Christ," without justifying such dating.

See *NRT* 63 (1936) 83-86; *JTS* 37 (1936) 85-87; *RB* 45 (1936) 263-65; *Scholastik* 11 (1936) 104-6.

612. Bonsirven, J., *Textes rabbiniques des deux premiers siècles chrétiens pour servir à l'intelligence du Nouveau Testament* (Rome: Biblical Institute, 1955). A collection of texts in French translation, excerpted from *Pirqe 'Abot, Tannaitic Midrashim*, the *Mishnah, Talmuds*, and *Tosephot*, arranged not according to passages of the NT, but according to the rabbinic tractates themselves. Useful indices facilitate the study of themes, OT passages cited, and the

NT passages which the rabbinic material may illustrate. The student should scrutinize the date of each text consulted in this collection and not be misled by the claim in the title that all these texts come "from the two first Christian centuries." Most of them are of a later date, and there has to be a reason for postulating an earlier dating.

See *CBQ* 17 (1955) 664; *RB* 63 (1956) 153-54; *NTS* 2 (1955-56) 209-12.

613. Bousset, W., *Die Religion des Judentums im späthellenistischen Zeitalter* (HNT 21; 3d ed.; ed. H. Gressmann; Tübingen: Mohr [Siebeck], 1926). Even though parts of this work are now outdated (largely because of the discovery of the Dead Sea Scrolls), it has long been the classic introduction to Jewish religion in the last pre-Christian centuries and to the theology and sects of Judaism and its apocryphal/deuterocanonical and pseudepigraphical writings.

See *RB* 12 (1903) 620-25.

614. Kasovsky (Kosowski), C. Y., *'ôṣar lĕšôn hammišnāh: Thesaurus Mishnae: Concordantiae verborum* ... (4 vols.; 2d ed.; Jerusalem: Massadah Publishing Co., 1967). This edition of a useful concordance to the Hebrew text of the Mishnah has been revised by the author's son Moshe.

615. *Moore, G. F., *Judaism in the First Centuries of the Christian Era: The Age of the Tannaim* (3 vols.; Cambridge, MA: Harvard University, 1927-30). This critical evaluation of Palestinian Judaism has become a classic, despite the fact that Moore sometimes dates some of the material too early and understands "Palestinian Judaism" solely from the viewpoint of the Pharisaic-rabbinic side. Some of this work's conclusions and observations are in need of revision, given the discovery of the Dead Sea Scrolls and the light shone on a quite different type of Palestinian Judaism, actually prior to and contemporary with the rise of Christianity. Hence, Moore's book is today to be used with discernment.

See *ExpTim* 39 (1927-28) 374-78; *JTS* 29 (1927-28) 60-65; *RHE* 24 (1928) 393-97; *RHPR* 7 (1927) 576-77.

616. *Neusner, J., *The Rabbinic Traditions about the Pharisees before 70 A.D.* (3 vols.; Leiden: Brill, 1971). Volume 1 presents passages attributed to pre-70 teachers in translation (with commentary), arranged according to sages; vol. 2, materials associated with the houses of Shammai and Hillel; vol. 3, literary and historical conclusions about these traditions. It is a modern attempt to use source- and form-criticism on the earliest parts of the rabbinic traditions. "For the present, NT scholars should carefully consider the preliminary results reached in N.'s study" (A. J. Saldarini).

See *CBQ* 35 (1973) 258-61; *JSJ* 3 (1972-73) 71-72; *Theology* 76 (1973) 269-70; *Bible Bibliography* (§ 7), 483.

617. Segal, M. H., *A Grammar of Mishnaic Hebrew* (Oxford: Clarendon, 1927; repr., 1958, 1978). This was intended to be a companion to GKC (§ 256) for the Hebrew language of the Mishnaic period. A revised form of it was later published in modern Hebrew, *Diqdûq lĕšôn hammišnāh* (Tel Aviv: Dvir, 1936).

(For a dictionary of Mishnaic Hebrew, consult § 221, 222, 222a.)

618. **Strack, H. L. and G. Stemberger, *Einleitung in Talmud und Midrasch* (7th ed.; Munich: Beck, 1982). This is a fully reworked edition of Strack's original *Einleitung in Talmud und Midraš* (Munich: Beck, 1887; 4th ed., 1907; 6th ed., 1976). It has become the standard introductory book for students who seek to initiate themselves into the mysteries of rabbinic literature. An English version of the earlier form exists: *Introduction to the Talmud and Midrash* (Philadelphia, PA: Jewish Publication Society of America, 1931; repr., New York: Atheneum, 1969). This version was produced from Strack's revision of the fifth German edition (1921). It is hoped that the new edition will be translated into English.

See *ZKT* 45 (1921) 293-97; *JTS* 23 (1921) 200-203; *TTZ* 92 (1983) 237-38; *TRu* 48 (1983) 387-88; *RelStRev* 8 (1982) 389; *TPQ* 130 (1982) 387; *RHPR* 64 (1984) 75-76; *TRev* 80 (1984) 18-21.

Str-B   **619.** *[Strack, H. L. and] P. Billerbeck, *Kommentar zum Neuen Testament aus Talmud und Midrasch* (6 vols.; Munich: Beck, 1922, 1924, 1926, 1928, 1924, 1956, 1961). Volume 4 appeared in two parts, the second before the first, vols. 1-4 are of the unchanged 4th edition. Volumes 5-6 were prepared by J. Jeremias (aided by K. Adolph) and contain a rabbinic index, a list of the sages quoted, and a geographical index. A 2d ed. of vols. 5-6 appeared in 1963, and the first four volumes were reprinted in 1965. Many modern scholars do not like to refer to this commentary as "Strack–Billerbeck," because in reality, as J. Jeremias writes in the preface to vol. 5, Billerbeck was "the sole author of the commentary" (der alleinige Verfasser des Kommentars). But "Str–B" has become such a commonly used siglum for this work that it is retained here. This commentary gives abundant citations from rabbinic writings to illustrate NT verses. The vast majority of the rabbinic material stems from a much later date, and students must learn to pay attention to the dates often supplied by Billerbeck after the citations or learn the dates of the sages quoted (see vol. 6), so that they will not simplistically predicate all such material of the first century A.D. Moreover, it should be recalled that the rabbinic writings used by Billerbeck were limited and that much more material can often be found in the targums (almost wholly neglected by him). Volume 4 (in two parts) contains some good excursus.

See *ZNW* 22 (1923) 156-57; *ZKT* 47 (1923) 577-80; *JBL* 81 (1962) 93-94; *RB* 64 (1957) 148-49; 69 (1962) 467-68; *VC* 16 (1962) 53.

620. *The Study of Judaism: Bibliographical Essays* (New York: Anti-Defamation League of B'nai B'rith, 1972). Two sections in this work will be of interest to the student of NT writings: "Rabbinic Sources" (J. T. Townsend, pp. 37-80), and "Judaism in New Testament Times" (R. Bavier, pp. 7-34).

CHAPTER XXII

Greek and Roman Cultural and Religious Milieu of the NT

Since Christianity emerged in the Roman empire and in a part of the world that was heavily hellenized, the question of the bearing of that background, especially its cultural and religious aspects, on the writings of the NT has often been raised. Listed below are important works that discuss Greek and Roman religions about the time of the emergence of the NT.

621. Cumont, F., *Les mystères de Mithra* (3d ed.; Brussels: H. La-mertin, 1913). This has been the classic discussion of the Mithra mysteries, which formed part of the religious background of the NT in the roman empire. A translation of the second French edition was produced, *The Mysteries of Mithra* (Chicago: Open Court, 1903); its French form was published in Paris (A. Fonte-moing, 1902).

   See *REG* 27 (1914) 338-39.

622. Ulansey, D., *The Origins of the Mithraic Mysteries: Cosmology and Salvation in the Ancient World* (London/New York: Oxford University, 1990). Ulansey challenges the prevailing theory that Mithraism is derived from ancient Iranian religion and offers an impressive array of arguments — iconographic, geographic, mythological, numismatic, and literary — to show that the focus of the cult was based on an astronomical code, which began as a religious reaction to a new scientific discovery.

623. Finegan, J., *Myth & Mystery: An Introduction to the Pagan Religions of the Biblical World* (Grand Rapids, MI: Baker, 1989). The author treats of Mesopotamian, Egyptian, Zoroastrian, Canaanite, Greek, Roman, Gnostic, Mandaean, and Manichaean religions. A very useful and readable survey.

624. Cumont, F., *Les religions orientales dans le paganisme romain* (2d ed.; Paris: Geuthner, 1909); a 4th ed. of the French appeared in 1929. An English version of the 2d ed. was published: *The Oriental Religions in Roman Paganism* (Chicago: Open Court, 1911). The book is a condensed form of various lectures delivered by Cumont at the Collège de France, describing the influence of various oriental cultures and religions on that of Rome. The book discusses the influence of the cult of Cybele, Ma, Men, Sabazius of Asia Minor, of Isis and Serapis of Egypt, of *Dea Syria* and her

baals, and the Mithra of Persia, as well as of oriental astrology and magic. The book has been regarded as a classic for years.

See *REG* 21 (1908) 99-100; *PTR* 11 (1913) 130-33.

625. *Reitzenstein, R., *Die hellenistischen Mysterienreligionen nach ihren Grundgedanken und Wirkungen* (3d ed.; Leipzig/Berlin: Teubner, 1927; repr., Stuttgart: Teubner, 1956, 1973). Originally, this was a lecture delivered in 1909; it was subsequently published in 1910; the third edition retains the lecture format, although it is expanded (pp. 1-91), and 20 additional appendices or excursus have been supplied. They discuss many aspects of the Greek mystery-religions and their alleged influence on NT writers, especially on Paul. An English translation of this important treatment has at length been produced, *Hellenistic Mystery-Religions: Their Basic Ideas and Significance* (Pittsburgh Theological Monograph Series 15; Pittsburgh, PA: Pickwick, 1978).

See *RB* 37 (1928) 153-56.

626. Grant, F. C. (ed.), *Hellenistic Religions: The Age of Syncretism* (Library of Religion, 2; New York: Liberal Arts, 1953). This collection of texts in translation offers readings in four aspects of ancient syncretism: (1) institutional religion; (2) criticism of traditional religion; (3) major cults (Orphic, Oriental, Egyptian, Attis, Mithras); (4) religious ideas of the philosophers (Epictetus, Epicurus, Plotinus, Proclus, Iamblichus, and Sallustius). The collection is quite handy and useful, but one may not always agree with the interpretations of the editor.

See *JR* 35 (1955) 125-26; *JNES* 14 (1955) 195-96; *CBQ* 16 (1954) 501-2.

627. *Nilsson, M. P., *Geschichte der griechischen Religion* (Handbuch der klassischen Altertumswissenschaft [ed. I. von Müller] 5/2; 2 vols.; Munich: Beck, 1941, 1950; rev. ed., 1961², 1967³). Volume 1 treats of Greek religion until the time of Alexander; vol. 2, that of the Hellenistic and Roman period. This is the standard treatment of Greek religion in the classical, Hellenistic, and Roman periods. An English translation of an earlier edition exists, *A History of Greek Religion* (tr. from Swedish; Oxford: Clarendon, 1925; 2d ed., 1963; New York: Norton, 1964).

See *CP* (1965) 48-49.

628. Festugière, A.-J., *L'Idéal religieux des Grecs et l'évangile* (EBib; Paris: Gabalda, 1932). The book is divided into three parts: (1) La philosophie (Plato, Aristotle, Epicurus, the Stoics, Neo-Pythagorianism); (2) La religion (failure of the philosophers, fate, cultic and literary mysteries, mysticism, popular belief in immortality, deliverance); and (3) Excursus (The origin of the idea of God in

Plato; body-soul-spirit [1 Thess 5:23] and Greek philosophy; Aristotle in the Christian Greek tradition up until Theodoret; St. Paul and Marcus Aurelius; and the religious value of the magical papyri).

See *Etudes* 216 (1933) 102-3; *Greg* 14 (1933) 287-91; *NRT* 60 (1933) 448-53; *RB* 43 (1934) 610-11; *TLZ* 59 (1934) 3-5.

629. Places, E. des, *La religion grecque: Dieux, cultes, rites et sentiment religieux dans la Grèce antique* (Paris: Picard, 1969). Greek religion is discussed under three main headings: (1) the gods, demons, and heroes; their feasts and cults; (2) development of a religious sense in the poets and other writers; and (3) the spiritual climate among the Greeks at the time of the emergence of Christianity and (more specifically) of Paul's address on the Areopagus.

See *Gnomon* 44 (1972) 230-35: *CWorld* 64 (1971) 88-89; *EtClass* 38 (1970) 373-74.

630. Grant, F. C. (ed.), *Ancient Roman Religion* (Library of Religion 8; New York: Liberal Arts, 1957). This collection of texts in translation from ancient Latin writers and inscriptions illustrates various phases of Roman religion: (1) old agricultural religion; (2) foreign influences; (3) philosophy and religion; (4) religion under the imperial republic; (5) the Augustan restoration; (6) religion under the empire; (7) the Christian victory and the pagan reaction.

See *CBQ* 20 (1958) 130-32; *Gnomon* 31 (1959) 83-85.

631. *Latte, K., *Römische Religionsgeschichte* (Handbuch der klassischen Altertumswissenschaft 5/4; Munich: Beck, 1960). This is a standard reference work on Roman religion, replacing the older work in the same series by G. Wissowa, *Religion und Kultus der Römer* (1912). Latte's exposé is historical, not systematic, in its presentation.

See *Bib* 42 (1961) 381-82; *Mnemosyne* 15 (1962) 84-93; *EtClass* 29 (1961) 229-30.

632. Lohse, E., *Umwelt des Neuen Testaments* (GNT 1; 7th rev. ed.; Göttingen: Vandenhoeck & Ruprecht, 1986). This work was first published in 1971; a 4th revised ed. appeared in 1978. It is divided into two main parts: (1) Judaism in the time of the NT (the political history of Palestine since Persian times; religious movements among the Jews of Palestine and in the diaspora; Jewish life and Jewish beliefs); and (2) the Hellenistic-Roman world of the NT (society and politics in the Roman empire in the first century; religious movements in the Hellenistic-Roman world; gnosticism). A French version exists, *Le milieu du*

Nouveau Testament (Etudes annexes de la Bible de Jérusalem; Paris: Cerf, 1973).

See *Bijdragen* 32 (1971) 324; *CBQ* 34 (1972) 87-88; *ETL* 50 (1974) 346; *TRu* 37 (1972) 90-91.

633. Wendland, P., *Die hellenistisch-römische Kultur in ihren Beziehungen zum Judentum und Christentum* (HNT 2; 4th ed., rev. by H. Dörrie; Tübingen: Mohr [Siebeck], 1972). This book was first published by a professor of classical philology in 1912 and has become a classic (*Standardwerk*) in the field. The 4th ed. is expanded and provides modern bibliography. An Italian version exists: *La cultura ellenistico-romana nei suoi rapporti con Giudaismo e Cristianesimo* (tr. G. Firpo; Biblioteca di storia e storiografia dei tempi biblici 2; Brescia: Paideia, 1986).

See *BO* 31 (1974) 140-41; *Studia Monastica* 15 (1973) 544-45.

CHAPTER XXIII

Hermeneutics

The question of the philosophic presuppositions with which one approaches and interprets the Bible inevitably arises. It arises because of the variety of presuppositions, which cannot be easily grouped. The following aspects will be listed under these headings: (A) History of the interpretation of the OT and the NT; (B) Exegetical methods and principles; and (C) the relation of the interpretation of the Bible to Church teaching.

A. History of the Interpretation of the OT and the NT

634. Clements, R. E., *One Hundred Years of Old Testament Interpretation* (Philadelphia, PA: Westminster, 1976; the British title is: *A Century of...* [Guilford/London: Lutterworth]). This is a brief survey of "the main lines of interpretation which have affected the study of the Old Testament, with a particular emphasis upon questions of methodology" (p. vii). It concentrates "upon the work of a few scholars whose contributions appear... to have been particularly significant and interesting" (ibid.). The survey treats of the interpretation of the pentateuch, historical books, prophets, psalms, wisdom literature, and OT theology.

   See *ExpTim* 88 (1976-77) 120; *AUSS* 15 (1977) 227-28; *PSB* 2 (1978) 63-65.

635. *Kümmel, W. G., *Das Neue Testament: Geschichte der Erforschung seiner Probleme* (2d ed.; Freiburg: K. Alber, 1970). This book first appeared in 1958 and surveyed the fields of NT scholarship from 1700 to 1930. Though it is not an introduction in the strict sense of the term, this book is a very important tool for the student, since it enables one to gain something of a perspective about methodology in German Protestant NT scholarship. It is lean on contributions from British or French quarters. An English translation of the 2d ed. exists: *The New Testament: The History of the Investigation of Its Problems* (Nashville, TN: Abingdon, 1972).

   See *TRu* 36 (1971) 378-79; *CBQ* 35 (1973) 395-96; *ATR* 55 (1973) 234-37; *ExpTim* 84 (1972-73) 344; *Int* 27 (1973) 353-58; *TS* 34 (1973) 295-97.

636. Kümmel, W. G., *Das Neue Testament im 20. Jahrhundert: Eine Forschungsbericht* (SBS 50; Stuttgart: Katholisches Bibelwerk, 1970). This report originally formed part of *Bilanz der Theologie im*

20. Jahrhundert: Perspektiven, Strömungen, Motive in der christlichen und nichtchristlichen Welt (4 vols.; ed. H. Vorgrimler and R. VanderGucht; 2d ed.; Freiburg im B.: Herder, 1970) 2. 279-371.

637. Neill, S., *The Interpretation of the New Testament 1861-1961* (Firth Lectures, University of Nottingham 1962; London/New York: Oxford University, 1964). This is a survey of how NT problems have been analyzed and handled since the use of modern historical and critical scholarship, roughly since 1835, D. F. Strauss's *Leben Jesu.* It is a counterbalance to W. G. Kümmel's *Geschichte* (§ 635), because it covers much of the British contribution. But it is neglectful of American and Roman Catholic contributions. This has been remedied a bit in the new second edition, but not to the extent that it should have been. See S. Neill and T. Wright, *The Interpretation of the New Testament 1861-1986* (Oxford/New York: Oxford University, 1988).

See *JBL* 83 (1964) 427-28; *Bib* 45 (1964) 454; *RB* 72 (1965) 135-37; *Greg* 46 (1965) 124-27.

B. Exegetical Methods and Principles

638. *Kaiser, O. and W. G. Kümmel, *Einführung in die exegetischen Methoden* (2d ed.; Munich: Kaiser, 1964). The explanation of OT exegesis has been written by Kaiser, and that of NT exegesis by Kümmel. Part of it has been rendered into English, *Exegetical Method: A Student's Handbook* (New York: Seabury, 1967). The German original contained a third essay, "Zur wissenschaftlichen Arbeitsweise," which has not been translated, because it is oriented to the special circumstances of a German university. English-speaking students can find the counterpart of it elsewhere.

See *ZAW* 76 (1964) 229; *NTA* 8 (1963-64) 457.

639. Schreiner, J. (ed.), *Einführung in die Methoden der biblischen Exegese* (Würzburg: Echter-V.; Innsbruck: Tyrolia, 1971). Various German exegetes have contributed essays on aspects of biblical interpretation in this collaborative work. It covers methods for both Testaments.

See *MTZ* 22 (1971) 164-66; *TPQ* 119 (1971) 361-62; *ZAW* 83 (1971) 419-20; *TRev* 69 (1973) 9-11.

640. Marshall, I. H. (ed.), *New Testament Interpretation: Essays on Principles and Methods* (Grand Rapids, MI: Eerdmans, 1977). A series of 18 essays written by conservative evangelical NT scholars on the background of the interpretation of the NT, the use of critical methods in that interpretation, the task of exegesis, and the NT and the modern reader.

See *CBQ* 40 (1978) 660-61; *NTA* 22 (1978) 323; *Churchman* 92 (1978) 53-55.

641. Zimmermann, H., *Neutestamentliche Methodenlehre: Darstellung der historisch-kritischen Methode* (6th ed.; Stuttgart: Katholisches Bibelwerk, 1978). This book presents a thorough and systematic introduction into the methods of textual criticism, literary criticism, form criticism, and redaction criticism; and in each instance the formal discussion is followed by exercises, i.e., work on specific NT passages. A Spanish translation of it exists, *Los métodos histórico-criticos en el Nuevo Testamento* (BAC 295; Madrid: Edica, 1969); also an Italian, *Metodologia del Nuovo Testamento: Esposizione del metodo storico-critico* (Turin: Marietti, 1971).

See *CBQ* 30 (1968) 136-37; 33 (1971) 156-58; *RB* 77 (1970) 449-50; 79 (1972) 314.

642. Strecker, G. and U. Schnelle, *Einführung in die neutestamentliche Exegese* (3d ed.; UTB 1253; Göttingen: Vandenhoeck & Ruprecht, 1988). This is not an introduction to the NT, but rather a guide to NT exegetical method. It was first published in 1983, and revised in 1985. It deals with interpretative tools, textual criticism, textual analysis, source criticism, form criticism, comparative religions, redactional criticism, and hermeneutics.

643. Stuhlmacher, P., *Schriftauslegung auf dem Wege zur biblischen Theologie* (Göttingen: Vandenhoeck & Ruprecht, 1975). An attempt to get historical-critical interpretation of the Bible to come closer to the needs of Christian theology. One chapter, "Historische Kritik und theologische Schriftauslegung" (pp. 59-127), has been translated into English, *Historical Criticism and Theological Interpretation of Scripture* (Philadelphia, PA: Fortress, 1977).

See *CBQ* 39 (1977) 160-62; *JBL* 95 (1976) 325-26.

644. Koch, K., *Was Ist Formgeschichte? Neue Wege der Bibelexegese* (Neukirchen-Vluyn: Neukirchener V., 1964; 2d ed., 1967). It is "a first-rate introduction to the form criticism of the OT" (A. Di Lella). Part I deals with the fundamentals and implications of form criticism, and part II applies the form-critical method to selected OT examples. An English version exists, *The Growth of the Biblical Tradition: The Form-Critical Method* (New York: Scribner, 1969).

See *CBQ* 31 (1969) 575-78; *JBL* 89 (1970) 242-43; *Dialog* 5 (1966) 145-47; *NedTTs* 21 (1966) 47-48; *TP* 41 (1966) 112-15; *JTS* 18 (1967) 164-66; *RB* 74 (1967) 440; *TLZ* 92 (1967) 758-59.

645. Guides to Biblical Scholarship (Philadelphia, PA: Fortress, 1969-   ). This is a series of paperbacks which seeks to explain various methods employed in biblical interpretation today;

they are edited by D. O. Via, Jr. The series is a contribution
to biblical hermeneutics, but not all the booklets are of equal
value, nor is each method described of equal effectiveness. Some
of the methods are of dubious merit. The series includes the
following studies: *What Is Form Criticism?* (E. V. McKnight,
1969); *What Is Redaction Criticism* (N. Perrin, 1969); *Literary
Criticism of the New Testament* (W. Beardslee, 1970); *Literary
Criticism of the Old Testament* (N. C. Habel, 1971); *Form
Criticism of the Old Testament* (G. Tucker, 1971); *Tradition
History and the Old Testament* (W. E. Rast, 1972); *Letters in
Primitive Christianity* (W. G. Doty, 1973); *Textual Criticism of
the Old Testament* (R. W. Klein, 1974); *The Historical-Critical
Method* (E. Krentz, 1975); *The Old Testament and the Historian*
(J. M. Miller, 1976); *What Is Structural Exegesis?* (D. Patte,
1976); *The Old Testament and the Literary Critic* (D. Robertson,
1977); *Literary Criticism for New Testament Critics* (N. R.
Peterson, 1978).

646. Bultmann, R. and K. Kundsin, *Form Criticism: Two Essays on
New Testament Research* (New York: Harper & Row, 1962;
originally, Chicago: Willet, Clark & Co., 1934). The first essay is
Bultmann's "The Study of the Synoptic Gospels," a translation of
Die Erforschung der synoptischen Evangelien (2d ed.; Giessen:
Töpelmann, 1930), a popular exposé of the methods used in his
History of the Synoptic Tradition (Oxford: Blackwell, 1968; from
the German 2d ed., *Geschichte der synoptischen Tradition*
(Göttingen: Vandenhoeck & Ruprecht, 1931]). Bultmann con-
tributed a special preface to the Torchbook edition. The second
essay is Kundsin's "Primitive Christianity in the Light of Gospel
Research," a translation of *Das Urchristentum im Lichte der
Evangelienforschung* (Giessen: Töpelmann, 1929). Both set forth
the principles of form criticism.

See *RB* 39 (1930) 623-25.

647. Gadamer, H. G., *Wahrheit und Methode* (Tübingen: Mohr [Sie-
beck], 1965). In English: *Truth and Method* (New York: Seabury,
1975; Crossroad, 1982). An overrated discussion of biblical interpretation produced by a philosopher.

See *TP* 41 (1966) 450-51; *TTZ* 75 (1966) 360-62; *TS* 37 (1976) 490-92;
BT 28 (1977) 335-42.

648. Ricœur, P., *Essays on Biblical Interpretation* (ed. L. S. Mudge;
Philadelphia, PA: Fortress, 1980). This is a collection of four
essays originally published elsewhere (two of them in French) that
try to cope with the problem of biblical interpretation. Yet Ricœur
is neither a theologian nor a biblical scholar, but rather a philosopher who tries to bring to biblical interpretation philosophy,

psychology, text-linguistics, and literary criticism. Many hope that the study of such disciplines will shed light on the interpretation of the Bible. But the real question is, "Can the special problems of Bible and theology be solved through absorption into the general intellectual culture, without commencing a fresh circle of uncertainty?" (J. Barr).

See *ATR* 63 (1981) 314-16; *RevExp* 78 (1981) 418-20; *Theology* 84 (1981) 462-64.

649. Palmer, R. E., *Hermeneutics: Interpretation Theory in Schleier-macher, Dilthey, Heidegger and Gadamer* (Evanston, IL: Northwestern University, 1969). Palmer is a professor of comparative literature, but since he came to the study of these theorists through the study of Bultmann, the reader will find that he puts the problem of biblical interpretation in the context of these other German theorists. *Cui bono?*

See *Int* 25 (1971) 232-33; *TToday* 26 (1969-70) 478-80; *WTJ* 34 (1971-72) 101-2.

650. McKnight, E. V., *Meaning in Texts: The Historical Shaping of a Narrative Hermeneutics* (Philadelphia, PA: Fortress, 1978). A good survey of recent attempts to forge a new hermeneutics for interpreting the Bible. Building on the poetics and hermeneutics of W. Dilthey, the book studies the later work of M. Heidegger and H. G. Gadamer about language and hermeneutics and the developments from Russian formalism to current investigations in the area of narrative, exploring the relation between structural study of narrative and existential hermeneutics. An application of the method is made to NT study, especially to Luke 5:1-11.

See *TS* 40 (1979) 178-80; *NTA* 23 (1979) 88; *Int* 34 (1980) 189-91; *JR* 60 (1980) 242-43; *RevExp* 76 (1979) 263-64.

651. Barthes, R. et al., *Exégèse et herméneutique* (Parole de Dieu; Paris: Editions du Seuil, 1971). An attempt on the part of nine French-speaking NT interpreters to present the new hermeneutics, which makes use of structuralism and modern psychology as a means to understand the biblical text. "It remains to be seen how many will really understand Scripture better after reading some of the more abstruse essays contained in the volume" (L. Sabourin).

See *NRT* 94 (1972) 963-64; *BLE* 73 (1972) 281-82; *BTB* 2 (1972) 95; *TRev* 68 (1972) 99.

652. Trible, P., *God and the Rhetoric of Sexuality* (Overtures to Biblical Theology Series; Philadelphia, PA: Fortress, 1978). This book has been hailed as a good example of advocacy interpretation, for it sets forth a modern feminist interpretation of the OT.

See *CBQ* 41 (1979) 463-65; 48 (1986) 609-16; *JBL* 99 (1980) 131-33.

C. The Relation of the Interpretation of the Bible to Church Teaching

EnchBib   **653.** *Enchiridion biblicum: Documenta ecclesiastica sacram Scripturam spectantia, auctoritate Pontificiae Commissionis de re biblica edita* (4th ed.; Naples: M. d'Auria; Rome: A. Arnodo, 1961). A collection of documents of the Roman Catholic church issued throughout the centuries on matters concerning the interpretation of Scripture. Some of these have been translated in *Rome and the Study of Scripture* (7th ed.; St. Meinrad, IN: Grail Publications, 1962); but beware of a glaring omission on p. 175 of the latter (about the Roman Catholic exegete's "full liberty" of interpretation) (see *NJBC* [§ 372], art. 72, § 25).

See *BenMon* 31 (1955) 49-50; *Antonianum* 30 (1955) 63-65; *CBQ* 18 (1956) 23-29.

654. Fitzmyer, J. A., *A Christological Catechism: New Testament Answers: Second Edition* (New York/Mahwah, NJ: Paulist, 1991). Appendix 1-3 contains a revised translation and commentary on the Biblical Commission's Instruction "On the Historical Truth of the Gospels." This instruction of 1964 is an important hermeneutical guide for the interpretation of the canonical Gospels. It gives official recognition to form criticism and distinguishes stages of the gospel tradition. The translation and commentary originally appeared in *TS* 26 (1964) 386-408 and was reprinted as a pamphlet, *The Historical Truth of the Gospels: The 1964 Instruction of the Biblical Commission, with Commentary* (Glen Rock, NJ: Paulist, 1964). A fuller form of the pamphlet was issued in German as *Die Wahrheit der Evangelien* (SBS 1; 2d ed.; Stuttgart: Katholisches Bibelwerk, 1966).

See *EstBib* 27 (1968) 87-88; *America* 110 (1964) 844-46; *RB* 74 (1967) 632; 90 (1983) 300-301; *TPQ* 114 (1966) 369; *TTZ* 75 (1966) 378; *TRev* 63 (1967) 4-7.

655. Tuya, M. de and J. Salguero, *Introducción a la Biblia* (BAC 262, 268; 2 vols.; Madrid: Edica, 1967). Volume 1 treats of biblical inspiration, the canon, the text, and versions; vol. 2, of biblical hermeneutics, history of interpretation of the Bible, institutions of ancient Israel, and geography of Palestine.

See *CBQ* 30 (1968) 640-41; *Bib* 49 (1968) 555-56; *JBL* 87 (1968) 350-51.

CHAPTER XXIV

Miscellany

Here will be listed a number of important publications that do not fit conveniently into the categories of the foregoing chapters. The items will be grouped as follows: (A) Ancient Near Eastern texts (or pictures) illustrating the OT and NT; (B) Studies of the institutions of ancient Israel; (C) Patristic literature and the study of the Bible; and (D) All else.

A. Ancient Near Eastern Texts (or Pictures) Illustrating the OT or NT

ANEP   **656.**   **Pritchard, J. B., *The Ancient Near East in Pictures Relating to the Old Testament* (Princeton, NJ: Princeton University, 1954; 2d ed., with supplement, 1969). A collection of over 750 pictures arranged according to such topics as daily life, writing, gods and their emblems, etc. Nearly one hundred pages of text explain the pictures and supply information and bibliography about their origins and discussions of them. This is a companion volume to *ANET* (§ 657; see also § 658). An abridged from of *ANET* and *ANEP* can be found in the author's *The Ancient Near East: An Anthology of Texts and Pictures* (2 vols.; Princeton, NJ: Princeton University, 1958, 1975).

See *Int* 9 (1955) 216-18; *ZAW* 67 (1955) 129-30; *JBL* 75 (1956) 77-78; *JSS* 1 (1956) 186-87; *RB* 63 (1956) 307-9.

ANET   **657.**   **Pritchard, J. B., *Ancient Near Eastern Texts Relating to the Old Testament* (3d ed.; Princeton, NJ: Princeton University, 1969). This valuable collection of ancient Near Eastern texts in translation first appeared in 1950. An expanded 2d ed. was put out in 1955 (along with a fascicle containing the added texts, *New Material from the Second, Revised Edition of Ancient Near Eastern Texts* ...; this fascicle made it possible to continue to use the first edition). The third edition (1969) not only contains further new material but offers translations of the existing texts that have been revised; when the additions were such that they could not be fitted into the existing space in the book's format, they were gathered in a supplementary section (some printings of the third edition lack some of the addenda on p. 676). The original texts are selections from Egyptian, Sumerian, Akkadian, Hittite, Ugaritic, South Arabic, Canaanite, and Aramaic documents, translated by experts in each field. The selections are grouped according to literary form: (1) myths, epics, legends; (2) legal texts (now including Akkadian treaties from Syria and Assyria); (3) historical texts; (4) rituals, incantations, and descriptions of festivals; (5) hymns and prayers; (6) didactic and wisdom literature; (7) lamentations; (8) secular songs and poems; (9) letters; (10) miscellaneous texts; and (11) supplement (the addenda which would not fit into existing space). The work is a real library of ancient Near Eastern literature, which is indispensable in the study of the OT.

See *JAOS* 71 (1951) 259-64; *JCS* 6 (1952) 124-28; *Or* 22 (1953) 221-23; *JSS* 1 (1956) 400-402; *Bib* 37 (1957) 365-67; *JNES* 16 (1957) 68-71; also the reviews mentioned in § 656.

ANESTP   **658.**   **Pritchard, J. B., *The Ancient Near East: Supplementary Texts and Pictures Relating to the Old Testament* (Princeton, NJ: Princeton University, 1969). This volume supplies the added materials in the 3d ed. of *ANET* (§ 657), which enables one to use the older editions of *ANET* and *ANEP*; 55 new pages of material are added to the latter. The new materials are from more recently excavated sites in Palestine, Syria, Jordan, and Iraq. They expand almost every section of the original edition; and some of the translations are revised forms of what is found in earlier editions.

See *RB* 77 (1970) 612-13; *JBL* 89 (1970) 347-50; *CBQ* 32 (1970) 298-99.

   659.   Beyerlin, W. et al. (eds.), *Religionsgeschichtliches Textbuch zum Alten Testament* (GAT 1; Göttingen: Vandenhoeck & Ruprecht, 1975). This is a collection of ancient Near Eastern texts (or excerpts from them) which are representative of the cultures surrounding ancient Israel and are so presented as to illustrate various OT passages. The material is gathered into five parts, each under the editorship of a different scholar: Egyptian texts (H. Brunner); Mesopotamian (H. Schmökel); Hittite (C. Kühne); Ugaritic (K.-H. Bernhardt); and Northwest Semitic (E. Lipiński). This book is not a rival of *ANET* (§ 657), but in many ways it does what *ANET* does not do by its mode of presentation and notes. An English form of it has been prepared by J. Bowden, *Near Eastern Religious Texts Relating to the Old Testament* (OTL; Philadelphia, PA: Westminster, 1978).

See *CBQ* 38 (1976) 547-48; 42 (1980) 230-31; *JBL* 98 (1979) 414-15; *RB* 86 (1979) 623-24.

   660.   Briend, J. and M.-J. Seux, *Textes du proche-orient ancien et histoire d'Israël* (Paris: Cerf, 1977). A slender collection of texts of extrabiblical material bearing on the study of Palestinian and Israelite history during the second and first millennia B.C. down to the time of Antiochus IV Epiphanes. It is explicitly patterned after K. Galling's *Textbuch* (§ 661), but contains more texts. Seux presents the Akkadian material; Briend, that of Egyptian, North-west Semitic, and Greek origin (no Hittite or Ugaritic material is included). Some texts are included here that are not found in either *ANET* (§ 657) or Galling's *Textbuch* (§ 661).

See *CBQ* 42 (1980) 230-31; *RB* 86 (1979) 622-24.

TGI **661.** Galling, K. (ed.), *Textbuch zur Geschichte Israels* (Tübingen: Mohr [Siebeck], 1959; 3d ed., 1979 (in collaboration with E. Edel and R. Borger]). A collection of ancient Near Eastern texts which illustrate the OT; they extend down into the first Christian centuries. The Egyptian and Akkadian texts have been translated into German; the rest are given in the original Hebrew, Aramaic, or Greek (and are supplied with brief notes).

See *JBL* 70 (1951) 164; *RB* 58 (1951) 273-74; *TZ* 7 (1951) 131-33; *ZDPV* 86 (1970) 103-4; *TP* 44 (1969) 294.

662. Labat, R. et al., *Les religions du Proche-Orient asiatique: Textes babyloniens, ougaritiques, hittites* (Le trésor spirituel de l'humanité; Paris: Fayard-Denoël, 1970). R. Labat edits the collection of Babylonian texts; A. Caquot and M. Sznycer the Ugaritic texts; and M. Vieyra the Hittite and Hurrian texts.

See *BO* 28 (1971) 287; *ETR* 47 (1970) 313-14; *RB* 78 (1971) 470-71; *ZAW* 82 (1970) 325.

663. Pettinato, G., *The Archives of Ebla: An Empire Inscribed in Clay* (Garden City, NY: Doubleday, 1981). A popular account of the discovery of Eblaite and its significance for the study of the OT.

See *AO* 1 (1983) 127-30; *BARev* 7/6 (1981) 10-12; *TToday* 38 (1981-82) 527-28; *CurTM* 9 (1982) 314-15; *ETR* 57 (1982) 618-20.

KAI **664.** **Donner, H. and W. Röllig, *Kanaanäische und aramäische Inschriften* (3 vols.; Wiesbaden: Harrassowitz, 1962, 1964, 1964; 2d ed., 1966, 1968, 1969; 3d ed., 1971). Volume 1 includes Phoenician, Punic, Neo-Punic, Moabite, Hebrew, and Aramaic texts; vol. 2 contains a German translation, bibliography, and commentary on the texts; and vol. 3 glossaries, plates, and indices. This is a highly praised collection of Northwest Semitic texts valuable for the study of the Hebrew Scriptures.

See *JSS* 17 (1972) 137-39.

TSSI **665.** Gibson, J. C. L., *Textbook of Syrian Semitic Inscriptions* (3 vols.; Oxford: Clarendon, 1971, 1975, 1982). A valuable collection of Northwest Semitic inscriptions that are important for the interpretation of the Hebrew Scriptures. Volume 1 is devoted to Hebrew and Moabite inscriptions; vol. 2 to Aramaic inscriptions (including those of Zenjirli); vol. 3 to Phoenician inscriptions (including those of Arslan Tash).

See *JBL* 91 (1972) 109-12; 96 (1977) 425-27; 103 (1984) 453-55; *JSS* 17 (1972) 139-43; 24 (1979) 115; *IEJ* 22 (1972) 187-89; 28 (1978) 287-89; *JAOS* 94 (1974) 509-12.

CTA   **666.**   Herdner, A., *Corpus des tablettes en cunéiformes alphabétiques découvertes à Ras Shamra-Ugarit de 1929 à 1939* (2 vols.; Mission de Ras Shamra, 10/1-2; Paris: Imprimerie Nationale/Geuthner, 1963). This is an important collection of Ugaritic texts in nine groups: (1) mythological texts (Baʿal and ʿAnat, Keret, Danel and Aqhat, Poem of the Rephaim, Birth of Saḥar and Šalim, Hymn to Nikkal); (2) religious texts; (3) letters; (4) diplomatic text; (5) economic texts; (6) hippological texts; (7) Akkadian texts in alphabetic writing; (8) Hurrian texts; (9) Varia.

PRU   **667.**   Schaeffer, C. F. A., *Le palais royal d'Ugarit II, III, IV, V, VI* (Mission de Ras Shamra 6/1-2,7, 9/1-2,11,12; Paris: Imprimerie Nationale/Klincksieck, 1957, 1955, 1956, 1965, 1970).

Ugaritica   **668.**   Schaeffer, C. F. A., *Ugaritica: Etudes relatives aux découvertes de Ras Shamra I-II, IV-VI* (Mission de Ras Shamra 3,5,15-17; Paris: Geuthner, 1939, 1949, 1962, 1968, 1969).

See *OLZ* 67 (1972) 356-58; *Or* 43 (1974) 145; *PEQ* 106 (1974) 170-71; *Syria* 48 (1971) 231-32.

    669.   Caquot, A., M. Sznycer, and A. Herdner, *Textes ougaritiques I: Mythes et légendes* (LAPO 7; Paris: Cerf, 1974). This first volume contains the French translation of the Baʿal-ʿAnat cycle, Aqhat, Keret, Rephaim and other small poems.

See *NRT* 97 (1975) 278; *RevThom* 74 (1974) 462-63; *AION* 35 (1975) 283-87; *RB* 82 (1975) 309-10.

CML   **670.**   Gibson, J. C. L., *Canaanite Myths and Legends* (Edinburgh; Clark, 1978). This is a revision of a book with the same title by G. R. Driver, published in 1956. The transliteration and translation are provided on the same page; the text-critical notes have been revised and the bibliography has been updated. "Overall it is the most usable and reliable translation with commentary now available in English" (R. J. Clifford).

See *JBL* 98 (1979) 580-82; *BSOAS* 42 (1979) 376; *Muséon* 92 (1979) 395; *RSO* 53 (1979) 411-13.

    671.   Dietrich, M. et al., *Die keilalphabetischen Texte aus Ugarit einschliesslich der keilalphabetischen Texte ausserhalb Ugarits: Teil 1. Transkription* (AOAT 24/1; Kevelaer: Butzon & Bercker; Neukirchen–Vluyn: Neukirchener-V., 1976).

RSP   **672.** Fisher, L. R. (ed.), *Ras Shamra Parallels: The Texts from Ugarit and the Hebrew Bible* (3 vols.; AnOr 49-51; Rome: Biblical Institute, 1972, 1975, 1981). Fischer prepared vols. 1-2; S. Rummel, vol. 3. The work discusses the parallels in Ugaritic and Akkadian literature to the OT. In vol. 1, A. Schoors treats literary phrases; M. Dahood, Ugaritic–Hebrew parallel pairs; and J. M. Sasson, flora, fauna, and minerals; in vol. 2, Dahood continues his treatment of parallel pairs; T. Yamashita treats professions; A. Rainey, family, civil, and military parallels; F. B. Knutson, political and foreign affairs and literary parallels; L. R. Fisher, literary genres; D. E. Smith, wisdom genres; M. Astour, place names; and J. Khanjian, Wisdom.

  See *CBQ* 38 (1976) 103-5; 39 (1977) 112-13; *BeO* 31 (1974) 3-26.

673. Dietrich, M. et al., *Ugarit-Bibliographie 1928-1966* (4 vols.; Kevelaer: Butzon & Bercker; Neukirchen-Vluyn: Neukirchener-V., 1973). Volume 1 covers the years 1928-50; vol. 2, 1950-59; vol. 3, 1959-66; vol. 4 contains indices.

674. Martinez, E. R. (ed.), *Hebrew–Ugaritic Index to the Writings of Mitchell J. Dahood: A Bibliography with Indices of Scriptural Passages, Hebrew and Ugaritic Words, and Grammatical Observations* (SPIB 116; Rome: Biblical Institute, 1967). This bibliography lists in chronological order Dahood's 135 books, articles, notes, and reviews that appeared between 1952 and 1966. There are a 30-page index of scriptural passages, a 64-page index of Hebrew and Ugaritic words, and lastly an index of grammatical observations.

  See *CBQ* 29 (1967) 632; *JBL* 87 (1968) 117.

TAD   **675.** Porten, B. and A. Yardeni, *Textbook of Aramaic Documents from Ancient Egypt: Newly Copied, Edited and Translated into Hebrew and English, 1. Letters, 2. Contracts* (2 vols.; Jerusalem: Hebrew University, 1986, 1989 [distributed by Eisenbrauns, Winona Lake, IN]). This is an excellent edition of the Aramaic texts from Egypt (Elephantine, Saqqarah, etc.) based on a new reading of the originals and supplied with wonderful facsimiles. More volumes are planned. The study of Biblical Aramaic is enhanced by the study of such texts.

  See *RB* 95 (1988) 294-99.

MPAT   **676.** Fitzmyer, J. A., and D. J. Harrington, *A Manual of Palestinian Aramaic Texts (Second Century B.C. — Second Century A.D.)* (BibOr 34; Rome: Biblical Institute, 1978). A collection of 150 texts (often fragmentary) from the period indicated, which give the student an idea of the kind of Middle Aramaic that was in use in Palestine about the turn of the Christian era. An appendix supplies the text of 56 other inscriptions, dating from the third to the sixth centuries A.D. (or Late Aramaic). Brief descriptive notes, bibliography, and glossaries are supplied.

See *TS* 40 (1979) 742-43; *PEQ* 111 (1979) 132-33; *RevQ* 10 (1979-81) 115-18; *RHR* 196 (1979) 207-8; *BO* 37 (1980) 81-82; *JBL* 100 (1981) 142-43; *TRev* 77 (1981) 15-16.

677. Beyer, K., *Die aramäischen Texte vom Toten Meer samt den Inschriften aus Palästina, dem Testament Levis aus der Kairoer Genisa, der Fastenrolle und den alten talmudischen Zitaten* (Göttingen: Vandenhoeck & Ruprecht, 1984). An interesting collection of Aramaic texts that covers more than is mentioned in the title. However, the readings should always be checked against the *editiones principes* and the grammatical analyses, especially the vocalizations, should be used with discernment.

See *RB* 92 (1985) 441-45; *ETR* 60 (1985) 626-29; *JBL* 105 (1986) 347-49; *Judaica* 41 (1985) 245-47; *JSJ* 16 (1985) 257-63.

NTB **678.** Barrett, C.K., *The New Testament Background: Selected Documents, Revised Edition* (London: SPCK, 1987; San Francisco, CA: Harper & Row, 1989). This book was first published in 1956 (repr., 1961). It contains a compilation of 280 documents in translation, most of them from Latin and Greek sources, which illustrate significant aspects of the civilized world in which the NT took shape. The texts come from historians, papyri, inscriptions, philosophers, mystery religions, Jewish history, rabbinic writings, Philo, Josephus, the LXX, apocalyptic literature, and the Dead Sea Scrolls. German translation: *Die Umwelt des Neuen Testaments: Ausgewählte Quellen* (WUNT 4; tr. C. Colpe; Tübingen: Mohr [Siebeck], 1959).

See *ExpTim* 68 (1956-57) 161-62; *ATR* 39 (1957) 281-82; *RSPT* 41 (1957) 250.

679. Sherk, R.K., *Roman Documents from the Greek East: Senatus consulta and epistulae to the Age of Augustus* (London/Baltimore, MD: Johns Hopkins University, 1969). This is "a work of immense value to the historian" (E.R.A. Sewter). It has two parts: (1) 32 decrees of the Roman senate in Greek, with bibliography, commentary, and notes; (2) letters written by Roman officials.

See *AJP* 91 (1970) 223-28; *Greece & Rome* 17 (1970) 233.

680. Tcherikover, V.A. and A. Fuks (eds.), *Corpus papyrorum judaicarum* (3 vols.; Cambridge, MA: Harvard University, 1957, 1960, 1964). In the third volume, published after the death of Tcherikover, M. Stern was added as an editor, and D.M. Lewis authored an "epigraphical contribution." This is an invaluable collection of Greek papyri, not all written by Jews, but relating "to Jews and Jewish affairs." They come from the Ptolemaic, Roman, and early Byzantine periods and contain much material for the history of the Jews in these times.

See *JBL* 78 (1959) 173-74; *Gnomon* 31 (1959) 422-29; 40 (1968) 250-59; *JJS* 9 (1958) 91-93; *Aegyptus* 44 (1964) 111-12; *RB* 66 (1959) 467-69; 68 (1961) 625-26; 73 (1966) 296-97.

681. Vermaseren, M. J., *Corpus inscriptionum et monumentorum religionis mithricae* (2 vols.; The Hague: Nijhoff, 1956, 1960). A modern collection of inscriptions and monuments related to Mithraic religion in the ancient Roman empire. In vol. 1 items are cited and discussed from Asia/Syria, Egypt, Africa, Italy, Spain, Great Britain, and France; in vol. 2 another 1375 items are presented from Germany, Rhetia, Pannonia, Dalmatia, Thrace, Macedonia, and Greece. This is an indispensable tool for the study of this religious phenomenon in the Roman world in which Christianity also took shape.

See *BO* 14 (1957) 251-53; 20 (1963) 331-33.

B. Studies of the Institutions of Ancient Israel

682. Dalman, G. H., *Arbeit und Sitte in Palästina* (7 vols.; Gütersloh: Bertelsmann, 1928-42; repr., Hildesheim: Olms, 1964). This classic study of life and customs in ancient and modern Palestine is outdated, but it contains much information that cannot be readily found elsewhere. The information is strictly speaking not archaeological, but could be revised by a proper use of modern archaeological data.

See *RB* 37 (1928) 474-75.

683. Jeremias, J., *Jerusalem zur Zeit Jesu: Kulturgeschichtliche Untersuchung zur neutestamentlichen Zeitgeschichte* (3d ed.; Göttingen: Vandenhoeck & Ruprecht, 1962). This study of Jewish life in Jerusalem in the first century A.D. has gathered much detail about economic and social conditions there. Though it uses archaeological and extrabiblical literary material correctly, it has not always distinguished the latter evidence from rabbinical literature as it should have. Not all that is found in rabbinical writings of A.D. 200 and later was necessarily in vogue in the time prior to the two revolts of Palestinian Jews against Rome (A.D. 66-70, 132-35), when Jesus would have been in Jerusalem. An English translation exists based on the 3d German edition, "with author's revisions to 1967": *Jerusalem in the Time of Jesus: An Investigation into Economic and Social Conditions during the New Testament Period* (Philadelphia, PA: Fortress, 1969).

See *RB* 39 (1930) 296; 67 (1960) 303-4; *CBQ* 32 (1970) 455-56; *JBL* 79 (1960) 194.

684. *Noth, M., *Die Welt des Alten Testaments: Einführung in die Grenzgebiete der alttestamentlichen Wissenschaft* (Sammlung Töpelmann 2/3; 4th ed.; Berlin: Töpelmann, 1964). This work, originally published in 1940, appeared in a considerably revised 2d ed. in 1952; the fourth has been again augmented. In compact form, it contains a mass of reliable information on Palestinian geography and archaeology, non-Israelite peoples, cultures, languages, and so on, as well as on the text and versions of the OT. It is an extremely valuable introduction to the background of the OT. It has been translated into English, *The Old Testament World* (Philadelphia, PA: Fortress, 1966).

See *RB* 60 (1953) 430-31; *BA* 16 (1953) 44; *TLZ* 81 (1956) 155; *ArOr* 22 (1954) 485-86; *BO* 11 (1954) 211-12; *JR* 47 (1967) 175-77; *JSS* 12 (1967) 128-30; *WTJ* 29 (1966-67) 192.

685. Pedersen, J., *Israel, I-II: Sjaeleliv og Samfundsliv* (Copenhagen: V. Pios, 1920 [parts 1-2I], 1934 [parts 3-4]). Some revision was made for the English version, *Israel: Its Life and Culture* (2 vols.; Copenhagen: P. Branner; London: Oxford University, 1936, 1940; repr., 1953-54). This is a permanently valuable contribution to the study of Israelite life, thought, and institutions, even though R. de Vaux's *Ancient Israel* (§686) may parallel it and outstrip it in modern references. The poor quality of the English translation, however, makes the reading of the book somewhat difficult.

See *JPOS* 6 (1926) 222-24; *JTS* 48 (1947) 72-75.

686. **Vaux, R. de, *Les institutions de l'Ancien Testament* (2 vols.; Paris: Cerf, 1958, 1960; 2d ed., 1961, 1967). This is an excellent survey of such topics as nomadism and its survival, family institutions, civil institutions, military institutions, and religious institutions as these are reflected in the OT, ancient history, and archaeology. Though the work is intended for the non-specialist, it is the product of the author's profound scholarship and balanced judgment and is an indispensable handbook for biblical study. An English translation, not as good as it should be, exists: *Ancient Israel: Its Life and Institutions* (New York/Toronto/London: McGraw-Hill, 1961; repr., 1965). The translation has been updated by the use of notes, corrections, and additions supplied by de Vaux himself.

See *BASOR* 168 (1962) 43; *TS* 19 (1958) 415-16; 22 (961) 111-12; 23 (1962) 681; *CBQ* 20 (1958) 556-57; *JSS* 4 (1959) 169-71; *VT* 8 (1958) 321-26; *JBL* 79 (1960) 64-65; 80 (1961) 275-76; 81 (1962) 410-11.

C. Patristic Literature and the Study of the Bible

687. **Altaner, B., *Patrologie: Leben, Schriften und Lehre der Kirchenväter* (9th ed., rev. A. Stuiber; Freiburg im B.: Herder, 1980).

This is a famous one-volume German introduction to patristic literature. "There exists no better bibliography for the exegesis of the Fathers; it is a quite indispensable tool for study" (P. Nober). An English translation of the 5th ed. was prepared by H. C. Graef, *Patrology* (London/Edinburgh: Nelson; New York: Herder and Herder, 1960). There is also a French adaptation of the same edition by H. Chirat, *Précis de patrologie* (Editions Salvator Mulhouse; Paris/Tournai: Casterman, 1961).

See *Bib* 40 (1959) 31*; J. L. Stewardson, *A Bibliography* (§ 694), 1.

688.   **Quasten, J., *Patrology* (3 vols.; Westminster, MD: Newman; Utrecht/Brussels: Spectrum, 1950, 1953, 1960 [dates of later reprintings vary]). The first volume of this important survey of patristic literature will interest the student of the NT, since it treats not only of the writings of the Apostolic Fathers, but the apocryphal literature of the NT, the beginnings of Christian poetry, the early Acts of the Martyrs — all of which has a bearing on the immediate aftermath of the NT itself. Chapter 7 is devoted to the beginnings of heretical literature and gnosticism. Quasten's *Patrology* was translated into French by J. Laporte, *Patrologie* (Paris: Cerf, 1955, 1957, 1963); into Italian (*Patrologia* [Turin: Marietti, 1980-81]) in two volumes. Then A. di Bernardino supervised the work of eight scholars who produced in Italian the last volume that Quasten was never able to finish: *Patrologia Vol. III* (Casale/Rome/Turin: Marietti, 1978). The three English volumes were also translated into Spanish in two volumes by I. Oñatibia: *Patrología* (BAC; Madrid: Editorial Católica, 1961, 1962; 4th ed., 1985), and also (from the Italian) *Patrología III: La edad de oro de la literatura patrística latina* (BAC 422; Madrid: Editorial católica, 1981; 2d ed., 1986). This Italian volume has also been translated into English by P. Solari, *Patrology: Volume IV: The Golden Age of Latin Patristic Literature from the Council of Nicea to the Council of Chalcedon* (Westminster, MD: Christian Classics, Inc., 1986). The last mentioned has been published in both cloth and paperback. The Spanish translation has a number of additions that do not appear in the English.

See *CBQ* 14 (1952) 88-90; 23 (1961) 396-97; *TS* 13 (1952) 603-5; 15 (1954) 649-50; 49 (1988) 340-42; 50 (1989) 642-43; *Bib* 39 (1958) 519-21; *Gnomon* 25 (1953) 547-49; 34 (1962) 524; J. L. Stewardson, *A Bibliography* (§ 694), 8-10.

689.   *Allenbach, J. et al. (eds.), *Biblia patristica: Index des citations et allusions bibliques dans la littérature patristique* (4 vols.; Paris: Centre National de la Recherche Scientifique, 1975-   ). This index has been produced by a computer and is an excellent key to all the biblical quotations and allusions in early patristic literature. Volume 1 (1975) covers the origins up to Clement of Alexandria and Tertullian; vol. 2 (1977) deals with the third century; vol. 3 (1980) covers Origen; and vol. 4 (1987) treats the writings of Eusebius of Caesarea, Cyril of Jerusalem, and Epiphanius of Salamis. The work has been done by a team of international scholars working at the Centre d'Analyse et de Documentation Patristiques in Strasbourg–Cronenbourg.

See *JBL* 98 (1979) 469-70.

690. Kraft, H., *Clavis patrum apostolicorum: Catalogum vocum in libris patrum qui dicuntur apostolici non raro occurrentium* (Darmstadt: Wissenschaftliche Buchgesellschaft, 1963). With the aid of U. Früchtel, Kraft composed this valuable index to the Greek vocabulary of the Apostolic Fathers.

See *NRT* 86 (1964) 1112; *RB* 74 (1964) 338; *RHPR* 44 (1964) 247.

691. Ortiz de Urbina, I., *Patrologia syriaca* (2d ed.; Rome: Oriental Institute, 1965). This small introduction to Syriac patristic writings, which first appeared in 1958, is very valuable and covers five main areas: (1) the Syriac Fathers and orthodox writers; (2) Nestorian theologians; (3) Monophysite theologians; (4) anonymous historical works; and (5) Syriac writers of the post-patristic age. At times the biblical student will raise questions about how the OT or NT was understood in the later Christian centuries of the Mesopotamian world; this book will help to locate writers and texts.

See *OrChr* 31 (1965) 494-95; *OrSyr* 4 (1959) 122-23; *Bib* 40 (1959) 111-14; *Muséon* 72 (1959) 473-76; J. T. Stewardson, *A Bibliography* (§ 694), 46.

692. McCullough, W. S., *A Short History of Syriac Christianity to the Rise of Islam* (General Series; Chico, CA [now Atlanta, GA], Scholars, 1982). This book provides the historical background of Syriac Christianity: Part I, in the Roman (Byzantine) world (in Parthian times [to A.D. 224], in Sasanian times [A.D. 224-651]); Part II, in the Parthian and Persian worlds (in Parthian times [to A.D. 224], in Sasanian times). It thus describes for the beginner the world in which Syriac interpreters of the Bible lived and worked.

See *JSS* 28 (1983) 371-73; *RelStRev* 10 (1984) 179; *Syria* 61 (1984) 147-48; *CHR* 71 (1985) 453-54.

BP   **693.** Schneemelcher, W. (ed.), *Bibliographia patristica: Internationale patristische Bibliographie* (Berlin/New York: de Gruyter, 1959-). So far 28 vols. of this valuable bibliography have appeared, produced by the best patristic scholars in the world. The NT student will find invaluable information in it on the early patristic writers (e.g., the Apostolic Fathers) and their use of the NT.

694. Stewardson, J. L., *A Bibliography of Bibliographies on Patristics* (Evanston, IL: Garrett Theological Seminary Library, 1967). This very good bibliography is only mimeographed; most of the items entered are annotated.

D. All Else

CHCLG   **695.** **Easterling, P. E. and B. M. W. Knox, *The Cambridge History of Classical Literature: I. Greek Literature* (Cambridge, UK: University Press, 1985). This well-written volume contains contributions of many renowned classical scholars and covers Greek literature from its beginnings to the end of Greco-Roman civilization in the 3d century A.D. (but prescinds from Christian writers). It is an excellent guide to Greek writers, their works, and select secondary bibliography. Its counterpart for Latin literature is *CHCLL* (§ 697).

See *HZ* 243 (1986) 651-54; *REG* 99 (1986) 380-82; *JHS* 106 (1986) 219-21; *CWorld* 80 (1986-87) 65.

696. Schmid, W. and O. Stählin, *Geschichte der griechischen Literatur* (Handbuch der Altertumswissenschaft VII/I.1-5; VII/II.1-2; 7 vols.; Munich: Beck: 1929, 1934, 1940, 1946, 1948, 1920, 1924). A highly-regarded mammoth history of Greek literature. Volume VII/II.1 will be of interest to the student of the Greek Bible and Greek intertestamental literature.

CHCLL   **697.** **Kenney, E. J., and W. V. Clausen, *The Cambridge History of Classical Literature: II. Latin Literature* (Cambridge, UK: University Press, 1982). The book was issued in five parts; its purpose is "to make available to the widest possible public the results of recent and current scholarship" (p. xiii). The contributions have been written by many well-known classical scholars and they present a welcome guide to Latin literature. Its counterpart for Greek literature is *CHCLG* (§ 695).

See *Gnomon* 56 (1984) 103-7; *EtClass* 52 (1984) 86-87; *CP* 81 (1986) 173-79; *Mnemosyne* 38 (1985) 222-28.

698. Schanz, M., *Geschichte der römischen Literatur bis zum Gesetzgebungswerk des Kaisers Justinian* (Handbuch der Altertumswissenschaft VIII/1-4; rev. C. Hosius; 4 vols.; Munich: Beck, 1927⁴, 1935⁴, 1922³, 1920²). A comprehensive, highly-respected history of Latin literature. Volume VIII/2 will be of interest to the student of the NT.

699. Andresen, C. et al. (eds.), *Lexikon der Alten Welt* (Zürich/Stuttgart: Artemis, 1965). This lexicon tries to embrace all sorts of details in the life of the people of the ancient Near East and in early Christianity. It has much to recommend it, being produced by good scholars.

See *Gnomon* 39 (1967) 737-58.

700. Deissmann, A., *Licht vom Osten: Das Neue Testament und die neuentdeckten Texte der hellenistisch-römischen Welt* (4th ed.; Tübingen: Mohr [Siebeck], 1923). Though old, this book is still useful, for it shows how the discoveries of Greek texts in Egyptian papyri have shed light on the language of the NT; most of what is discussed here, however, has been incorporated in lexica such as B–A or BAGD (§ 224, 225). English translation: *Light from the Ancient East: The New Testament Illustrated by Recently Discovered Texts of the Graeco-Roman World* (2d ed.; London: Hodder and Stoughton; New York: Doran, 1927).

LAE

See *RB* ns 6 (1909) 626-28.

701. Cartlidge, D. R. and D. L. Dungan, *Documents for the Study of the Gospels: A Sourcebook for the Comparative Study of the Gospels* (Cleveland, OH: Collins, 1980). This is a collection of selected texts, newly translated from pagan, Jewish, and Christian authors which illustrate the form-critical categories of the gospel tradition. The texts enable one to study the various gospel forms in comparison with other ancient similar writings (e.g., parables, miracle stories). An earlier form of the book appeared in SBLSBS 1 (Missoula, MT: Scholars, 1973).

See *CBQ* 36 (1974) 98-99; 37 (1975) 247-48.

702. Francis, F. O. and J. P. Sampley (eds.), *Pauline Parallels* (SBLSBS 9; Philadelphia, PA: Fortress; Missoula, MT [now Atlanta, GA]: Scholars, 1975). The English text of ten Pauline letters (minus the Pastorals) is set in parallel columns to facilitate "synoptic" study of the Pauline literature. The text used is that of the *RSVCB* (§ 182a). This is a very useful tool for Pauline interpretation.

See *JBL* 95 (1976) 673-74; *CBQ* 38 (1976) 378-79; *RTB* 6 (1976) 313, *RB* 84 (1977) 305-6.

703. Hüttenmeister F. and G. Reeg, *Die antiken Synagogen in Israel* (2 vols.; Beihefte zur Tübinger Atlas des Vorderen Orients, Reihe B, 12/1-2; Wiesbaden–Dotzheim: L. Reichert, 1977). An alphabetical catalogue of the sites and inscriptions of ancient Jewish and Samaritan synagogues, schools, and courts up to the seventh century. Volume 2 contains extensive indices that facilitate the use of this work.

See *RB* 88 (1981) 152-54; *ZDPV* 95 (1979) 211-13; *JJS* 31 (1980) 136.

704. Saller, S. J., *A Revised Catalogue of the Ancient Synagogues of the Holy Land* (Publications of the Studium Biblicum Franciscanum, coll. min. 6; Jerusalem: Franciscan Press, 1969; rev. ed., 1972). A survey of 113 sites, where ancient synagogues of Palestine were to be found. The book is a revision of an article that first appeared in SBFLA 4 (1953-54) 219-46. The list builds on that of E. R. Goodenough, *Jewish Symbols in the Greco-Roman Period* (13 vols.; New York: Bollingen, 1953-65) and that of J.-B. Frey, *Corpus inscriptionum iudaicarum* (2 vols.; Vatican City: Institute of Christian Archaeology, 1936, 1952).

See *BeO* 13 (1971) 94-95; *ZDPV* 89 (1973) 109-10.

SCHNT   **705.** Studia ad corpus hellenisticum Novi Testamenti (Leiden: Brill, 1970-   ). This series, edited by H.-D. Betz, is very important for the bearing of the language and literature of Hellenistic Greek writers on NT books. It is an area of NT background study that is at times too much overlooked. So far six volumes have appeared in this series: e.g., G. Petzke, *Die Traditionen über Apollonius von Tyana und das Neue Testament* (1970); G. Mussies, *Dio Chrysostom and the New Testament* (1972); H.-D. Betz (ed.), *Plutarch's Theological Writings and Early Christian Literature* (1975); *Plutarch's Ethical Writings and Early Christian Literature* (1978); W. C. Grese, *Corpus Hermeticum XIII and Early Christian Literature* (1979); P. W. van der Horst, *Aelius Aristides and the New Testament* (1980).

See *JBL* 92 (1973) 465-67; 94 (1975) 631-33; 99 (1980) 641-44; 100 (1981) 140-42.

WA   **706.** Fitzmyer, J. A., *A Wandering Aramean: Collected Aramaic Essays* (SBLMS 25; Missoula, MT [now Atlanta, GA]: Scholars, 1979). This collection of 12 essays on aspects of the study of Aramaic includes a number that bear directly on the question of the Aramaic background of the NT, the methodology that should govern the study of it, the respect for the kind of Aramaic to be used for comparison, the contribution that Aramaic texts from Qumran have made to this study, etc.

See *JBL* 98 (1979) 617-18; *TS* 41 (1980) 192-93; *ETL* 56 (1980) 167-68; *BL* (1980) 130; *Or* 50 (1981) 222-25; *TRu* 46 (1981) 186-87; *JSS* 27 (1982) 81-85; *TRev* 76 (1980) 276-77; *JNES* 39 (1980) 217-19; *TZ* 37 (1981) 62-63.

Index of Modern Authors

Numbers following the names refer to numbered paragraphs.

Reviews of the Second Edition of *IBSS*

Adris Newsletter	11 (1981) 7 (Anon.)
Bijdragen	42 (1981) 309 (W. Beuken)
ETL	57 (1981) 355-57 (F. Neirynck)
OTA	4 (1981) 269-70 (B. Vawter)
SBFLA	31 (1981) 403-4 (G. C. Bottini)
TD	29 (1981) 381 (Anon.)
BZ	26 (1982) 150 (R. Schnackenburg)
CBQ	44 (1982) 479-80 (J. I. Hunt)
Greg	63 (1982) 398-99 (G. L. Prato)
ITQ	49 (1982) 72 (Anon.)
NRT	104 (1982) 585 (J. L. Ska)
NTA	26 (1982) 74 (Anon.)
RB	89 (1982) 610-12 (J.-M. de Tarragon)
RelStRev	8 (1982) 278 (W. L. Humphreys)
TRu	47 (1982) 385-86 (W. G. Kümmel)
TS	43 (1982) 175 (F. L. Moriarty)
TvT	22 (1982) 87 (J. Lust)
ZKT	104 (1982) 205 (K. Stock)
Afer	25 (1983) 63 (P. Vonck)
BL	(1983) 14 (R. J. Coggins)
HeyJ	24 (1983) 490 (R. P. R. M.)
JTS	34 (1983) 693 (R. Morgan)
LTP	39 (1983) 363-64 (P.-E. Langevin)
Selecciones de libros	20 (1983) 255-56 (R. de S.)

Finito di stampare il 26 ottobre 1990
Tipografia Poliglotta della Pontificia Università Gregoriana
Piazza della Pilotta, 4 - 00187 Roma